Limits to Free Trade

To James, Carol, Steve and Dan

Limits to Free Trade

Non-Tariff Barriers in the European Union, Japan and United States

David Hanson

Associate Professor of International Business, Duquesne University, Pittsburgh, USA

Edward Elgar

Cheltenham, UK • Northampton, MA, USA

Published by
Edward Elgar Publishing Limited
The Lypiatts
15 Lansdown Road
Cheltenham
Glos GL50 2JA
UK

Edward Elgar Publishing, Inc.
William Pratt House
9 Dewey Court
Northampton
Massachusetts 01060
USA

A catalogue record for this book
is available from the British Library

Library of Congress Control Number: 2009936740

ISBN 978 1 84720 247 5

Printed and bound by MPG Books Group, UK

Contents

Tables

Abbreviations

ADA	Anti-Dumping Agreement
APHIS	Animal and Plant Health Inspection Service (US)
CEN	Comité européen de normalisation
DRU	Dispute Resolution Understanding
FAO	Food and Agriculture Organization
FCC	Federal Communications Commission (US)
FDA	Food and Drug Administration (US)
GATS	General Agreement on Trade in Services
GATT	General Agreement on Tariffs and Trade
GPA	Government Procurement Agreement
HLS	Homeland Security (US)
IPPC	International Plant Protection Council
IPPC	International Plant Protection Convention
IPR	Intellectual Property Rights
METI	Ministry of Economy, Trade and Industry (Japan)
MFN	Most-Favored Nation
NCSCI	National Center for Standards and Certification Information
OECD	Organisation for Economic Co-operation and Development
OIE	Office International des Epizooties
OSHA	Occupational Safety and Health Administration (US)
SCM	Subsidies and Countervailing Measures
SPS	Sanitary and Phytosanitary Standards
TBT	Technical Barriers to Trade
USTR	United States Trade Representative
WTO	World Trade Organization

1. Dilemmas of free trade

> Recognizing that their relations in the field of trade and economic endeavour should be conducted with a view to raising standards of living, ensuring full employment and a large and steadily growing volume of real income and effective demand, developing the full use of the resources of the world and expanding the production and exchange of goods,
>
> Being desirous of contributing to these objectives by entering into reciprocal and mutually advantageous arrangements directed to the substantial reduction of tariffs and other barriers to trade and to the elimination of discriminatory treatment in international commerce,
>
> Have through their Representatives agreed as follows . . .
>
> (Preamble, *General Agreement on Tariffs and Trade* (1947), at: www.wto.org/english/docs_e/legal_e/gatt47_01_e.htm)

1. INTRODUCTION

On 1 January 1948, delegates from 23 countries brought the UN Conference on Trade and Employment at Marrakesh, Morocco, to an apparently successful conclusion by signing the General Agreement on Tariffs and Trade (GATT). Unfortunately, the US senate refused to ratify the Convention, and it became a legal dead letter. The enforcing agency, the proposed International Trade Organization, was never organized.

Fortunately, President Truman decided to proceed as if GATT were the law of the land. The results have been spectacular. The nations of the world have negotiated tariff reductions through a 50-year series of multinational negotiating "rounds". A toothless GATT has been replaced by a far more powerful World Trade Organization (WTO). A series of companion agreements have been negotiated that extend the trading rules to cover a wide range of issues, from intellectual property to the international protection of animal health. International trade has grown explosively.

Unfortunately, the world community may be seeing the limits of political support for free trade. Both the OECD and the World Bank have been pointing to the rising impact of 'non-tariff trade barriers' on international trade (Laird and Yeats, 1988, Laird and Yeats, 1990). The countries of the world are turning to international litigation through the WTO Dispute Resolution Process. The rhetoric and resistance in these disputes have been surprisingly stringent. The last Doha Round collapsed without any major agreement (*New York Times*, 2008, p. 1). Has the impetus for trade liberalization run out of steam?

2. THE ISSUE OF FREE TRADE

2.1 Thesis: Trade is Fundamental

For most economists, the argument is obvious. The goal of economic policy should be to maximize national welfare. The measure of welfare is the value of goods and services produced and consumed in the economy. Expanding trade should increase economic welfare. This economic expansion is pareto optimal. There will be winners and losers, but the winners will win more than the losers will lose. On average, everyone is better off.

The policy position associated with this analysis might be termed "classic free trade". For countries adopting the classic free trade position, the overriding goal would be trade liberalization. Merchandise trade surpluses and deficits would not be regarded as serious problems. Floating exchange rates would eventually bring the resources leaving the country into equilibrium with the resources being brought in. Winners and losers could be sorted out with internal transfer payments (Krugman, 1997).

If this analysis is correct, then national support for free trade should be a given. There are few policies in public life that, on average, benefit everyone. In fact, one economist concluded that trade expansion accounted for one-third of the economic growth in the world economy since World War II. The other factors, innovation and declining production costs, may be also promoted by trade expansion (Baier and Bergstrand, 2001).

The reasons for a relation between trade and economic development are easy to see. Without trade, we would all have to be self-sufficient, producing everything that we use. No schools, no cars, no McDonalds; life would be intolerable. Trade allows each of us to specialize in areas in which we can be most productive. As we enjoy the goods and services offered by others, they can also enjoy our contributions to the common weal.

We all have areas in which we are comparatively efficient. Through markets, we all have an opportunity to focus on our competitive advantages. If the Chinese can make dinnerware better than we can, let them have the market. They in turn, will buy the corn in which we have a comparative advantage. With specialization through markets, we can all be better off.

The economics of capital investment also play a role. To a large extent, the process of industrialization has involved replacing human effort with machine processing. Hand labor is a marginal cost item: the more you make, the more you are paid. As a result, there are few economies of scale in hand-made goods. Costs tend to be relatively proportional to production.

Machines though are a capital investment. A stamping press will cost almost the same regardless of whether it is used to make one or a thousand widgets. As a result, there are major economies of scale in capital investments. The cost per widget is far less if the machine is used to make a thousand copies than for ten. However, I won't want to produce a thousand widgets unless I know the market is sufficiently large to absorb them at a profit. The greater the cost of my stamping machine, the larger the market must be before I can make money on the investment.

The economics of innovation are becoming ever-more capital intensive with the rapid increases in development costs. It would be impossible to consider the development of a modern computer chip fabrication plant or a new commercial airliner if the products could not be sold on a global marketplace. Thus a rule of thumb: if markets don't keep growing then it will be harder to justify the increasing investments in new technologies that could lead to better, cheaper products (Ostry, 1997).

The logic of marketing and the product life cycle also play a role in the need for free trade and expanding markets. Prices and profits tend to be high for new products with little competition. Profit margins drop as competitors come into a now crowded field.

A common response? Look for new profits with new products. Companies developing new products might look for a niche that their competitors have not yet exploited. A focus on a niche though means that a company is trying to reach a smaller segment of the potential marketing universe. To compensate, companies often try to grow the universe by considering foreign markets. Another general conclusion: if the scope of commerce isn't growing, it will be hard to find market niches that could support more specialized products.

The combination of expensive new technologies, rising development costs and stringent market requirements has been pushing up the capital requirements for new product development in many product areas. The marginal cost of building an automobile is relatively small; it takes around ten hours of labor to build a new car (Womack, Jones and Roos, 1997). However, the average costs are far higher. These have to include product research and development and company overheads, and these expenses can be quite high. Engineers designing new cars have to balance the competing requirements of government-mandated safety and gas economy requirements with market demands for attractive, comfortable, reliable, economical vehicles. Developing cars that can meet these competing demands has become a very expensive process.

Because the costs of developing new designs have become so high, car manufacturers have been forming international alliances for sharing designs and technologies. New automobile manufacturing plants are likely to cost well over a billion dollars. These investments can only be justified if the manufacturers can sell to global markets.

The pressures for niche marketing and the rising capital costs of design, development and production are likely to be even greater in the future. If so, the capital investments required to be competitive in manufacturing will continue to increase. The resulting pressures for market expansion and company consolidation are likely continue for the indefinite future.

Finally, trade may dampen national interest in war and international adventures (Barbieri and Levy, 1999; Hegre, 2000; Anderton and Carter, 2001a, 2001b; Barbieri and Levy, 2001; Dorussen, 2002). Friedman (1999) has argued that modern capitalism imposes its own set of restrictions. If, as a country, you want the prosperity, you must obey the rules, which includes getting along with your neighbors. Business leaders who have staked their company's future on international trade and investment are likely to resist political demands for cutting ties with trading partners. This logic has been put to the test in a very practical way: the European Union was created in part to finally put an end to the seemingly endless cycles of European wars (Fischer, 2000).

2.2 Antithesis: Governments Limit Trade

Reality may not be quite so supportive. Many economists slide over the fact that trade expansion is likely to bring economic competition and competition brings winners and losers in the marketplace (Schumpeter, 1950). The pain of losing is often more concentrated and more apparent than the mild and diffuse gains enjoyed by the winners. Many people are likely to benefit from the low prices charged by Wal-Mart. However, the gains are relatively modest and the winners are not likely to be either vocal or organized. The pain from Wal-Mart's success might be seen in the (hypothetical) closing of a neighboring Sears department store. The employees who lost their jobs might not share a general enthusiasm for free trade.

A policy of "mercantilism" becomes the logical end of government efforts to cushion the damage caused by free markets, competition and economic dislocation. The goal of government becomes a policy of protecting domestic companies rather than increasing national welfare. Close working relations between business and government would be encouraged. Exports and outbound direct investment are likely to be encouraged while imports in inbound investment are likely to be discouraged. Trade surpluses would be squirreled away for strategic use by government and business rather than being used to fund imports that would enhance improvements in popular living standards.

Governments also tend to be organized in ways that encourage mercantilism. Viewed in its most basic form, most government funding usually comes from taxing commerce. Income from taxes is used to fund a capacity to coerce future tax payments. Any surplus income can then be used to advance other interests of government. The costs of tax collection can be reduced when governments use public power to do favors for private groups.

Government programs are often intended to limit trade. In politics, advantages generally go to the well-organized and strong. Groups under economic pressure are likely to use their political connections to redress a lack of market strength. Workers want minimum wage laws, consumer groups want product safety standards, domestic manufacturers may seek tariff protection and farmers often want subsidies. All of these programs involve restrictions on the free market. Governments also limit the benefits of trade. Taxation limits trade by moving resources from the exchange economy to the command economy. To the extent that transactions are less than voluntary, the participants are likely to view the results as less than satisfactory.

Governments are often organized in ways that encourage more attention to the passionate few than the modest many, even if economic progress is more tied up with the interests of the modest many. There may be a tragedy of the commons here. Relatively minor defections from a commitment to free trade may provide substantial relief to the passionate few with little injury to the modest many. However, a government that shields its citizens from too many of the shocks from the free market may end up by eliminating the benefits of trade as well.

Historically, enthusiasm for free trade has been an anomaly. Ever since the world was young, dominant countries have used military force to carve out regions for trading privileges. Alexander the Great's major motivation for conquering a substantial portion of the known world was probably to develop the tax and manpower base needed to support his armies and to expand the markets in which Macedonian and Greek merchants could trade without challenge. Similar motives prompted the British to conquer India and turn it into a source of cheap labor and materials and a guaranteed market for British manufacturers.

Some analysts have argued that trade does not bring peace (Barbieri, 2002; Barbieri and Levy, 2002). However, the phenomenon seems to be rather complex. Increasing levels of balanced trade between countries that are approximate commercial equals is associated with more conflict, not less. However, increased trade between countries that are not commercial equals is not likely to result in more conflict.

These conclusions are consistent with the mercantilist model. Since mercantilism is, in part, about enhancing national power, leaders are likely to accept economic subordination when they have little choice while enjoying power when they have it. Equality, though, would be likely to lead to more conflict (Conybeare, 1987).

We therefore have two models on which to base national trade policy. The assumptions chosen are likely to have an impact on the resolution of trade disputes. Governments that embrace the neoclassical assumptions about the benefits of free trade would, logically, seek to resolve trade disputes as soon as possible. Negotiations would probably be based in part on an implicit offer of "we will liberalize if you will liberalize".

In contrast, governments that embrace mercantilism, either explicitly or implicitly, would probably be in no rush to resolve disputes involving import restrictions. These disputes are more likely to depend on whether the complaining nations are in a position to inflict new harm on our exporters that is substantially greater than the domestic benefits provided by the trade restrictions in question.

2.3 Synthesis: Trade Policy Reflects a Balance Between Economic and Political Concerns

A working hypothesis: countries are likely to embrace free-market ideas as a general policy when they are forced into this position by circumstances. Deviations into an implicit mercantilism may be likely, especially if the overall political and economic costs seem to be low. Changing circumstances may lead to changes in the balance between trade and protectionism.

Prior to World War II, tariff negotiations were generally conducted on a bilateral basis. The US would offer to lower tariffs on shoes if Canada would lower the rate on socks. The result was a hodgepodge of different classifications and rates on similar items for different countries. "Tariff engineering" became a respectable profession.

The structure of the international tariff negotiations subtly favored higher tariffs. If the US and Canada were discussing tariffs on widgets, then the widget manufacturers on both sides would be expected to be out in force, generally lobbying for more protection. The lobby for lower-priced widgets through competition from international trade would be too small and too poorly organized to have much effect.

The period between 1914 and 1948 was the occasion for the development of major trade barriers. Although the United States did not enter the First World War until 1917, the European conflict led to the passage of major restrictions on trade, especially in Allied trade with Germany (Polanyi, 1944).

The political climate in the United States after the end of World War I was quite isolationist. The refusal of the US government to join the League of Nations, an organization that had been championed by the US president, is one famous example. More relevant for our purposes was the enactment of the Smoot Hawley tariff in 1930 (Schaffer, Earle and Agusti, 2008 p. 272). The goal was to protect US industries from foreign competition during the early stages of the Great Depression. Tariffs were raised to the highest level in US history (Schaffer, Earle and Agusti, 2008, p. 256). Tariffs on industrial goods approached 60 per cent *ad valorem* by 1938 (Irwin, 1999).

Predictably, US trading partners retaliated by raising their rates on US imports. The problems were compounded by a loss of international liquidity. The costs of the war had come close to bankrupting the British economy. American banks, which had capital to lend, withdrew from international markets. The result was a sharp decline in international trade. The expected post war recession soon became the Great Depression (Rolfe and Burtle, 1973).

The president was given authority to negotiate reciprocal tariff reductions and to offer unconditional most-favored nation status with the passage of the Reciprocal Trade Agreements Act of 1934 (Schaffer, Earle and Agusti, 2008, p. 272). This helped bring some order to the resulting mess. If the US granted most-favored nation status to Canada, then the US rate on widgets from Canada would not be any higher than the lowest rate imposed on widgets from any other country.

The promotion of national prosperity through international trade became a key element of Allied strategy after the end of World War II. The US and Britain had been able to keep the USSR out of Western Europe during the War. However, countering the threat of communism in a decimated post-war Europe required a rapid economic recovery. That required, in turn, dramatic progress in trade liberalization. The development of first the European Coal and Steel Community and then the European Economic Community began the process of trade liberalization within Europe.

The tangled development of the General Agreement on Tariffs and Trade was the first major step in liberalizing trade worldwide. The principles of GATT 1947 were implemented through a series of multinational trade negotiations, or 'rounds'. The results have been impressive. The number of participants has grown from 23 to 123 countries. Tariff reductions on over 50 000 items have been negotiated with an aggregate value of over $200b per year (Wikipedia, 2008). In the US, for example, average tariffs on industrial goods dropped to around 5 per cent *ad valorem* (Irwin, 1995). The US negotiating position on many electronic products is "zero for zero": the elimination of US tariffs in exchange for similar concessions from the other side (World Trade Organization, 1996).

GATT has been revised several times. The current version was ratified in connection with the creation of the World Trade Organization. It includes most of the sector-specific agreements that will be discussed below. However, the basic principles have been largely unchanged.

The creation of the World Trade Organization in 1995 led to the negotiation of a seemingly endless series of new multilateral agreements covering particular problems in trade and an extended series of generally successful multilateral trade negotiations.

The result of trade liberalization, the growing competences of Asian governments and the introduction of new technologies that substantially reduced the costs of moving people, goods and information have been spectacular. Trade has been increasing at a far more rapid rate than overall economic outputs. Consider, for example, the increasing importance of international merchandise trade for national economies. Our measure of trade penetration is the value of merchandise imports plus exports divided by GNP. Illustrative data are set forth in Table 1.1.

Unfortunately, the political imperative for free trade seems to be lessening. The Cold War is over. Russia is now (more-or-less) integrated into the global trading system. The threats of outside subversion and global war are (more-or-less) over. The political need for free trade as a global ideology seems to be waning. The European Union has gained some of the advantages of colonialism together with increased political security and power by bringing the Eastern European countries into the Union. These developments are paralleled in the western hemisphere with the development of NAFTA, CAFTA-DR and MERCOSUR. The collapse of the Doha Round and the proliferation of non-tariff trade barriers may simply be a reflection of the changing political realities.

All is not well in the field of free trade. "Non-tariff trade barriers" have proliferated almost as fast as international negotiations have led to new agreements to reduce tariff and non-tariff barriers. The World Bank noted in 1980 that some 40 per cent of the foreign trade of the Netherlands was "significantly compromised" by non-tariff trade barriers (Laird and Yeats, 1990; see also Laird and Yeats, 1988).

A review of national trade barriers will illustrate how our three countries have struck different balances between free trade and protectionism. We will need to understand why the patterns of non-tariff balances are different if we are to approach the issue of what could be done to improve the prospects for resolving them.

A search for the causes of international trade barriers in different states will involve an analysis of how the balance between the demands

Table 1.1 The growing importance of trade for national economies

		1978	1988	1998	2006
US	GNP	2118	4886	7903	13202
	Exports	119	320	880	1037
	Imports	157	441	944	1918
	Trade/GNP	13%	16%	23%	22%
France	GNP	423	933	1465	2231
	Exports	64	162	301	496
	Imports	71	177	286	542
	Trade/GNP	32%	36%	40%	47%
Germany	GNP	597	1218	2180	2907
	Exports	118	323	544	1108
	Imports	101	291	472	907
	Trade/GNP	37%	50%	47%	69%
Italy	GNP	214	810	1157	1845
	Exports	45	129	242	417
	Imports	46	138	216	443
	Trade/GNP	43%	33%	40%	47%
Japan	GNP	785	2851	4089	4340
	Exports	81	256	388	647
	Imports	71	188	281	380
	Trade/GNP	19%	16%	16%	24%

Notes: All figures are in $b US.

Sources: *Statistical Abstracts of the United States*, 101st ed., 1980, table 1583, p. 907; 110th ed., 1990, table 1446, p. 840; 120th ed., 2000, table 1364, p. 831; World Bank Statistical Database, online).

for political protection and the demand for unfettered market access are struck in different governments.

3. QUESTIONS AND A METHODOLOGY

To understand how the balance between free trade and protectionism is struck in a particular country, we should look at the trade disputes, not just at the stated trade policy. The stated policy for GATT signatories is most likely to embrace neoclassical economics and free trade. However, the real commitment comes when international objections are raised about local breaches of the overall policy. Are these lapses common? Will the defaulting country rectify local mistakes to promote free trade? Or is it more likely to defend key industry protectionism to the bitter end?

Answers to these questions will illuminate a lot about the real national commitments to free trade.

This analysis will review the status of the charges of protectionism raised by the governments of the US, the EU and Japan against each other between 2002 and 2007. Our goal is to use this analysis to say something interesting about the status and process of international trade negotiations in general.

There are several reasons for focusing on the US, the EU and Japan. They are the political and legal leaders in the international trade regulation system. They are also the dominant economies in the global marketplace. As Table 1.2 shows, our three countries account for over 60 per cent of total world merchandise trade. Furthermore, the "developing" countries of the world generally trade more with the "developed" countries than with each other. The EU, Japan and the US are the major developed polities.

4. ON THE CLASSIFICATION OF TRADE ISSUES

We will generally be looking at trade issues raised in discussions among these three governments over a five-year period, between 2002 and 2007. By looking at trade issues over this period, we can identify the issues that have been resolved, those that have persisted and those that have emerged. Persistent issues are those that were raised in both 2002 and 2007. Resolved issues are those that were raised in 2002 but not in 2007. Emergent issues are those that appeared in the 2007 list but were not in the 2002 inventory. Looking at the similarities and differences among the issues that fall in each category for each government will provide insights into the types of trade restrictions that have strong national backing and are relatively resistant to international pressure.

Identifying trade issues involved a degree of judgment. Only issues that seem to constitute actual trade barriers have been included. Some of the issues raised in all three sources involve warnings that a particular government will be monitoring developments to see if trade barriers may emerge in the future. These have been omitted from the analysis, which will only include trade barriers involving decisions by the central government. Governance in both the US and the EU involves substantial delegation in strongly federated systems. Trade issues that are purely local have been dropped from the analysis. Finally, decisions as to whether the issues raised by different governments were similar or different and whether an issue had been carried over or resolved between 2002 and 2007 also involved a degree of judgment.

Table 1.2 The importance of the EU, Japan and the US in world trade: 2004

Exports from	Total value	% world	Exports to		% to developing countries
			Developing countries	Developed countries	
World	8566				
Europe	3828	45	2716.135	512.060	84
Japan	565	7	242.672	315.646	43
US	1015	12	180.343	357.410	34
Rest	3158	37			
Africa			121.418	42.015	74
S. America			503.997	117.143	81
Asia			1117.925	1188.264	48

Notes:
Figures are for all commodities. Values are in US$b.
Figures do not add up to 100% due to rounding.

Source: United Nations (2004) Special Table A, pp. 519, 558.

The machineries of the European Union will be referred to as the "government" of Europe. This is consistent with the lead role of the EU in setting external trade policies for the member states. It is also a convenient terminology. No implications are intended as to whether the EU is now sovereign state or an intergovernmental organization serving at the pleasure of the member states.

We want to consider the prospects for resolving some of these trade barriers through international negotiations. What are the differences among the persistent, emergent and resolved trade issues? What differences in the contexts of government seem to best account for these differences? Even approximate answers to these questions will offer some ideas about whether we can expect a future of global trade or the re-emergence of trade blocs and competing trade interests. For an extended discussion of this issue, see Trotman (2004).

We will also be interested in the results of comparisons among the types of trade barriers attributed to the three governments. How do trade barriers attributed to the Japanese government differ from the types that seem to emerge in the US import and export trades? Are there strong similarities between the US complaints about Japan and the issues raised by the EU about Japanese trading and investment practices? These comparisons will provide information about differences in how the three governments view the world and how they respond to it.

The major sources of information will be the public reports published by the three governments on trade and investment restrictions raised by the other two governments. Embassy and consular personnel are constantly holding discussions with their host government counterparts on trade issues. In many cases, these issues can be resolved quickly and with little fuss, without becoming matters for public debate. Issues become matters of public comment when a government goes public with trade complaints. Governments are not likely to post public complaints about the trade policies of allied nations unless it has been decided that the issue is both significant and is not likely to be resolved through confidential bilateral discussions.

The Office of the United States Trade Representative (USTR) is charged with representing the US government in international negotiations over tariffs and other trade and investment restrictions. The USTR publishes an annual *Report on Foreign Trade Barriers* which analyzes trade barriers according to the responsible country. Our analysis will be based in part on the reports on trade and investment barriers attributed by the USTR to Japan and the European Union; these include situations where alleged trade and investment restrictions are both burdensome and unreasonable to US businesses. They are not necessarily based on allegations that the restrictions constitute breaches of international agreements.

The *Report* carries some political and diplomatic weight. In Chapter 4, we will discuss the contentious issue of the claim by the US of unilateral rights to impose sanctions against alleged foreign trade barriers under the "Super 301" process. Before an action can be taken under Super 301, the issues must be listed in the USTR's Annual Report.

In Japan, the Ministry of Economy, Trade and Industry publishes an annual *Report on Compliance by Major Trading Partners on Trade Agreements*. Information for this analysis has been taken from the 2002 and 2006 reports on the US and the EU. The 2006 report is supplemented by a 2007 report from the Ministry on Japanese trade negotiation priorities. These reports ostensibly focus on situations where Japan's trading partners have taken measures that violate international agreements. The legal analyses they provide on these issues are very helpful. We have generally concluded though that the relevant international agreements have, in many cases, been interpreted with sufficient latitude to cover most Japanese trade interests.

In the EU, Directorate General Trade maintains the *Market Access Database* (European Union, Directorate General Trade, irregular) a file on foreign trade barriers. The database consists of a series of "fiches". Each fiche describes a specific type of foreign trade barrier that a European exporter may encounter. The emphasis is primarily on barriers to trade rather than investment. The fiches are periodically updated to assure currency and are deleted from the database when the underlying issues have been resolved.

Directorate General Trade invites European merchants to submit complaints about foreign trade practices through its website. Analysts in the Directorate then research and analyze the complaints. If a complaint is accepted as valid, then a fiche concerning the issue is added to the database and the issue is added to the EU's ongoing agenda for international trade negotiations.

Each fiche is assigned a unique number. The first two digits are the last two digits of the year the issue was first entered into the database. Each fiche also lists the most recent date on which the fiche contents were reviewed. For example. Fiche 960048 concerns the imposition of a "Merchandise Processing Fee" by the United States. The date given on the fiche for "last update/check" is 21/11/2006. We can infer that the issue was accepted for the database in 1996 and was not settled by November 2006. Issues discussed in fiches with serial numbers of 02xxxx or lower and last review dates of 2006 or later will be classified as "continuing".

Serious trade disputes may be adjudicated through the World Trade Organization's Dispute Resolution Process. The nations of the world have shown a surprising willingness to push for changes in trade policies through this process, which will be described in detail in the next chapter.

We will be looking at the WTO cases arising between 2002 and 2007 where the US, the EU and Japan were suing each other for alleged breaches of international trade agreements through the Dispute Resolution Process (World Trade Organization, n.d.). Cases arising between 2002 and 2004 will be considered in the 2002 category. Cases arising between 2006 and 2007 will be grouped together as later cases.

For the purposes of classifying whether an issue listed in the Market Access Database was under discussion in 2002 and/or 2007, fiches with dates of 2002, 2003 and 2004 or earlier will be classified as 2002. Fiches with dates of 2005, 2006 and 20 07 will be classified as 2007. According to the dates on the fiche for the Merchandise Processing Fee, this issue would therefore be classified as under discussion in both 2002 and 2007.

Unfortunately, there is no public record of the positions of the European Union on issues that were settled between 2002 and 2007. The relevant fiches are simply removed from the Market Access Database. This may create an undercount of "settled" issues for the United States and Japan. The discussion in Chapter 9 will address this issue.

To facilitate comparisons, trade issues listed in these four data sources will be organized according to a common set of criteria. The classification system consists of subheadings under three major categories:

1. Issues that address the importation of goods and services. Subheadings include:
    a. Trade administration issues. This includes the administration of the international trade process, including the collection of any associated fees. It also includes tariffs, tariff quotas and the associated product classification system. The world has largely harmonized national systems for defining and classifying tariff items. However, definitions for the various levels of tariff classification are necessarily general, leaving room for ambiguities in classification. Although this book primarily considers non-tariff trade barriers, these issues have been considered for several reasons. There are only a few of these tariff-based issues. The disputes are usually not on whether the published tariffs are too high or too low, but whether the agreed-upon rates are in fact being applied.
    b. Government procurement issues. Explicit limits on foreign vendors and set-asides for national companies clearly limit international trade. Other types of vendor qualification requirements and/or set-asides that do not mention nationality may also limit foreign participation in government procurement markets.

Outside the United States, it is not uncommon for national markets for pharmaceuticals and medical devices to be dominated by buyers from the national health system. Vendor qualification requirements, bidding procedures and pricing policies may limit foreign participation.

   c. Sanitary and phytosanitary inspection requirements. Virtually every developed country has a system in place for inspecting and rejecting plants and animals at the border that could harbor undesirable pests. Sanitary requirements apply to animals. Plants are covered by phytosanitary requirements.
   d. Issues concerning access to service markets. The entry of individuals into the medical, legal, financial and educational service markets is commonly regulated through a licensing process. Corporations that want to open banks, provide power or invest in transportation or communications are typically required to go through a licensing or permitting process. These requirements may serve to limit foreign participation in these areas.
   e. Issues concerning safeguards, countervailing duties and anti-dumping policies. GATT allows countries to safeguard domestic interests against foreign competitors that buy their way in by under-pricing their products. To companies that are kept out of foreign markets, these rules may seem like trade barriers.

2. Issues related to the regulation of domestic commerce. Subcategories include:
   a. Issues concerning standards and technical requirements. Government regulation of product design, manufacturing or performance usually involves the development and enforcement of standards and/or technical requirements. For an analysis of the major systems, see Zuckerman (1997).

      A standard is a description of some aspect of a product or process that has been developed by the private sector for general use on a voluntary basis to achieve some goal. ISO 9000 is a standard. A technical requirement is a set of requirements governing some aspect of a product or process that has been developed by the government. Compliance is generally required.

      The OECD has summarized the results from a series of business surveys on exporter attitudes towards trade barriers (OECD, 2003). From the exporters' perspective, the most serious barriers are based on international differences in national product development and documentation requirements (OECD, 1999). In the US, for example, the UL logo is generally regarded as an indicator of a safe product. In the EU, it is the CE mark.

Although the UL and CE mark systems assure comparable levels of product safety, the two systems are designed around entirely different strategies. US manufacturers which are interested in selling their products in the EU will probably have to master the CE marking system.

In the US, the regulations issued by the Environmental Protection Agency are filled with technical requirements. The distinction between a standard and a technical requirement is being blurred by the growing tendency for government to mandate conformity to standards as if they were technical requirements.

Other national differences in standards and technical requirements can pose serious barriers to international trade. For example, the United States is the only major country to draft its requirements in the imperial system of measurement. Everyone else uses the metric system. This difference impedes trade.

b. Issues concerning the regulation of pharmaceuticals and medical devices. Most governments regulate the introduction of new pharmaceuticals and medical devices in national markets. The use of these products may create serious health risks. The review process is generally intended to make sure that the risks are well understood and that the potential rewards outweigh the risks. These are complex tasks, so the review process can be long and expensive. Trade disputes usually arise when the importing government refuses to accept the product data and certifications developed by the exporting government.
c. Issues concerning intellectual property rights. Virtually every country recognizes legal rights in patents, trademarks, copyrights and trade secrets. However, there are national differences in how these rights are defined and enforced, and these can clog up trade. National differences in intellectual property laws and their enforcement represent another major concern to the exporters in the surveys summarized by the OECD study (OECD, 2003). Exports to offending countries may be easy, even encouraged. However, the results can be a loss of major markets as faux products come back tenfold from the countries where the genuine articles were first sent.
d. Issues concerning business regulation. There are also several issues involving the administration of the trade process that cut across discrete product categories. These will be discussed as we compare national patterns in trade issue development and resolution. They include the taxation of foreign source income

and a failure to enforce non-discriminatory, transparent business practices, Corruption is the third major barrier to trade for most exporters identified in the OECD study (OECD, 2003). It is not as easily captured in studies such as this. The process of clearing customs can be lengthy and expensive, if everyone has their hand outstretched. The problems facing ethical exporters can be compounded if their national governments have penalties for participation in foreign corruption.

3. Issues concerning the regulation and promotion of exports. These include:
    a. Issues concerning export restrictions. Many countries restrict the export of selected products; this may be prompted by a desire to avoid domestic shortages or to safeguard critical technologies. As a result of the rising tide of international trade, many national economies are becoming increasingly dependent on exports from other countries.
    b. Issues concerning export subsidies. This includes direct subsidies, such as a payment for exporting, and export-based offsets, such as tax credits that are based on export performance.

5. THE POLITICAL ECONOMY OF TRADE POLICIES

The balance between free trade and mercantilism will be influenced by the organization of the political process. Who gets to decide an issue, what commitments have they made and how will the outcomes affect them? These factors will have a major impact on what decision alternatives are chosen. There are two levels to this review of the political process. One is "constitutional": what are the enduring patterns in the organization of decision making? The other is "political": how have recent changes in the economic and political circumstances of the country affected the pressures on the decision makers?

Achieving mutual advantage through commerce is not the only motivator for social behaviors. From time to time, we all act to promote social harmony or to avoid government coercion. Underlying the search for social harmony though, is the power of widely shared expectations on how we should relate to each other. These patterns of "culture" will also affect how we conduct our trade and organize our companies. In a very real sense, they provide a fundamental framework for the entire social system. National differences in the patterns of business culture have a real impact on national differences in economic competencies. If we want to account for national differences in trade barriers, we have to be ready to include analyses of cultural differences in the explanation.

6. CLOSING THOUGHTS

We have argued above that government decisions and policies often reflect the culture and organization of governance. This leads to questions about the nature of the trade barriers most often associated with each of our three polities. We would like to know what types of domestic interests are reflected in the emergence of these trade barriers. Can these barriers be effectively addressed? If not, is free trade possible? To understand these issues, we must examine them in the economic, political and social contexts in which they develop. We want to know if there are any patterns to the types of protectionist interests that are being advanced by governments. We can learn a lot by simply looking for patterns in the types of market restrictions that are promoted by a government.

So what? Comparative information on trade complaints and responses will be more interesting if we can tie it to differences among the three governments. We posed questions relating to why these disputes arise, their long-term effects and how they can be more easily resolved. To address these questions, we will be considering three pieces of the puzzle: the responses of the countries, the nature of the issues and the processes of trade policy harmonization. This general line of inquiry can point to specific sub-questions. Examples are:

1. An inquiry into the responses of the countries raises the question of whether the trade complaints that are raised against each of the three economies tend to fall into any particular pattern. Is there any evidence that the governors of each economy tend to place exceptional weight on specific types of interests in either defending against foreign competition or promoting access to the other economies? If so, why? Does there seem to be any relation between governments' trade concerns and any pressing issues in the national economy and polity?
2. An inquiry into the nature of the issues under contention raises the question of whether any particular facet of the international trade process is more prone to generate trade disputes. The governments of the world seem to be placing a renewed emphasis on environmental issues. Are trade disputes emerging because the development of new programs is affecting international trade? Have these issues been addressed through GATT agreements, or do they point to the need for additional agreements?

3. A concern for the process of trade policy harmonization leads to questions about the types of trade issues that tend to be raised, which ones tend to be resolved and how resolution best occurs. Gross counts of issues raised and issues resolved are important here. We will be looking for guesstimates as to whether issues are being resolved more rapidly than they are being raised. If so, then we may be sailing into calm seas and trade expansion. However, if trade issues are being raised more rapidly than they are being resolved, then we may be looking at some limits to the political appetite for further trade liberalization.

Our three issues are related. If we consider national responses together with trade harmonization processes, we come to questions about the impact of differences in national policy processes on relative success or failure in trade harmonization. Governments are not unitary creatures. Agencies that are charged with international responsibilities are likely to have different perspectives on international trade from interests representing businesses that are facing ever-stiffening international competition. Who is involved in the decisions in each polity that affect international trade? Do these processes tend to be dominated by trade advocates or trade opponents? An observation that the emergence of trade restrictions reflects the special nature of the policy processes would suggest that further trade liberalization may require more than stronger diplomacy in Geneva. We may have to rethink the processes of government decision making.

Consider the nature of the issues and the process of trade policy harmonization together. Does the nature of the agreement affect the prospects for discord? Consider international agreements on tariffs and tariff nomenclature. This is a very complex area. However, the government commitments in the relevant agreements are very specific. Does this make discord more or less likely? In contrast, government commitments in areas such as sanitary and phytosanitary (SPS) regulation can be very general, often consisting of little more than a pledge to use scientific evidence in making SPS decisions. Does the imprecision of the language contribute to the intractability of the disputes? If so, then our way out may be to continue developing an international consensus on the factual bases for these disputes.

Given the limitations of the scope of the study, we will be looking for suggestions rather than conclusions. To take even this first stab though, we will be looking at the current system of international agreements (Chapter 2), patterns of national decision-making (Chapters 3, 5 and 7) and the actual trade disputes involving each economy (Chapters 4, 6 and 8). We will return to the questions raised here about the implications for international trade in Chapters 9 and 10.

REFERENCES

Anderton, C. and J. Carter (2001a), "The impact of war on trade: an interrupted time series study", *Journal of Peace Research*, 38(4), pp. 445–457.
Anderton, C. and J. Carter (2001b), "On disruption of trade by war: a reply to Barbieri and Levy", *Journal of Peace Research*, 38(5), pp. 625–628.
Baier, S. and J. Bergstrand (2001), "The growth of world trade: tariffs, transport costs and income similarity", *Journal of International Economics*, 53(1), pp. 1–27.
Barbieri, K. (2002), *The Liberal Illusion: Does Trade Promote Peace?* Ann Arbor, The University of Michigan Press.
Barbieri, K and J. Levy (1999), "Sleeping with the enemy: the impact of war on trade", *Journal of Peace Research*, 36(4), pp. 463–479.
Barbieri, K. and J. Levy (2001), "Does war impede trade? A response to Anderton and Carter", *Journal of Peace Research*, 38(5), pp. 619–624.
Conybeare, J. (1987), *Trade Wars: The Theory and Practice of International Commercial Rivalry*, New York, Columbia University Press.
Dorussen, H. (2002), "Trade and conflict in multi-country models: a rejoinder", *Journal of Peace Research*, 39(1), pp. 115–118.
European Union, Directorate General Trade (irregular), *Market Access Database*, at http://madb.europa.eu/madb_barriers/barriers_select.htm, accessed 30 May 2009.
Fischer, Thomas (2000), *The United States, The European Union and the "Globalization" of World Trade: Allies or Adversaries?* Westport, Quorum Books.
Friedman, T. (1999), *The Lexus and the Olive Tree*, New York, Farrar, Straus and Giroux.
Hegre, H. (2000), "Development and the liberal peace: what does it take to be a trading state?" *Journal of Peace Research*, 37(1), pp. 5–30.
Irwin, D. (1999), "Historical perspectives on U.S. trade policy", National Bureau of Economic Research at www.nber.org/reporter/winter99/irwin.html, accessed 28 May 2009.
Krugman, P. (1997), *Pop Internationalism*, Cambridge, MA, MIT Press.
Laird, S and A. Yeats (1988), *Trends in Non-Tariff Barriers in Developing Countries*, Washington, the World Bank.
Laird, S. and A. Yeats (1990), *Quantitative Methods for Trade Barrier Analysis*, New York, New York University Press.
New York Times (2008), "Global trade talks said to collapse", 30 July, p. 1.
OECD (Organisation for Economic Co-operation and Development), Working Party of the Trade Committee (1999), "An assessment of the costs for international traders meeting regulatory requirements", TD/TC/WP(99) 8/FINAL.
OECD (Organisation for Economic Co-operation and Development), Working Party of the Trade Committee (2003), "Overview of non-tariff barriers: findings from existing business surveys", TD/TC/WP(2002) 38/FINAL, Paris: OECD.
Ostry, S. (1997), "Globalization, domestic policies and the need for harmonization", in L. Waverman, W. Comanor and A. Goto (eds) *Competition Policy in the Global Economy: Modalities for Cooperation*, London, Routledge.
Polanyi, K. (1944), *The Great Transformation*, New York, Farrar and Rinehart.
Rolfe, S. and J. Burtle (1973), *The Great Wheel: The World Monetary System, A Reinterpretation*, New York, Quadrangle.

Schaffer, R., B. Earle and F. Agusti (2008), *International Business Law and its Environment (7th edn.)*, Ohio: South–Western Cengage.
Schumpeter, J. (1950), *Capitalism, Socialism and Democracy*, New York, Harper.
Trotman, L. (2004), "The WTO: the institutional contradictions", in M. Moore (ed.) *Doha and Beyond: The Future of the Multilateral Trading System*, Cambridge, Cambridge University Press, pp. 19–25.
United Nations (2004), *International Trade Statistics Yearbook*, vol. II.
United States Trade Representative (annual), *Report on Foreign Trade Barriers*, Washington at www.ustr/gov/Document_Library/Reports_Publications/Section_Index.html, accessed 30 May 2009.
Wikipedia (2008), "General Agreement on Tariffs and Trade" at en.wikipedia.org/wiki/General_Agreement_on_Tariffs_and_Trade, accessed 30 May 2009.
Womack, J., D. Jones and D. Roos (1997), *The Machine That Changed the World: The Story of Lean Manufacturing*, New York, The Free Press.
World Trade Organization (1947), *General Agreement on Tariffs and Trade*
World Trade Organization (1996), "Ministerial declaration on trade in information technology products" at www.wto.org/english/docs_e/legal_e/itadec_e.htm, accessed 30 May 2009.
World Trade Organization (n.d.), "Dispute settlement: the disputes" at http://www.wto.org/english/tratop_e/dispu_e/find_dispu_cases_e.htm, accessed 30 May 2009.
Zuckerman, Amy (1997), *International Standards Desk Reference: Your Passport to World Markets, ISO 9000, CE Mark, QS-9000, SSM, ISO 1400, Q 9000, American, European and Global Standards Systems*, New York, Amacon.

2. International agreements

1. INTRODUCTION

International trade does not take place in a legal vacuum. An elaborate system of international agreements has been developed since 1945 that is intended to protect and promote the emergence of a global market in goods and services. Even when the provisions of these agreements are not directly on point on a particular trade issue, they frame the expectations of the international community in the area of free trade and intergovernmental relations. In some cases, the complaints that each of our three polities raise about the other two can only be understood in the context of these agreements.

The most ambitious period of international negotiations took place during the Uruguay Round. The final agreement for the Round was signed on 15 April 1994. In total, there were about 60 agreements approved during the Round. The 15 most important were listed as annexes to the master agreement establishing the World Trade Organization. In addition, there were a series of "plurilateral" trade agreements that only included some of the WTO membership, as well as a series of unilateral ministerial decisions. This chapter will focus on the 15 agreements included in the annexes to the Final Act (World Trade Organization, 1994k).

The number, scope and detail of these agreements is one indication of the complexity of the international marketplace. This situation relates to an issue mentioned in Chapter 1: are the institutions and procedures supporting international trade up to the political issues and regulatory challenges posed by government policies affecting international trade?

The reader may note that the Uruguay Round agreements are, in general, more concerned with national actions affecting the import process. Our review of the actual trade disputes will suggest that many arise from the application of measures that seem to be directed at domestic regulations. The causes and consequences of this discrepancy will be discussed in Chapter 10.

2. THE FRAMEWORK AGREEMENTS

2.1 The General Agreement on Tariffs and Trade

The original GATT agreement (World Trade Organization, 1947) rests on a few fundamental principles. The first is a preference for tariffs over quotas. All restrictions on imports from another GATT member are to be based only on duties, taxes or other charges. By implication, quotas are to be phased out (GATT, Article XI).

The signatory states are also pledged to a policy of non-discrimination. Once a product is admitted through customs, it is expected to be treated in the same manner as a product of national origin (GATT, Article III). The national regulations governing the manufacture, handling and use of products should not afford protection to domestic production. However, government procurement of products for government purposes are exempt from this requirement (GATT, Article III, paragraph 8a).

Probably the most significant provision is the ban on discriminating among other GATT signatories. In effect, every member state is to extend most-favored nation status to all other signatories. "Any advantage, favour, privilege, or immunity granted by any contracting party to any product originating in or destined for any other country shall be accorded . . . unconditionally . . . for . . . all other contracting parties" (GATT, Article I).

This provision had two major consequences. Tariffs were slashed as every country benefited from the lowest tariffs extended to any country. Furthermore, subsequent tariff reductions had to be negotiated in multilateral "rounds" since a reductions granted to any country was equally applicable to all other countries. The "rounds" or trade negotiations resulting in dramatic tariff reductions mentioned in Chapter 1 constituted the successful implementation of the promise implicit in Article I of GATT.

The GATT offers several grounds for limiting the application of the non-discrimination principles. There is a general exception for any measure adopted by a contracting party to protect public morals, protect human, animal or plant life or health, related to the importation of gold or silver, or that is related to the conservation of exhaustible natural resources (GATT, Article XX).

GATT also authorizes the contracting parties to impose extra duties in the event that exporting countries are "dumping" their exports. Dumping is defined as selling for "less than the comparable price in the ordinary course of trade in the exporting country" (GATT, Article VI). However, there are some restrictions. The country imposing the anti-dumping duty must first determine that it is causing material injury to domestic industry (Article 6a). The magnitude of the anti-dumping duties is limited to the margin of dumping. Similar provisions limit the application of "countervailing duties", which can be imposed by importing countries to offset the impact of subsidies granted by the exporting states.

Finally, the terms of GATT authorize the negotiation and organization of customs unions and free trade areas. However, "the purpose of a customs union or of a free trade area should be to facilitate trade between the constituent territories and not to raise barriers to the trade of other contracting parties" (GATT, Article XXIV).

The results from the GATT agreement have been impressive. Over the course of 50 years, major reductions in tariffs were negotiated. In the US, for example, average tariffs on industrial goods dropped to near 5 per cent *ad valorem* (Irwin, 1995). The US negotiating position on many electronic products is "zero for zero": the elimination of US tariffs in exchange for similar concessions from the other side (World Trade Organization, 1996b).

GATT has been revised many times. The most comprehensive expansion of international trade agreements took place in the 1986–1994 Uruguay Round of trade negotiations (World Trade Organization, 1994k). The Final Act of the Uruguay Round wraps a refinement of the GATT agreement around the creation of the World Trade Organization and the conclusion of 15 other general agreements on specific trade sectors or issues. However, the basic principles of GATT have remained unchanged.

2.2 The World Trade Organization

The major breakthrough of the 1994 Uruguay Round was authorization for creation of a World Trade Organization. This is the successor to the ill-fated International Trade Organization that was expected to implement the original version of GATT.

The WTO has three major functions. It provides a neutral venue for negotiating international trade agreements. It is the depository for international agreements affecting trade and it hosts the dispute resolution process (World Trade Organization, n.d.c).

There are three major levels of organization within the WTO hierarchy. All 150+ members of the WTO participate in all levels of the organization. However, the terms of participation and the scope of issues considered varies according to the organizational level. WTO members periodically meet as the Ministerial Conference to consider all major issues. Between meetings of the Ministerial Conference, the WTO membership is organized into the General Council, the Dispute Resolution Body and the Trade Policy Review Body. The differences in the organization and functioning of these groups reflects the differences in their responsibilities. Both the Dispute Resolution Body and the Trade Policy Review Body report to the General Council (World Trade Organization, n.d.c.).

2.3 The Dispute Resolution Process

The General Agreement on Tariffs and Trade (1947) sets forth a basic system for resolving trade disputes. Article XXIII, "Nullification or Impairment", states that if any party believes that "any benefit accruing . . . under this Agreement is being . . . impaired . . . as the result of . . . the failure of another contracting party to carry out its obligations under this Agreement" it should start by making "written representations" to the offending party suggesting ways of resolving the issue.

If these consultations do not resolve the issue, then the matter may be referred to Contracting Parties to the GATT Agreement. The Contracting Parties are then charged with investigating the matter and making recommendations to the countries involved. If the matter is considered to be sufficiently serious, then the offended country may suspend any concession extended to the offending country under GATT (Article XXIII).

This system in short, didn't work. Countries charged with violating GATT agreements were not required to participate in the process. Panel decisions did not have the weight of either international or domestic law. The prevailing parties could not implement the awards in their favor, which often involved imposing additional duties on imports from the losing party, until the decision had been adopted by the GATT Council of Ministers. Under the original organization of the Contracting Parties, every country in the Council, including the offending party, had a veto over Council decisions. Participation and compliance with a panel decision was, in effect, voluntary (Schaffer, Earle and Agusti, 2008, p. 299).

In the absence of a strong multilateral process for resolving trade disputes arising under GATT, the member states tended to resort to unilateral measures to defend their interpretations of their GATT rights. This has been especially true for the US. International resistance to US claims to unilateral enforcement rights will be discussed at length in Chapter 4. The problem is that mutual compliance with multilateral agreements is at the core of the GATT process. As long as enforcement is handled on a unilateral basis, then states are implicitly free to interpret their GATT obligations in ways that favor their actions and interests.

The acceptance of the Dispute Resolution Understanding (World Trade Organization n.d.b) with the organization of the WTO greatly strengthened the process for resolving disputes over national interpretations of international trade agreements (World Trade Organization, 1994k, Annex

2). International disputes over national compliance with GATT are now referred to committees, or "panels", that are drawn from representatives from countries that are not involved in the dispute. The panels are organized by the WTO Office of the General Council, which is also responsible for managing the subsequent processes. As a result, the offending parties are no longer able to veto the effective initiation of dispute resolution procedures. The process is conducted on behalf of the Dispute Resolution Body, which consists of all WTO members sitting as a committee of the whole (Shaffer, Earle and Agusti, 2008, pp. 293–294).

The process is initiated when one country asks another for WTO consultations over a trade dispute. A DS file is opened when a formal request has been made to refer an issue to the dispute resolution process. However, the complainant may ask for a delay in the appointment of a panel if there is a chance that the dispute could be resolved informally. If the parties do not report within 60 days that the issue has been resolved, the complaining party may request that a panel be appointed to hear the case. A panel consists of three to five members who are appointed by the General Council. Either party may protest the panel nominations, but only for compelling reasons.

A dispute resolution panel is charged with making an objective assessment of the facts and determining whether either party has violated a WTO obligation. Decisions are based on submissions of facts and arguments on law by the parties. A dispute resolution panel can also call on outside experts for scientific and technical advice. Other countries with substantial interests in the issue can request the right to make presentations to the panel. The panel must make a written report on the case to the Dispute Settlement Body within six months.

If the losing side wants to appeal an unfavorable panel decision, then it may ask for the appointment of an appellate panel. Such panels have an ongoing organization: the members are appointed for four-year terms. The appellate panel can only consider the issues of law raised in the original dispute resolution panel proceedings on which the contending parties disagree.

Regardless of whether a decision is appealed or not, the panel decision will include a recommendation as to the measures that the prevailing party may take against the losing party because of its violation of international obligations. The panel decision must then be adopted by a majority vote of the WTO members. If the decision is ratified, the offending state is given a period of time in which to come into compliance. If it does not comply with the terms of the decision, an arbitrator is appointed who will specify the time period for compliance. If the offending state does not take the actions set forth in the decision within the compliance period, then the wronged party may take retaliatory steps against the offending country. These retaliatory measures will consist of suspensions of the WTO obligations that would otherwise be owed to the offending state. The goal is to compensate the prevailing party for the losses incurred by the violations by the offending state of GATT benefits. The sanctions can be maintained until the offending state has come into compliance with its WTO obligations (World Trade Organization n.d.b).

The WTO Dispute Resolution Process has proven to be quite popular. A total of 397 disputes were taken to the WTO during the 13-year period between 1994 and 2007. The US has been the country most involved in the process, both as complainant and as respondent. We will discuss a number of these WTO cases in the following chapters. Data on the frequencies with which our three governments filed suit in the WTO Dispute Resolution Process are set forth in Table 2.1. For Europe, this table only includes cases in which the EU was either a complainant or a respondent. The table does not include the many cases involving EU member states as separate countries.

3. AGREEMENTS GOVERNING IMPORT ADMINISTRATION

The basic principles of GATT have been supplemented by the ratification of a series of additional intergovernmental agreements on trade policies and practices. The terms of many of these agreements are relevant for the trade disputes that are discussed in the balance of this book.

The primary focus in this book will be on the failures of efforts to liberalize international trade. However, the very fact that the governments of the world have negotiated these agreements speaks to the power of their commitment to free trade. A balanced view of the successes and failures in trade liberalization must therefore cover the agreements that seem to be working (because, in part, no trade complaints have been filed on the basis of these agreements) as well as those agreements that are the subject of international conflict and dispute.

The process of international trade negotiations contributes to the necessity for the Dispute Resolution Process. The critical provisions of international agreements must be sufficiently broad to cover foreseeable contingencies and contending points of view. A willingness to fudge points of conflict with ambiguous language is likely to be a useful negotiating strategy. Once the agreement has been ratified, the differences can be ironed out through negotiations and, if necessary, litigation. Fighting over a few points after an agreement has come into force may be an acceptable

Table 2.1 Number of dispute resolution cases involving the three governments

Japan complainant		Japan respondent	
United States	8	European Union	6
Indonesia	2	United States	6
Brazil	1	Korea	2
Canada	1	Canada	1
Total	12	Total	15
European Union complainant		European Union respondent	
United States	31	United States	17
India	9	Canada	8
Argentina	7	Brazil	6
Japan	6	India	5
Canada	5	Thailand	4
Brazil	4	Argentina	3
Korea	4	Guatemala	3
Chile	3	Honduras	3
Mexico	3	Korea	3
China	1	Mexico	3
Australia	1	Australia	2
Indonesia	1	Chile	2
Pakistan	1	Norway	2
Total	76	Peru	2
		Columbia	1
		Ecuador	1
		New Zealand	1
		Uruguay	1
		Total	67
United States complainant		United States respondent	
European Union	17	European Union	31
Japan	6	Canada	14
Korea	6	Brazil	9
Mexico	6	Japan	8
Canada	5	India	7
China	5	Mexico	7
Argentina	4	Korea	7
Australia	4	Thailand	4
Brazil	4	Argentina	3
India	4	Australia	2
Belgium	3	Chile	2
Ireland	3	China	2
Philippines	3	New Zealand	2

Table 2.1 (continued)

France	2	Taipei	1
Greece	2	Aruba	1
Chile	1	Columbia	1
Denmark	1	Costa Rica	1
Egypt	1	Ecuador	1
Hungary	1	Indonesia	1
Netherlands	1	Malaysia	1
Pakistan	1	Norway	1
Portugal	1	Philippines	1
Romania	1	Switzerland	1
Total	82	Venezuela	1
		Total	109

Source: World Trade Organization (n.d.d).

cost for achieving multilateral commitment on the many points on which everyone agrees.

In short, most of the international trade agreements commit signatory states to trade policies that are to be evaluated in accordance with such criteria as "reasonableness", or "international harmonization". Agreements relying on terms such as these do not really reflect an understanding about what the signatory states should be doing. Rather, they constitute an international consensus on the issues that should govern policies in these trade areas together with a vague commitment to better define the contents of these evaluative terms in some future negotiations. Many of the disputes we will be discussing can be viewed as volleys in these negotiation wars. We will return to the question of whether these processes are the best avenues for conducting these negotiations at the end of this book.

There are several agreements addressing the importation and customs processes. These are not directly relevant for the issues discussed in this book. The WTO has a general policy of trade facilitation through encouraging member states to harmonize, simplify and promote the transparency of their trade processing systems. Several formal agreements have come out of these efforts.

The *Agreement on Rules of Origin* (World Trade Organization 1994g) marked a substantial advance in international efforts to develop basic principles governing the process of defining national origin for goods undergoing import review. The 1994 *Agreement on Customs Valuation* (World Trade Organization, 1994d) is intended to unify national practices in the process of calculating dutiable value on the basis of transaction value. The

Agreement on Preshipment Inspection (World Trade Organization 1994f) is intended to prevent importing countries from using pre-shipment inspection requirements as a basis for discriminating among exporting countries; pre-shipment inspection requirements must be applied in a non-discriminatory manner. The Agreement also sets up a system for adjudicating disputes between exporters and inspection agencies. Some countries require importers to obtain a government license. This policy is subject to the *Agreement on Import Licensing Procedures* (World Trade Organization, 1994e). Neither the US, the EU nor Japan licenses importers.

Several agreements address various aspects of national policies concerning anti-dumping and safeguard procedures. *The Agreement on Implementation of Article VI (Anti-dumping)*, (World Trade Organization, 1994c; Schaffer, Agusti and Earle (2008) pp. 358–362) defines "dumping" as exporting products for sale below "normal" prices. The normal price is usually considered to be the price in the home market. Dumping is prohibited under the GATT rules (Schaffer, Agusti and Earle, 2008, p. 358; Anti-Dumping Agreement Article 2.1). Countries subject to dumping can impose countervailing duties on the offending products.

The original agreement on anti-dumping procedures was concluded in the Tokyo Round of the GATT talks. The new agreement negotiated during the Uruguay Round built on this prior agreement. Before measures can be taken, a state must prove that dumping occurred and that it caused injury to a domestic industry. The new Anti-Dumping Agreement (ADA) tightens up the provisions in the Tokyo Agreement on how these findings can be made. It also clarifies the relation between actions taken by domestic authorities and any international actions taken through the WTO's Dispute Resolution Process.

The new provisions on the process of initiating an anti-dumping case include a requirement that all interested parties must be given meaningful opportunities to present evidence. Proceedings can't go forward if the dumping margin is less than 2 per cent of the "normal" product value or if the value of dumped products is less than 3 per cent of the total value of imports of that product into the complaining country.

The revised ADA includes new rules on how to determine whether a product has been dumped. New rules are set forth governing how comparisons must be made between the export price and the "normal" price of the product (ADA, 2.2 and 2.4). Sometimes the normal price can't be assessed directly. The revised ADA includes new rules on how a "constructed" or estimated price can be developed. Calculations of dumping, product equivalencies and dumping margins must recognize the differences among national markets in cost and demand factors in order to come up with a fair comparison.

The importing country must also show that the dumping caused injury to domestic industry producing like products (ADA, Article 3.5). "Domestic industry" is defined in the revised ADA as the domestic producers of like products as a whole or as the industries whose production constitutes a majority of total domestic production. It is not enough, in other words, to just find injury to a small group of companies. The impact of dumping must essentially be felt industry-wide.

Anti-dumping tariffs can only be imposed on goods of the type that were dumped which originate from the company that is responsible for the dumping. The magnitude of the anti-dumping duties is limited to the dumping margin.

A new provision requires countries initiating anti-dumping procedures or imposing sanctions on dumped products to give a prompt and detailed notification to the Committee on Anti-dumping Practices. The Committee is an arm of the WTO. It is intended to provide all involved parties with an opportunity to consult on any issues related to the anti-dumping action. Any measures taken must expire within five years unless there is a finding that dumping would be likely to continue if the sanctions were removed.

The Agreement on Subsidies and Countervailing Measures (SCM) (World Trade Organization, 1994j) builds on the *Agreement on Interpretation and Application of Articles VI, XVI and XXIII*, which was negotiated during the Tokyo round.

The Agreement defines a subsidy as a benefit provided by a government for a domestic firm or industry through income or price supports, by providing funds, grants or loans at less than non-guaranteed market rates, by not collecting taxes, by providing investment capital, goods or services, or by purchasing goods or services at above-market rates.

The SCM Agreement only applies to a "specific subsidy", which is defined as a subsidy that is only available to an enterprise or group of enterprises that are within the jurisdiction of the authority granting the subsidy. A tax provision favoring US shipping companies, for example, would not normally be regarded as a specific subsidy since the US Internal Revenue Service (IRS) does not have jurisdiction over the maritime industry. Subsidies provided to US flag carriers by the Maritime Administration (Marad) would be regarded as a subsidy, since Marad is responsible for promoting the US maritime industry.

Specific subsidies are classified under the SCM Agreement into three categories. Any arrangement which ties the availability of a subsidy to a particular level of import substitution or export performance falls in the "prohibited" category.

"Actionable" subsidies are those arrangements which are not prohibited, but create serious prejudice to the interests of other member states.

"Serious prejudice" is defined as injury to the domestic industry of another country or the impairment of some benefit that would otherwise accrue under GATT to another member state. Serious prejudice is assumed to exist if the subsidy exceeds 5 per cent of the value of the product. The burden of proof is on the sponsoring nation to show that the subsidy in question does not cause serious prejudice to the complaining nation.

Member states affected by actionable subsidies may refer the matter to the WTO's Dispute Resolution Process. If this concludes that serious prejudice exists, the offending state must either withdraw the subsidy or remove the adverse effects.

"Socially beneficial subsidies" are not actionable under the Subsidies Agreement. These include subsidies that are intended to promote the expansion of knowledge, subsidies to depressed regions and subsidies to companies to meet new environmental requirements. A member nation which believes that a non-actionable subsidy causes serious prejudice may ask for a determination of the matter.

If a member country finds that a prohibited or actionable foreign subsidy has seriously prejudiced national economic interests, then it may impose a countervailing duty on the imported good in an amount equal to the value of the subsidy. All relevant economic factors must be taken into account in making a determination about the presence of a subsidy and the extent of the prejudice.

Export subsidies and import substitution subsidies are explicitly prohibited under the Agreement. An export subsidy is one that is contingent on export performance. An import substitution subsidy is contingent on using domestic products or services in lieu of imported ones. An importing country can invoke a WTO dispute resolution procedure when facing subsidized imports, even without a showing of domestic injury. The importing country can also impose countervailing duties against the subsidized goods. However, there first has to be a finding of domestic injury.

The Subsidies Agreement allows governments to offer a wide range of subsidies for domestic business operations. However, domestic subsidies may be banned under the Subsidies Agreement if they have an "adverse effect" on international trade. An adverse effect exists if a domestic subsidy causes injury to the domestic industries of another WTO member, impairs the rights of another country under GATT, or causes "serious prejudice" to another WTO member. Domestic subsidies must be industry- or product-specific before they can be reviewed under the Subsidies Agreement.

"Serious prejudice" is presumed to exist if the domestic subsidy exceeds 5 per cent of subsidized product value, if the subsidy covers a firm's operating losses or if the government forgives a debt owed by the subsidized company. "Serious prejudice" may exist if the domestic subsidy impedes world trade in a particular product, leads to lost sales due to price undercutting, or causes an increase in the subsidizing country's world market share for primary products.

The SCM Agreement establishes a rebuttable assumption that any subsidy with per product values in excess of 5 per cent causes serious prejudice. On the other hand, countervailing duty investigations must be terminated if the level of subsidy is 1 per cent of the product value or if the volume of subsidized imports is negligible. All countervailing duty investigations must be completed within 18 months of initiation and any countervailing duty that is imposed must be terminated within five years.

Special rules are set forth in the Agreement on SCM for developing countries and for civil aircraft. The assumption that subsidies that are more than 5 per cent per exported product cause serious prejudice does not apply to civilian aircraft. State funding that becomes available only if aircraft sales are below expectations does not give rise to an assumption of serious prejudice.

The Agreement on Safeguards (World Trade Organization, 1994h) states that even if there is no dumping by exporting companies or subsidies by exporting countries, importing countries are entitled to impose "safeguards" to protect domestic industries from an unforeseen increase in imports which are likely to cause serious injury to domestic industry or dislocations caused by foreign competition (GATT, Article XIX).

The Agreement on Safeguards prohibits the use of "grey area" measures, such as voluntary restraint agreements that involve "voluntary" pledges by the exporting country to unilaterally limit exports and to undertake other types of "orderly marketing arrangements". Any such agreements had to be phased out by 31 December 1999.

Safeguard investigations must give all interested parties opportunity to present evidence, including evidence on whether a safeguard measure would be in the public interest. If the situation is critical, a provisional safeguard measure can be imposed immediately, but for no longer than 200 days.

The Agreement on Safeguards limits safeguard measures to those which are necessary to prevent or remedy serious injury or to facilitate industry adjustment. In general, safeguard measures should not last longer than four years. Quantitative safeguards, such as quotas, should be applied equitably among all relevant exporting countries. Any safeguards that are imposed should not reduce imports below their average for the last three years, unless there is clear justification for such a measure.

The Agreement assumes that the country imposing safeguards will offer compensation to affected countries. If consultations over the compensation are not successful, then the affected countries may withdraw equivalent concessions under GATT agreements from the country imposing safeguards. However, these retaliation measures can't be taken if the safeguard measure was taken as a result of an absolute increase in imports, conformed to the terms of the Safeguard Agreement and is less than three years old.

4. AGREEMENTS COVERING TRADE IN SPECIFIC GOODS

4.1 The Agreement on Agriculture (World Trade Organization, 1994a)

This is a framework agreement that is primarily intended to define the agenda for future negotiations. The Agreement addresses two conflicting policy initiatives. On the one hand, some countries (usually the major agricultural exporters) are looking for reforms that will promote market access, limit the use of market-distorting policies and establish a greater reliance on free-market pricing mechanisms. Other nations, generally the less-developed countries (LDCs), want to maintain a strong commitment to policies intended to promote market stability and to protect rural employment and income.

In the area of promoting free markets in agricultural goods, the countries signing the Agreement are pledged to replace market-limiting measures such as quotas with tariffs at a level that provides the same level of protection. The developed countries will then have six years in which to reduce their agricultural tariffs by at least 36 per cent. The less-developed counties will have ten years in which to reduce their agricultural tariffs by at least 24 per cent. Domestic agricultural support measures, such as technical support services and SPS requirements, are excluded from the tariffization and tariff reduction requirements.

Tariff quotas that currently account for less than 3 per cent of domestic consumption can be increased to account for at least 6 per cent. Special "safeguard" tariffs can be imposed where quotas have been "tariffized" to protect against sudden import surges.

Developing countries signing the Agricultural Agreement are also required to reduce the value of their agricultural export subsidies to a level that is 36 per cent and the quantity of subsidized agricultural exports 21 per cent below the 1986–1990 base period. This reduction is to take place over the six-year implementation period. Developing countries are committed to reducing their export subsidies by 21 per cent over a ten-year period.

In addition to the tariff and quota commitments, the countries signing the

Agricultural Agreement are also committed to reducing their "Aggregate Measure of Support" (AMS) for agriculture. The developed countries are to reduce their AMS by at least 20 per cent and the developing countries by 13.3 per cent over their implementation periods.

The Agreement on Agriculture was never meant as more than a statement of policy and a partial liberalization that would lead to a more comprehensive and detailed set of reforms in the next set of negotiations. Agricultural reform has been a major agenda item for the current Doha Round of GATT/WTO multilateral negotiations. Unfortunately, the negotiations seem to have collapsed without agreement because the leading countries have not been able to come to agreement on measures to reform international trade in agricultural goods. In broad terms, the developed countries have not been willing to make sufficient reductions in their agricultural subsidies. In turn, the developing countries have refused to open their markets to subsidized exports (*New York Times*, 2008).

4.2 The Agreement on Sanitary and Phytosanitary Measures (World Trade Organization 1994i)

Virtually every set of complaints by each of our three parties against the other two includes vigorous denunciations of their adoption of sanitary and phytosanitary measures that discriminate against imported agricultural products. "Sanitary" measures are concerned with the health and safety of animals and animal products. Measures taken to protect against the introduction or spread of bovine spongiform encephalopathy (BSE) are an example of sanitary measures. "Phytosanitary" measures are intended to protect plants and plant by-products. The quarantine of oranges grown in California to prevent the spread of the Mediterranean fruit fly is an example of a phytosanitary measure.

The rights of governments to impose these types of measures is explicitly defended in the Agreement on Sanitary and Phytosanitary Measures as long as they are consistent with the provisions of the agreement (Art. 2.1). However, these measures should only be applied when and to the extent that they are necessary to protect human, animal or plant life or health (Arts 2.3 and 2.4). Sanitary and phytosanitary measures must be based on scientific principles and a comprehensive evaluation of the contexts in which they are to be applied (Arts 2.2 and 5.2). They must not provide a basis for unjustified discrimination against imported agricultural products (Art. 2.3). The measures adopted must not arbitrarily or unjustifiably discriminate against member states where the same or similar conditions prevail.

Members are encouraged to base their measures on internationally accepted standards, guidelines or recommendations where they exist. More stringent measures may be taken if they result in a higher level of protection. These decisions must be based on scientific justifications or on consistent risk analyses that are based on appropriate risk assessments.

Several intergovernmental institutions have been developed to coordinate and support national efforts to ensure the safety and health of agricultural resources. The Food and Agriculture Organization provides the overall umbrella. Research and promotion of sanitary measures is sponsored by the OIE, the Office International des Epizooties (also known as the World Animal Health Organization). The safety and health of plants are addressed by the IPPC, the International Plant Protection Convention. Activities carried out under the IPPC are governed by the Commission on Phytosanitary Measures. One of the activities is the development of a series of draft technical requirements which are listed in the International Standards for Phytosanitary Measures. Measures that have been approved by the OIE or the IPPC for international adoption are codified in the Codex Alimentarius by the Codex Commission. National measures that are based on the Codex are considered to be in compliance with the GATT Agreement.

4.3 The Agreement on Textiles and Clothing (World Trade Organization 1994n)

One major success has been the phasing out of the Multi-Fiber Arrangement (MFA). Under the original MFA, the countries that import textiles were involved in a complex series of bilateral quotas and other trade restrictions with the countries that were exporting textiles. These arrangements seriously impeded world trade in textiles. The was no mechanism for adjusting the quota arrangements to reflect international changes in national development and textile production terms. The MFA was also not responsive to the growing complexity of the international textile supply chain. It was not uncommon to find that the spinning of yarn, cloth weaving, cloth cutting, basic garment assembly and putting the final details on a piece of clothing were done in different countries. The MFA did not provide an efficient mechanism for optimizing these arrangements.

The Agreement on Textiles and Clothing was intended to bring trade in textiles and clothing into the GATT/WTO framework. The shift in the trading rules took place in stages. The negotiations were based on three lists of products: yarns, textiles, and textile products and clothing. On 1 January 1995, each importing country that was party to the Agreement selected products from the three lists that accounted for not less than 16 per cent of their relevant imports by value. An additional 17 per cent of textiles imports were integrated into the normal WTO system on 1 January 1998. Another 18 per cent were integrated into the normal trading rules on 1 January 2002. The remaining 49 per cent were shifted over to the normal GATT rules on 1 January 2005.

The Agreement balanced the interests of the textile importers and the exporting countries. The prior MFA rules were maintained for the trades that were not yet covered by the Agreement. However, the quotas covered by these prior rules were allowed to increase more rapidly than had been allowed under the old rules. The expansion factor for the old quotas was 16 per cent in the first stage, 25 per cent for the second stage and 27 per cent for the third stage. Although the exporting countries were losing their quotas over the ten-year period of the Agreement, they were allowed to ship more under the old quotas before the MFA expired. However, there were potential limits to this growth. The Agreement allowed the importing countries to take safeguarding measures if the expansion of the import quotas threatened domestic industries.

The operation of the Agreement on Textiles and Clothing was managed by a new body, the Council for Trade in Goods, which also sponsored the Textile Monitoring Body. Disputes are adjudicated through the Dispute Settlement Understanding. Although the Council continues in a general role, the Agreement and the Textile Monitoring Body lapsed on 1 January 2005.

4.4 The Information Technology Agreement (ITA) (World Trade Organization 1996b)

This is not, strictly speaking, a result of the Uruguay Round. The ITA was negotiated during the Singapore Ministerial Conference by 29 countries in 1996. It came into force on 1 April 1997 after it was signed by a sufficient number of countries to account for 90 per cent of international trade in information technology products. This was one of the major trade initiatives sponsored by the United States (Fischer, 2000).

The sole focus of the ITA is on cutting tariffs. There are three basic principles: all products listed in the Agreement must be covered, all tariffs on covered items must be reduced to zero and any other applicable duties and charges must also be reduced to zero. These concessions are covered by the most-favored nation provision of GATT. The benefits therefore must also accrue to other WTO members, even if they did not sign the ITA. Although the ITA provides for the review of non-tariff trade barriers, there are no binding commitments in the Agreement to reduce or eliminate these barriers.

A Committee of Participants on the Expansion of Trade in Information

Technology Products was organized by the ITA signatory countries to monitor the implementation of ITA commitments. The Committee has considered such issues as national differences in tariff classifications for information technology products, consultations on non-tariff trade barriers and bringing new members into the Agreement.

In 1997, 40 countries participating in the Information Technology Agreement, including the European Union and the United States, agreed to eliminate all tariffs on computer and telecommunications components by 1 January 2000.

4.5 The 1994 Agreement on Trade in Services (GATS) (World Trade Organization 1994o)

This parallels the major provisions of GATT regarding trade in goods. GATS is intended to cover a very wide range of services including services in the areas of architecture and engineering, legal and consulting, travel and tourism, rental and leasing, distribution and courier services, entertainment, education, franchising and others.

There are three major components to the GATS Agreement. The first part sets forth the basic rights and responsibilities of the signatory states. The second part lists the areas and schedules for implementing the commitments made by the signatory states. The third component of the GATS Agreement contains a series of annexes listing the special circumstances for specific sectors in specific countries.

The Framework Agreement (the first part of GATS) establishes the legal relevance of the basic "most-favored nation" principle for international trade in services. The service providers from every signatory country shall be treated on terms no less favorable than those accorded to service providers from any foreign country. However, the condition of national treatment is not included.

The basic agreement addresses the terms for recognizing the credentials required for entry into a licensed profession. The countries signing the GATS Agreement are committed to a goal of basing the recognition of professional qualifications for admission into the professions on internationally accepted criteria. The parties must make sure that any organizations controlling admission to licensed professions do not abuse their positions.

The parties may also specify specific derogations from the basic non-discrimination principle. These exceptions from basic GATS principles should be reviewed in five years and cancelled in ten years. The terms of the derogations are set forth in the third part of the GATS Agreement. There is also a transparency agreement: the parties must publish the texts of all relevant laws and regulations affecting foreign access to domestic service markets.

Countries signing the *GATS Agreement on Trade in Financial Services* (World Trade Organization 1995) pledged to apply free-trade principles to commercial banking, insurance and securities industries. Signatory countries pledged to remove specific barriers to international trade in financial services. The US, for example, agreed to eliminate a number of nationality requirements that had been imposed at the level of state regulation. Unfortunately, the EU members each signed as separate entities so there are no EU-wide policies for implementing the Trade in Financial Services Agreement.

The GATS *Annex on Telecommunications Services* (World Trade Organization, 1996a) covers voice and facsimile telephone services, transmissions, fixed and mobile satellite services, data services, mobile paging services and related areas. The US, the EU and Japan are signatories to the Agreement. Foreign carriers should be allowed to supply any service that is in the host country carrier's schedule. Access to the telecommunications networks must be provided to foreign service providers on terms that are reasonable and non-discriminatory. The terms and conditions imposed on the foreign service providers should be no more than are necessary to safeguard public responsibilities, to ensure the technical integrity of the network and to make sure that foreign providers only supply services under a specific commitment.

4.6 The Agreement on Government Procurement (GPA) (World Trade Organization, 1994b)

This establishes international rules governing international access to government procurement, which was not covered in the initial GATT agreement. The forerunner to the present GPA was negotiated during the Tokyo Round in 1979 and came into force in 1981. The current version of the GPA was negotiated during the Uruguay Round and signed in 1994. Many countries signed with reservations that limited the application of the GPA to selected areas of government procurement.

Where the GPA is applicable, it mandates the same sort of transparency and non-discrimination that are in force for the other areas covered by GATT. There is a lot of emphasis in the GPA on transparency in setting up the request for proposals and the bidding process (GPA, Articles XIX:1, Appendix IV, IX:lll). Discrimination against foreign vendors is prohibited. Only developing countries can establish offset requirements and then only for qualifying vendors, not for awarding contracts. Disputes arising under the GPA can be referred to the WTO Dispute Resolution Process.

The GPA was signed by relatively few WTO members. Most countries signing it limited the application of the Agreement to specific agencies and products. Many countries entered into side-bar agreements with their major trading partners that specified that their understandings on the GPA would be applied; see, for example, European Union (1995). This process is resulting in a tendency to base national interpretations of GPA obligations on reciprocity in government procurement with partner states.

4.7 Agreement on Trade Related Investment Measures (TRIMS) (World Trade Organization, 1994q)

The core of the TRIMS agreement is a commitment to apply the GATT principles to international investment. The Annex lists a few examples that are to be regarded as violations of GATT and TRIMS. They include:

- obligations to use domestic products or that tie the permissible value of imports to some quantity of domestic purchases
- obligations to use domestic products that are related to the value of exports
- limitations to access to foreign exchange that are based on the value of the foreign exchange that has been generated, and
- limits on the terms of exports that are based on the value of local consumption.

On the other hand, the Agreement carries over all the exceptions in GATT into TRIMS (Article 3). Furthermore, developing nations can deviate from the TRIMS requirements if it is necessary to address balance of payments issues (TRIMS, Article 4). Any derogations from the TRIMS obligations must be transparent and notified to other signatory states.

5. AGREEMENTS INVOLVING THE DOMESTIC REGULATION OF BUSINESS

5.1 The Agreement on Technical Barriers to Trade (TBT) (World Trade Organization, 1994m)

Many of the issues raised by each of the three parties considered in this book against the other two included complaints about standards, testing and certifications. These requirements and procedures are covered by the Technical Barriers to Trade Agreement.

First a bit of nomenclature: a "standard" is a description of some attribute or process that has been developed by the private sector and is intended for voluntary use. The specifications for formatting data for inscription on a DVD would be one example of a standard. The testing procedures and performance criteria used by Underwriters Laboratory for evaluating fire extinguishers would constitute another set of standards. A "technical requirement" is similar to a standard. However, compliance with a technical requirement is required by the government. The Corporate Average Fuel Economy rules that set minimum fleet mileage requirements in the US are one example of a technical requirement.

The distinction between a standard and a technical requirement is legally important since governments, in theory, can't be held accountable for the development of standards. However, the distinction has become blurred by the widespread government practice of using standards as the basis for technical requirements. In the US, for example, the National Technology Transfer Act (1996) requires agencies of the Federal government to use (private sector) standards as the basis for (government-mandated) technical requirements.

Under the terms of the TBT, technical requirements must not discriminate against imported or foreign-designed products. They must not be any more trade restrictive than is necessary to achieve their legitimate objective. The provisions of the TBT also require signatory governments to notify other states of proposed changes in standards and technical requirements, if possible, and to develop a procedure for receiving the notifications issued by other countries. The goal is to promote international comments on potentially difficult standards and technical requirements before they have become set in stone.

The National Center for Standards and Certification Information (NCSCI) is the US contact point for notifications under the TBT. The NCSCI has a computerized system for sending e-mail notifications on specified subjects to anyone requesting the service. The European Union and Japan have similar systems in place.

Countries that have signed the TBT are also pledged to use "international standards" for domestic regulatory purposes wherever feasible. The strategy of pushing for national convergence around international standards has not worked out well in practice. One issue is to define what constitutes an "international standard". This has been a subject of extended debate between the US and the EU. The EU argues that only standards developed by truly international institutions, in this case, the International Standards Organization and the International Electrotechnical Commission, can be considered "international". The US defines an "international standard" as any standard that is accepted internationally. A significant number of standards developed in the US would qualify under that definition.

Another barrier to implementation is created by the legacy of products and processes that have been developed in each country on the basis of national standards. Most standards evolve over time. Radical changes are hard to make.

Since standards are developed in the private sector, the TBT is limited to exhorting governments to use their best offices to make sure that standards developed in their countries comply with the technical requirements set forth.

5.2 The Agreement on Trade Related Aspects of Intellectual Property Rights, Including Trade in Counterfeit Goods (TRIPS) (World Trade Organization, 1994p)

The negotiation of the TRIPS Agreement reflected a widespread conclusion that national practices varied widely and that the lack of any broad acceptance of a unifying set of principles was presenting significant barriers to international trade.

The TRIPS is based on the core principles that are basic to GATT but have rarely been applied to intellectual property issues. The first is an acceptance of the most-favored nation principle. Any Intellectual Property Right (IPR) privilege extended to any other TRIPS signatory must be also be made available to all other TRIPS signatories (TRIPS, Part I: Article 4). There is also a non-discrimination requirement in domestic regulation: there must not be any discrimination between the intellectual property rights granted to domestic products and those inherent in imported products (TRIPS, Part I, Article 3).

The signatories to the TRIPS Agreement are also pledged to adopt the provisions of the basic IPR agreements that have been negotiated outside the WTO framework. Copyrights are to be covered by the provisions of the Berne Convention of 1971 (TRIPS, Part II, Article 9). Exceptions are made for laws governing authors' moral rights, and copyrights on computer programs. Trademarks are to be covered by the provisions of the Paris Convention of 1967 (TRIPS, Part II, Article 15).

For the first 10 years after the ratification of TRIPS, intellectual property rights in printer circuit designs are to be based on the *Washington Treaty on Intellectual Property with Respect to Integrated Circuits* 1989 (TRIPS, Part II, Articles 34, 35).

Special rules are set for "geographical indications" that try to differentiate between uses that refer to generic categories and uses that are intended to point up specific origins. Greater protection is extended to the use of geographical indications for wines and spirits. Procedures are also established for international consultations regarding the use and restrictions on geographical indications (TRIPS, Part II, Articles 22–24).

The TRIPS agreement addresses many other aspects involved in the protection of intellectual property rights and the prevention of their abuse. For example, the terms of the Agreement do not cover the patentability of diagnostic, therapeutic or surgical procedures. Patent protection can also be denied to animals and plants, not including microbiological processes (TRIPS, Part II, Article 27).

The TRIPS Agreement does not bar signatory states from passing measures needed to protect morality and public order (TRIPS, Part I, Article 8): signatory countries can take measures to bar the implementation of anti-competitive practices in contractual leases. However, the countries involved should first be in consultation about the situation (TRIPS, Part II, Article 40). On the other hand, the TRIPS Agreement also contains provisions protecting trade secrets (TRIPS, Part II, Article 39).

Part V of TRIPS sets forth the major dispute resolution procedures. Signatory states are required to ensure transparency in the governing laws, regulations and administrative or legal decisions. A WTO Council for Trade Related Information Property Rights was organized. The Council was charged with reviewing the extant international disputes over intellectual property rights and to make the appropriate recommendations to the WTO General Council. The WTO Dispute Resolution Process was made available to resolve conflicts among signatory states over their TRIPS obligations five years after the organization of the WTO (TRIPS, Part V, Articles 63 and 64).

The malaria and AIDS epidemics placed a special strain on the TRIPS Agreement. Drugs that are effective against these diseases have been developed and manufactured in the West. However, their market prices are often far more than local public health budgets can afford. Several developing countries responded by refusing to grant patent protection on the needed pharmaceuticals. They were, in effect, inviting local companies to manufacture pirated copies.

In 2001, the WTO Trade Negotiation Committee addressed this problem with the development of the *Doha Declaration on the TRIPS Agreement and Public Health* (World Trade Organization, 2001). Developing countries now are authorized to grant compulsory licensing for pharmaceuticals if it is necessary to address a national emergency. HIV/AIDS, TB and malaria epidemics were explicitly mentioned as possible reasons for declaring a national emergency. The Doha Declaration also noted that many countries might not have the resources needed to analyze and manufacture the needed drugs. This is a problem that will be considered at a later date.

In effect, a deal had been struck. Authorization for compulsory licensing of pharmaceuticals requires a finding of a national emergency. The pharmaceutical companies are being invited to lower their prices on the required drugs to a point where compulsory licensing would cease to be attractive. Since any company bidding on a compulsory license would probably expect to make a profit, the clearing price would also be profitable for the original manufacturers.

REFERENCES

European Union (1995), "Agreement in the form of an exchange of letters between the European Community and the United States of America on government procurement", *Official Journal*, L 314, 20 June 1995, pp. 0026–0036.

Fischer, T. (2000), *The United States, the European Union and the "Globalization" of Free Trade: Allies or Adversaries?* Westport Conn., Quorum Books.

Irwin, D. (1995), "The GATT in historical perspective", *The American Economic Review* 85(2), pp. 323–328.

New York Times (2008), "Global trade talks said to collapse", 29 July, p. 1.

Rolfe, S. and J. Burtle (1973), *The Great Wheel: The World Monetary System, A Reinterpretation*, New York, Quadrangle.

Schaffer, R., F. Agusti and B. Earle (2008), *International Business Law and its Environment* (7th ed), Ohio: South–Western Cengage.

United States (1996), *National Technology Transfer Assistance Act*, Public Law 104-113 of 7 March 1996.

World Trade Organization (n.d.a), "Information Technology Agreement: introduction" at www.wto.org/english/tratop_e/inftec_e/itaintro_e.htm, accessed 30 May 2009.

World Trade Organization (n.d.b), "Understanding on rules and procedures governing the settlement of disputes", at www.wto.org/english/res_e/bocksp_e/analytic_index_e/dsu_09_e_htm, accessed 30 May 2009.

World Trade Organization (n.d.c), "Understanding the WTO" at www.wto.org/english/thewto_e/whatis_e/tif_e/tif_e.htm, accessed 30 May 2009.

World Trade Organization (n.d.d) "Dispute settlement: Find dispute cases" at www.wto.org/english/tratop_e/dispu_e/find_dispu_cases_e.htm, accessed 30 May 2009.

World Trade Organization (1947), 'General Agreement on Tariffs and Trade' at www.wto.org/english/docs_e/legal_e/gatt47_e.pdf, accessed 30 May 2009.

World Trade Organization (1994a), "Agreement on Agriculture", Document LT/UR/A-1A/2.

World Trade Organization (1994b), "Agreement on Government Procurement" at www.wto.org/english/doc_e/legal_e/gpr-94_e.pdf, accessed 30 May 2009.

World Trade Organization (1994c), "Agreement on Implementation of Article VI of the General Agreement on Tariffs and Trade 1994" at: www.wto.org/english/docs_e/legal_e/19-adp.pdf, accessed 30 May 2009.

World Trade Organization (1994d), *Agreement on Implementation of Article VII of the General Agreement on Tariffs and Trade* (Agreement on Customs Valuation), Document LT/UR/A-1A/4.

World Trade Organization (1994e), "Agreement on Import Licensing Procedures" at www.wto.org/english/docs_e/legal_e/23-lic.pdf, accessed 30 May 2009.
World Trade Organization (1994f), "Agreement on Preshipment Inspection" at www.wto.org/english/docs_e/legal_e/21-psi.pdf, accessed 30 May 2009.
World Trade Organization (1994g), *Agreement on Rules of Origin*, Document LT UR/A-1A/7.
World Trade Organization (1994h), *Agreement on Safeguards*, Document LT/UR/A-1A/8.
World Trade Organization (1994i), *Agreement on Sanitary and Phytosanitary Measures*, Document LT/UR/A-1A/12.
World Trade Organization (1994j), *Agreement on Subsidies and Countervailing Measures*, Document LT/UR/A-1A/9.
World Trade Organization (1994k) "General Agreement on Tariffs and Trade 1994" at www.wto.org/english/docs_e/legal_e/06-gatt.pdf, accessed 30 May 2009.
World Trade Organization (1994l), "General Agreement on Tariffs and Trade, Annex 1A: Multilateral Agreement on Trade in Goods" at www.wto.org./english/docs_e/legal_e/05-anx1_e.pdf, accessed 30 May 2009.
World Trade Organization (1994m), *Agreement on Technical Barriers to Trade*, Document LT/UR/A-1A/10.
World Trade Organization (1994n), *The Agreement on Textiles and Clothing*, Document LT/UR/A-1A/11.
World Trade Organization (1994o), *General Agreement on Trade in Services*, Document LT/UR/A-1B/s/1.
World Trade Organization (1994p), *Agreement on Trade Related Aspects of Intellectual Property Rights*, Document LT/A-1C/IP/1.
World Trade Organization (1994q), *Agreement on Trade Related Investment Measures*, Document LT/UR/A-1A/13.
World Trade Organization (1995), *Second Protocol to the General Agreement on Trade in Services*, Document S/L/11.
World Trade Organization (1996a), *Fourth Protocol to the General Agreement on Trade in Services*, Document S/L/20.
World Trade Organization (1996b), *Ministerial Declaration on Trade in Information Technology Products*, Document WT/MIN(96)/16.
World Trade Organization (2001), *Declaration on the TRIPS Agreement and Public Health*, Document WT/Min(01)/Dec/2.

3. Background to trade policy in the US

1. INTRODUCTION

The purpose of this chapter is to provide some background on the ways in which trade-relevant decisions are made in the United States. We will be looking at the trade policy decision processes from three perspectives: cultural, constitutional and administrative. Following the themes that were sketched out in Chapter 1, we will be considering three major groups of participants: business, government and voters. This simple scheme will provide a common framework as we consider the decision-making process in the European Union in Chapter 5 and in Japan in Chapter 7.

The following discussions will expand on three simple themes about the politics of trade in the United States. Business is important, government is mistrusted and regulations are viewed suspiciously. However, the cumulative impact of international competition on US industries and communities has led to a widespread mistrust of free trade. Finally, the president controls international trade negotiations but Congress controls anti-dumping laws, countervailing duties and other government responses to international trade pressures. The conflicts between the president and Congress have contributed to a certain incoherence in United States trade policies.

2. THE CONTEXT OF GOVERNANCE IN THE UNITED STATES

2.1 A Cultural Perspective

As Tocqueville pointed out, Americans are a mobile people, often lacking firm identities of family and place. Business becomes very important; we are what we do (Tocqueville, 1835; Boorstin, 1965). Our foremothers could adopt new identities as they came to the country. It is common for people to change cities as they change jobs. The question "Who are you?" can often be best answered in terms of terms of a job, an employer or a profession (Stewart and Bennett, 1972).

The prospects for business in the US have, from an historical perspective, been excellent. The US grew on the edge of an open frontier for 300 years. The first successful settlements in Massachusetts began in 1617. The Oklahoma Territory became a state in 1917. The centuries in between were characterized by almost constant expansion from the East Coast to the West. An open frontier was a constant factor in American society for over 300 years.

The open frontier was characterized by almost constant economic expansion and endemic labor shortages. The myth of the American Dream has carried some historical power: if you were willing to work hard and use your intelligence, your prospects for getting ahead were generally excellent.

The geographic expansion of the US contributed greatly to a growing, modernizing American economy. As Schumpeter (1950) pointed out, economic growth is generally characterized by creative destruction: less uncompetitive companies are likely to die as more competitive companies come to the fore.

In the US, this process of creative destruction has been an important factor in national expansion. The positions of the prosperous landowners of central New York States were effectively ended by the opening of the Erie Canal. The process of constant renewal made it easier for the innovators to seemingly emerge from nowhere. The American Dream goes further; with talent and some luck, the sky is the limit. Bill Gates and Warren Buffett are not the first Americans to rise to the stars through business.

For substantial periods in American frontier history, settlers were likely to pass outside US territory. The French and Indian Wars (1754–1763) took place in part because English colonists were moving into French territory. Texas became first a country and then a state because American settlers moved into Northern Mexico and declared their independence. Similar patterns emerged in California and Hawaii. Oklahoma is called the "Sooner" state because it was settled by people who got there sooner than the territory was open for settlement (Boorstin, 1965). As a result, government has often been viewed in the United States as an inefficient, unwelcome source of interference in the business of empire building. Free trade is welcome.

These experiences left an imprint on the attitudes of Americans towards business and government. Private enterprise is the engine of civic development and should be left unregulated (unless, of course, business needs help). Community comes before government. Government is generally suspect and should be kept under firm limits. Overall, the attitude is that the government should stay out of the affairs of business and the people, unless it is needed to protect our communities and way of life (Fukuyama 1995).

These attitudes towards government have been tempered by the experiences of the Great Depression, World War II, the Cold War and the space race. There are some things that only the government can do. Only the government can provide the social safety net to cushion against shocks too big for the individual to handle. Government, almost regretfully, has come to be the insurer of last resort (Lodge, 1987; Bennett and Bennett, 1990).

2.2 A Business Perspective

The politics of international trade are almost inevitably influenced by the realities of economic growth and contraction. In general, the last thirty years have been a time of prosperity in the United States. On average, the economy grew at an annual rate of 5.4 per cent. Per capita incomes in chained 2000 dollars rose from $18,391 in 1970 to $38.987 in 2006 (United States, 2008, table 645).

Traditionally, international trade has not been a particularly important sector of the American economy. It has been generally easier to look for sales in a large and dynamic domestic market than to wade through the difficulties involved in going international. However, the rising tide of globalization has inevitably had an impact on the US economy. The data in Table 3.1 document the growth of international trade in merchandise and services. All sectors have been growing more rapidly than the overall economy with one exception: merchandise exports.

Inevitably, not everyone benefited equally from prosperity. Most of the income gains went to the people who were already in the top quarter of the income hierarchy. At the top of the spectrum, the number of households reporting incomes over $75,000 increased from 24.1 per cent to 28.3 per cent between 2000 and 2005. At the other end, the fraction of households with an income of less that $15,000 also rose from 13.7 per cent to 14.7 per cent (United States, 2008, table 668).

The boom years in the 1990s affected different industries in different ways. The Clinton Administration released technologies for general civilian use that had been developed with government funding (United States, 1996). The result was an impressive boom in the commercialization of digital technologies. Investments, employment and value-added in the digital sector soared.

The traditional manufacturing sectors did not fare so well. One problem was caused by the successes of the new technologies. Overall, the value of manufacturing output remained more-or-less constant. However, worker

Table 3.1 International trade and the US economy

		1995	2000	2006	change (%) 1995–2006
Exports	Goods	575	772	1 026	+78
	Services	219	299	423	93
Imports	Goods	749	1 227	1 861	148
	Services	141	224	343	143
GDP		7 398	9 817	13 241	79

Note: Figures $b, 2006.

Source: United States (2008), table 645.

Table 3.2 Relative prosperity and decline in manufacturing

	1998	2005	Change (%)
GDP	9 470	10 049	6
Manufacturing	1 286	1 523	18
Computers	96	310	223
Motor vehicles	112	125	12
Metals	46	48	4
Machinery	114	109	−4

Note: Figures in $b, 2000.

Source: United States (2008), table 969.

productivity soared. As a result, manufacturing employment dropped from 18 million jobs in 1990 to 14 million in 2006 (Table 3.2).

The changing patterns of international trade didn't help. The strong dollar encouraged cheap imports. The merchandise trade deficit grew from $96 billion in 1995 to $258 billion in 2006. The volume of imports grew the most in non-high technology sectors. US imports from China, mostly in low-technology goods, grew from $18 billion in 2001 to $71 billion in 2006.

Problems were particularly acute in the auto and metals sectors. Japanese, Korean and European car manufacturers took ever larger sectors of the US automobile market. The value of auto imports grew from $157 billion in 2000 to $212 billion in 2006. A substantial number of the car companies built manufacturing plants in the US. However, these plants were generally located in the low-cost, non-unionized southern

Table 3.3 Winners and losers in US urban population: 1990–2006

	Population change: 1990–2006 (%)
Las Vegas, Nevada	104.8
Fort Collins, Colorado	95.9
Naples, Florida	90.5
Phoenix, Arizona	69.5
Austin, Texas	68.8
Boise, Idaho	67.5
Fayette, Arkansas	67.2
Dayton, Ohio	−0.06
Charlottesville, West Virginia	−0.07
Huntington, West Virginia	−0.09
Scranton, Pennsylvania	−0.43
Syracuse, New York	−1.5
Pittsburgh, Pennsylvania	−4.0
Buffalo, New York	−4.4
Youngstown, Ohio	−4.4
Utica, New York	−6.2

Note: Entries are calculated from data for 1990–2000 and 2000–2006.

Source: United States (2008), table 20.

regions of the United States. These new plants did not, in general, hire the people who were laid off when the American car companies cut back.

The problems in the steel industry were especially acute. Imports rose from $16 billion to $31 billion between 2001 and 2006. The industry had already gone through a horrific contraction due to competition from foreign producers and the new domestic mini-mills. Throughout the industry, peripheral facilities were shut down first to protect company investments in their major plants. This did not always work. In the Pittsburgh region alone, 11 out of 12 steel mills were shut down forever in 1984.

These processes of progress and retrenchment left a crazy-quilt pattern of prosperity and depression in the US. The high-technology centers in California, Texas and Massachusetts boomed. The flood of money being generated by these ventures brought new prosperity to financial centers such as New York and Chicago. On the other hand, regions that had based their economies on more traditional manufacturing industries often went into sharp decline. Some sense of the extent of regional differences in economic prosperity and pain can be gained from Table 3.3, which tracks population changes in US cities.

2.3 A Voter Perspective

Few people consider free trade to be an essential bedrock of economic policy, outside of government policy makers, university economics departments and a few free-floating intellectuals. Even for boom industries, our major initiatives are primarily in domestic markets. However, our cultural traditions provide general support for free trade. A vigorous people will welcome a challenge and can compete in any market. Furthermore, trade protection smacks of government interference, which is a bad thing. However, these arguments become a lot harder to sell in the US in regions that are facing the collapse of their manufacturing base and a long-term decline. These experiences support a pragmatic compromise: free trade is acceptable but don't disrupt our markets or block us from yours.

The tragedy of 11 September 2001 also had an impact on public attitudes and government policies that has spilled over into trade restrictions. Nineteen Islamic radicals, mostly from Saudi Arabia and Egypt, hijacked four commercial airliners that had taken off from Boston, Newark and Washington. Two of the planes were flown into the World Trade Towers during the height of the business day. The third plane was crashed into the Pentagon in Washington. The passengers on the fourth plane revolted against their captors and their plane crashed in a field in rural Pennsylvania. This was the worst attack on US territory in history. Over 3000 people were killed or missing and presumed dead.

The attack on 9/11 became the basis for a series of new trade security initiatives such as the Patriot Act and the Container Security Act. These have become the basis for some of the complaints about trade restrictions that were subsequently raised against the United States by allied countries.

2.4 A Government Perspective

The American colonies were settled by the refugees from the frequent and often bloody bouts of religious persecution in the UK. When the Catholics were in power, refugees flooded into the Protestant settlements in New England. When Protestants returned to government, emigration to the Catholic colony of Maryland grew. When the Parliamentary armies were winning in the civil war, Royalist supporters were more likely to emigrate to Virginia. When religious orthodoxy of any stripe was being enforced, nonconformists were more likely to seek refuge in Pennsylvania.

These realities ensured that a strong federal system would emerge in the US. The different colonies not only had different histories, but were also generally settled by people who had been mortal enemies with the residents of neighboring colonies. The legacy of this history persists. There are still significant cultural and political differences among the different regions of the United States (Fischer, 1989; see also Philips, 1999).

The problem in drafting the Constitution was how to preserve democracy when your mortal enemies were in power. The solution was to promote gridlock. As Hamilton, Jay and Madison argued in *The Federalist* (1788 [1941]), power was divided in the new Constitution among the president, Senate, House and Supreme Court. Officials in each entity represented a different constituency and achieved office through different routes. Members of the House of Representatives are elected directly by the voters. Senators were originally to be elected by the state legislatures. The president is technically elected by an electoral college that was to be drawn from a national upper class. The justices of the Supreme Court have life tenure and are expected to uphold the primacy of the Constitution and common law in the face of partisan enthusiasms. This system made it very difficult to pass legislation only addressing the interests of a narrow constituency.

Regionalism in the electorate and fragmentation in government has left an imprint on political decision making. All politics, as Tip O'Neil pointed out, (O'Neill, 1987) are local. Although there are only two major party labels in use in the US, there are hundreds of state party organizations. In general, local political coalitions have to raise their own monies. Businesses are major contributors. Politicians are far more likely to represent local cultural and economic interests rather than any national political agenda (Hershey, 2009). As a result, local short-term business interests are likely to trump long-term party program or ideology in Congress.

These realities have an effect on decision making in the US government. A diffusion of power has led to a fragmentation of authority. There are four major centers of authority in the US system: state governments, Congress, the presidency and the regulatory commissions.

As the Constitution was originally conceived, the states and federal governments would have almost exclusive jurisdictions over different areas of policy. What has evolved is a system of "marble cake" federalism. State and Federal governments work together in the development and administration of national programs. The Federal government usually provides most of the money and defines the requirements. State governments participate on a voluntary, cost-sharing basis. The protection of state interests is ensured by the power of the senators, who are elected on a state-wide basis (Zimmerman, 2005).

Presidents are reluctant to override what are perceived as important state interests. For example, state policies restricting government procurement are generally not challenged by the Federal government. Occupational licensing is generally handled at the state level. In general, the Federal government does not challenge these policies as long as they are not abusive.

At the Federal level, all legislative authority comes ultimately from Congress. However, the fragmentation of political representation has led to a slow process of political decision making. Congress has a hard time fine-tuning existing policies in response to short-term changes; the process is simply too slow to respond effectively. Furthermore, legislation generally offers limited responses to specific problems, because there are limits to what can be passed. Only rarely can the US legislative process provide sweeping changes in overall policy in response to major long-term issues.

As a result, Congress has tended to delegate authority to make short-term policy adjustments to the president and to the regulatory agencies. Since the president serves as the representative of the country in international negotiations, Congress has delegated a lot of authority to him to negotiate and conclude international trade agreements (Foley, 1990). The regulation of the domestic economy has largely been delegated to a host of government agencies and independent regulatory commissions.

3. JURISDICTION AND DECISION MAKING ON TRADE-RELATED ISSUES

The key issue is the extent to which Congress has been willing to delegate authority to the offices that must carry out the related administrative tasks. This varies by topic and agency. In general, Congress will keep substantial control over policies if they do not have to be adjusted rapidly to meet new regulatory threats and the implementation procedures are relatively routine. In these areas, policy changes affecting US trade relations will have to be made through Congressional legislation. In other situations, agencies must be free to adopt new policies and procedures in response to new situations. In these situations, Congress tends to defer to the experts. The agencies responsible for policy implementation are more likely to be able to make the necessary changes on their own authority through the regulatory process.

Congress often contends with the president for control over policy. In Congress, power is generally wielded through the committee system. The committee chairs can shape the agenda for the committee work, including the all-important question of which version of which legislative initiatives will be taken up for consideration. Members of Congress vie to get on the committees that are the most relevant for their most important political supporters. These committees generally conduct "oversight hearings" to review the policies and decisions of the relevant executive agencies. As a result, "The essence of the Federal bureaucracy . . . is a many splintered thing". The bureaucracy is "riddled by . . . clienteleism . . . and crippled by a profound lack of co-ordination and continuity" (Williams, 1990). Power inevitably flows to Congress (Cammisa, 1995; Brady and Volden, 1998).

There are two major factors that shape that struggle. The Office of Management and Budget (OMB) offers a more potent tool. Agencies reporting to the president are expected to get the approval from their OMB desk officer before releasing any statements, draft regulations or legislative proposals to the public. OMB must also review and approve all agency budgets and financial requests. OMB is reasonably effective. However, it is limited by the complexity of government programs and a tendency to focus on new initiatives rather than on old policies. Agencies that don't do very much rarely have difficulties with OMB.

The Administrative Procedures Act (APA) (5 USC 500 *et seq.*) provides another check on the autonomy of administrative agencies. The provisions of the APA generally force the agencies to stay close to established policies and to their legislative mandate. Agencies that want to issue new regulations or make new licensing decisions must first put a notice of proposed administrative activities in the *Federal Register*. Interested parties must have an opportunity to comment on the proposals on the record. Outside parties can also gain access to virtually all official documents under the Freedom of Information Act. The agency must base the final decision "on substantial evidence in the record as a whole". Finally, outside parties can challenge the agency decision in court as outside the legislative mandate or unsupported by the record. As a result of these requirements, administrative agencies and regulatory commissions have a strong incentive to operate in accordance with established policies and processes.

The president's third source of authority, the power to send nominations for political positions in the government to Congress, is a relative weak reed. Political administrators are generally under strong pressure to go along with the programs, policy preferences and professional cultures of the agencies they are expected to manage. From the agency perspective, presidents come and go, but Congress is forever.

Control of trade policy in the United States is split between the president and Congress. Congress has given the president control over trade policy negotiations, especially over tariffs. The Office of the United States Trade Representative (USTR) represents the US in international trade negotiations; it is a part of the Office of the President and is under his direct control.

The president signs international agreements on behalf of the US. However, treaties do not become binding US law until they are ratified by a two-thirds affirmative vote of the Senate. Tariff schedules, and other domestic laws affecting US international trade, have to be approved by both houses of Congress through the normal legislative channels.

The tug of war between the president and Congress for control of trade policy has changed over time. Legally the president is dependent on the support of Congress, especially the Senate, in setting trade policy. However, Congress delegated substantial authority to the president during the early days of the Cold War. The prospects for defeat in the struggle with the Soviet Union were significant. If the United States was going to push back effectively, the president needed the freedom to move rapidly and he needed the backing of a united country.

These considerations became far less pressing for Congress after the collapse of the Soviet Union and the gradual erosion of US manufacturing. Trade protection became a politically more acceptable topic for debate between Congress and the president. The problems encountered by the US in enforcing concessions gained in the GATT negotiations before the creation of the WTO trade Dispute Resolution Process also contributed to the more assertive role taken by the US Congress since the 1990s (Foley, 1990; Milner, 1993).

In reality, the Congress has delegated a lot of authority over formal trade policy to the president. Presidents have to move quickly in international tariff negotiations, so Congress has largely delegated authority to set tariffs to the president. This is an ongoing delegation. The president must have the authority to enter into binding agreements in the GATT rounds. Congress will therefore delegate "fast track" authority to the president in anticipation of upcoming multilateral negotiations. Under the "fast track" provisions, Congress agrees to give a yes or no vote on the negotiated deal, and to vote any agreement within a set period of time and without insisting on amendments. This is a limited delegation of authority. The president must receive a new grant of fast track authority before every new set of negotiations.

Authority over government procurement has largely been ceded to Congress and the bureaucracy. The Federal agencies with the largest procurement budgets are the Department of Defense, the Department of Transportation and the General Services Administration. Although all three agencies are under presidential control, difficulties emerge in trying to open up government procurement to international bidding. The resource requirements for developing new defense systems can be very high. Project officers usually work with a limited number of companies in the development of new proposals. Protecting these alliances becomes a way to ensure the stability of the essential defense manufacturing base. New entrants to the party are generally not welcome.

The Department of Transportation works closely with state and local governments in the development of new transportation initiatives. These projects can be very important for local contractors and manufacturers. Local and national businesses will often use their influence over their Congressional delegations to keep foreign competition at an arm's length. The General Services Administration manages the business dealings of the Federal government, which has offices throughout the country. Local service is often an important criterion on qualifying GSA bidders. National firms often have an advantage.

Anti-dumping and safeguard proceedings are initiated by the US Department of Commerce and implemented by the International Trade Commission. The major policies and procedures are set forth in statutes passed by Congress. The ITC is nominally independent of presidential control. The commissioners are nominated by the president, are approved by the Senate and serve for fixed terms. The president has some control over the initiation of anti-dumping procedures through the Secretary of Commerce. However the major policies and procedures of the ITC can only be changed through Congressional legislation. Since the nuances of anti-dumping policies do not have to reflect any subtle changes in the international trade environment, Congress keeps fairly tight control over the policies and procedures under which the ITC has to operate.

Congress has given the Food and Drug Administration (FDA) responsibility for assuring the safety of foodstuffs, pharmaceuticals, cosmetics and medical devices that are used in the United States. The FDA is primarily responsible for reviewing and approving materials for use. Primary responsibility for administering sanitary and phytosanitary (SPS) issues within the US is given to APHIS, the Animal and Plant Health Inspection Service. APHIS is an agency of the US Department of Agriculture (DoAg), which is also responsible for promoting US agricultural exports. As a result, the management of DoAg tends to be quite sensitive to the impact of foreign SPS requirements on US agricultural trade.

The two agencies work closely together. Although the FDA provides formal representation for the US to the IOE, the IPPC and the Codex Commission, they are closely advised by experts from APHIS. As a result, both agencies have strong international commitments.

Given the importance of international trade in plants and animal products and the speed with which diseases and pests can migrate from country to country, the major agricultural countries have a high incentive to share information and collaborate in control measures. The FDA and APHIS must be able to respond rapidly to new SPS threats and changes in international regulations, and also to implement new developments in SPS control measures. As a result, Congress has delegated broad authority over these policies to the FDA. The key trade decisions can usually be made at the agency level.

Congress has delegated the enforcement of intellectual property (IP) rights to the Library of Congress. However, the administration of IP rights has not, in the past, required close international cooperation. This is a field that requires predictability. There is little need to make rapid changes in IP processes in response to a fast-changing environment. As a result, the core IP policies are firmly under Congressional control. The core IP policies were enacted over a hundred years ago to meet the needs of a rapidly developing domestic economy. Given the need for stability and predictability in IP laws, it is not surprising that significant differences between US laws and international practices have persisted.

REFERENCES

Bennett, L. and S. Bennett (1990), *Living with the Leviathan: Americans come to Terms with Big Government*, Lawrence, University of Kansas Press.

Boorstin, D. (1965), *The Americans: The National Experience*, New York, Random House.

Brady, D. and C. Volden (1998), *Revolving Gridlock: Politics and Policy from Carter to Clinton*, Boulder, Westview Press.

Cammisa, Anne Marie (1995), *Governments as Interest Groups: Intergovernmental Lobbying and the Federal System*, Westport, Praeger.

Fischer, D.H. (1989), *Albion's Seed: Four British Folkways in America*, New York, Oxford University Press.

Foley, Michael (1990), "Congress and policy making: can it cope with foreign affairs?" in Robert Williams (ed.) *Explaining American Politics: Issues and Interpretations*, London, Routledge, pp. 65–96.

Fukuyama, F. (1995), *Trust: The Social Virtues and the Creation of Prosperity*, New York, The Free Press.

Hamilton, A., J. Jay and J. Madison (1788 [1941]). *The Federalist*. New York, McLean.

Hershey, M. (2009), *Party Politics in America*, 15th edn., New York, Pearson/Longmans.

Lodge, C.C. (1987) "The United States: the costs of ambivalence", in George Lodge and Ezra Vogel (eds), *Ideology and National Competitiveness: An Analysis of Nine Countries*, Boston, Harvard Business School Press, pp. 113–139.

Milner, H. (1993), "Maintaining international commitments in trade policy" in R. Weaver and B. Rockman (eds) *Do Institutions Matter? Government Capabilities in the United States and Abroad*, Washington, Brookings Institution, pp. 341–369.

O'Neill, Tip (1987), *Man of the House: The Life and Political Memoirs of Speaker Tip O'Neill*, New York, St. Martin's Press.

Phillips, K. (1999), *The Cousins' Wars: Religion, Politics and the Triumph of Anglo-America*, New York, Basic Books.

Schumpeter, J. (1950), *Capitalism, Socialism and Democracy*, New York, Harpers.
Stewart, E. and M. Bennett (1972) *American Cultural Patterns: A Cross Cultural Perspective*, Boston, MA, Intercultural Press.
Tocqueville, Alexis de (1835: 2000 ed.) *Democracy in America*, Indianapolis, Hackett.
United States (1996), *The National Technology Transfer and Advancement Act*, Public Law 104–113, codified at 15 USC 3701, *et seq*.
United States Department of Commerce (2008) "Statistical abstract of the United States", at www.census.gov/compendia/statab2008/2008edition.html, accessed 30 May 2009.
Williams, R. (1990), "Policy, process and power in American bureaucracy" in Robert Williams (ed.) *Explaining American Politics: Issues and Interpretations*, London, Routledge, pp. 97–115.
Zimmerman, J. (2005), *Congressional Preemption and Regulatory Federalism*, Albany, State University of New York Press.

4. Issues concerning US trade practices

1. INTRODUCTION

There are three categories of issues that have been raised by the EU, Japan or both about alleged US trade barriers. The first group consists of "longstanding" issues that were raised in both 2002 and 2007. The second group consists of "emerging" issues that were first raised after 2002. The third category includes "settled" issues that were raised in 2002 but not in 2007.

Many of the issues discussed in this book are unique to each country. There are several distinctive characteristics to the trade issues raised about the United States. These include the sheer number and intensity of the complaints. The issues raised by Japan and the European Union about US trade policies also focused on the US claims for a right of unilateral enforcement of asserted trade rules and rights.

2. TRADE ISSUES RAISED ABOUT THE US IN 2002 AND 2007

Forty-eight trade issues were raised against the United States by one or both of the other partners in both 2002 and 2007. They are listed in Table 4.1.

2.1 Import-related Policies

2.1a Trade administration issues

The Harbor Maintenance Tax Since 1987, the US has levied an *ad valorem* tax of 0.125 per cent on most of the merchandise passing through US ports. The tax is levied on virtually all imports at the time of importation through the customs process. No tax is to be paid on domestic freight moving through Alaska, Hawaii and off-shore dependencies, or on fish or on crude oil from Alaska. Companies that would otherwise owe $10,000 or less per quarter are exempt from the obligation to pay. Collections on the movement of military goods are limited to $500,000,000 per year. The tax was originally applied to exports and the fee was to be paid voluntarily on

Table 4.1 Issues raised about US trade policies in 2002 and 2007

Issue	Complainant		WTO
	EU	Japan	
1. Import-related			
a. Trade administration issues			
Harbor Maintenance Tax	x	x	x
Merchandise processing fee	x		
Textiles rules of origin	x		
Rules of origin on clocks		x	
Failure to recognize EU as a country	x		
b. Sanitary, phytosanitary requirements			
Excessive quarantine for plant imports	x		
Stringent BSE quarantine rules	x		
Limits on importing uncooked meats	x		
c. Restrictions on foreign-sourced services			
Barriers to foreign financial services	x	x	
Barriers to foreign telecommunications	x		
Merchant Shipping Act (The Jones Act)	x		
d. Restrictions on foreign investments			
Barriers to foreign power facilities	x		
The Exon-Florio Amendment	x	x	
e. Government procurement issues			
Barriers to government procurement	x	x	
Barriers to defense procurement	x		
The Berry Amendment	x		
Limits on foreign satellite launchers	x		
Buy America for transportation projects	x		
Small business set-asides	x		
Minority business set-asides	x		
f. Safeguard policies			
The Helms-Burton Act	x	x	x
The Anti-Dumping Act of 1916	x	x	x
The Byrd Amendment	x	x	x
Zeroing methodology on anti-dumping duties	x	x	x
Retaliation on foreign discrimination	x	x	
Section 301 of the Trade Act, 1974	x	x	x
Carousel rule on retaliatory measures	x	x	
Iran and Libya Sanctions Act	x	x	
Countervailing duties on imported steel	x		x

Table 4.1 (continued)

Issue	Complainant		WTO
	EU	Japan	
2. Domestic-related			
a. Standards and technical requirements			
Motor Vehicle Content Disclosure Act	x	x	
Corporate Average Fuel Economy rules	x	x	
Failure to use metric system	x	x	
b. Intellectual property rights			
First to invent doctrine on patents	x		
The Hilmer Doctrine on Intellectual property	x	x	
Copyrights and videogame rentals	x	x	x
Limited recognition of Cuban trademarks		x	x
The barbershop exemption	x	x	x
Government use of patented materials	x		
Moral rights to copyright performances	x	x	
Handling of patent infringement cases	x		x
c. Market regulation			
Foreign corporation tax code requirements	x		
Fragmented markets for electrical products	x		
3. Export-related			
a. Export restrictions			
Export Management Systems		x	
Export restrictions on logs		x	
b. Export subsidies			
Export subsidies in the 2002 Farm Bill	x	x	
Aircraft development subsidies	x		x US
Maritime subsidy programs	x	x	
Foreign sales corporations	x		x

Note: Entries in the WTO column mean that a case has been referred to the WTO dispute resolution process.

a quarterly basis. However, the Supreme Court held in 1998 that exports were exempt from the tax in accordance with Article 1, section 9 clause 5 of the Constitution, which prohibits export tariffs. As a result, the fee falls disproportionally on imports.

Japan argued that the Harbor Maintenance Tax violates Article III of GATT, which pledges equal treatment for domestic and international goods. Since the tax has allegedly accumulated a surplus of $1.1 billion, it is also in violation of Article VIII of GATT, which limits trade transaction fees to the actual costs of a transaction. The EU asked the US for consultations over the Harbor Maintenance Tax under GATT Article XXII on February 1998. Japan participated in the consultations as a third party. At the time of writing the consultations have been inconclusive (European Union, 2006, fiche 960049; Japan, 2002, pp. 4–6; Japan, 2006, pp. 11–12; WTO *DS 118*).

Merchandise processing fee The US also imposes a 0.21 per cent fee to cover the costs of processing import transactions, up to a maximum charge of $485 per clearance. Canada challenged the fee in 1987 with an action before the GATT Council, which found that fees for customs processing should be based on actual costs. The merchandise processing fee is *ad valorem* and does not meet this criterion. The US has not acted on that finding (European Union, 2006, fiche 960048).

Textile rules of origin The trade documentation for fabrics traded in the US must specify their country of origin. For most products, this is where the product was assembled. However, the country of origin for textiles, table linens and some silk accessories is defined as where the fabric was made. The EU argues that this rule places an unreasonable burden on EU exports where the origin of the textiles was difficult to determine. Furthermore, the country of origin does not reflect the country where the bulk of the value was added to the product (European Union, 2006, fiche 960179).

Rules of origin on clocks and wristwatches According to the terms of the US Tariff Act of 1930, national origins must be declared for the separate components for watches and clocks, such as straps, cases, movements, batteries and the like. Although these rules do not infringe directly on any WTO agreements, Japan argues that they are inconsistent with GATT Article IX:2, which calls for the development of rules of origin that do not impede commerce (Japan 2002, pp. 10–11; Japan, 2006, p. 39).

Failure to recognize the EU as a country of origin For the most part, programs involving product regulations are developed and supervised at the EU level; examples include sanitary and phytosanitary requirements, product safety requirements and environmental regulations. However, US regulators may require separate certifications from each EU country.

The EU has repeatedly asked the US to recognize the EU as a separate country of origin. Thus far, the US has refused (European Union, 2006, fiche 970144).

2.1b Sanitary and phytosanitary requirements

Excessive quarantine periods for certain types of live ornamental plants Foreign companies shipping plants to the US are not allowed to include growing media in the exports unless a pest risk assessment has been carried out by the Department of Agriculture's Animal, Plant and Health Inspection Service (APHIS). The process of obtaining a risk assessment has proven to be very time consuming. The Department of Homeland Security (HLS), not APHIS, is now responsible for border inspection. The HLS inspectors do not seem to have the necessary expertise to carry out these tasks. Neither APHIS nor HLS have been diligent in notifying potential exporters of problems with their shipments (European Union, 2007, fiche 960081; European Union, 2007, fiche 960082).

Stringent BSE quarantine rules The EU argued that US has strongly backed the adoption of the rules for quarantining beef that may carry bovine spongiform encephalopathy that were developed by the Organization for International Epizootics (European Union, 2006, fiche 960083).

Limits on importing uncooked meats The EU argues that the US rules banning the importation of uncooked meats should be amended to allow companies to bring in some types of hams and sausages (European Union, 2007, fiche 960088).

2.1c Limitations on foreign-sourced services

US discrimination against foreign financial service providers Financial, insurance and banking services are regulated in the US at the state level. Some states prohibit foreign banks from opening branches or agencies. Only three states allow foreign banks to operate on a par with domestic banks in all areas of service. The US stipulated many reservations when it signed the Commitments on Financial Services. A degree of national harmonization in state licensing requirements was introduced with the passage of the Gramm-Leach-Bliley Act in 1999. Japan hopes that an extension of this initiative may help remove some of the discriminatory barriers facing foreign financial service providers seeking to enter US markets (Japan, 2002, pp. 43–45; Japan, 2006, pp. 44–45).

US discrimination against foreign telecommunications service providers The Federal Communications Commission (FCC) regulations of February 1998 barred foreign service suppliers from participating in the Economic Competitive Opportunity program. Foreign direct investment restrictions were maintained. Foreign applications for FCC licenses could be denied on the basis of the "public use" doctrine or because the application posed "extremely high threats to competition", or for "foreign policy or trade concerns". The guidelines governing these decisions are vague and the FCC has substantial latitude in making licensing decisions. The states have major responsibilities and discretion in implementing the FCC regulations and decisions at the operational level. According to the Japanese report, these policies have created a fragmented market and constitute substantial barriers to market entry for foreign telecommunications service providers. However, they are not in violation of WTO commitments (Japan 2002, pp. 45–47; Japan, 2006, pp. 45–46).

The Merchant Shipping Act of 1920 (the Jones Act) This states that only ships owned by US citizens, built in US yards and manned by US crews can be used in US domestic trade. Japan considers the Jones Act to be in violation of GATT Article III, guaranteeing national treatment of imported goods and services, and GATT Article XI, which prohibits the imposition of quantitative restrictions in general (Japan, 2002, pp. 6, 48–52; Japan 2006, pp. 46–47).

The US argues that the Jones Act supports national defense efforts because it provides work for shipyards and merchant marine crews that would constitute vital assets in the event of a a major mobilization. The US further argues that the Jones Act is covered by the special rule on the provisional application of GATT 1947. The US insisted in the Uruguay Round that the Special Rule should be carried forward into GATT 1994. Since then, the US has insisted that the provisions for a periodic review of the inclusion of the special rule in GATT 1994 should be terminated when there has been no change in the underlying circumstances (European Union, 2006, fiches 960098 and 060129).

2.1d Restrictions on foreign investments

Barriers to foreign participation in US energy markets Under the Federal Power Act, anyone who is involved in the construction, operation or maintenance of interstate power facilities must be licensed. Licenses are also required for facilities involved in the production or use of nuclear materials. Only US citizens can receive licenses. The European Union argues that these restrictions are unjustified (European Union, 2006, fiche 960066).

The Exon-Florio Amendment (United States, 1968 5 USC app 2170) The Exon-Florio Amendment to the Omnibus Trade and Competitiveness Act of 1988 authorizes the president to suspend acquisitions, mergers and take-overs of US firms by foreign firms if they threaten US national security. The Committee for Foreign Investments in the United States, an agency of the US Department of the Treasury, is responsible for reporting to the president on the potential impact of proposed transactions.

The EU and Japan argued that these procedures are creating an ever-more uncertain investment climate. Japan recognizes that the GATT rules on trade and investment permit national security exemptions, so the Exon-Florio Amendment does not violate international law. However, Japan asks for a lessened reliance on national security issues and for greater transparency in the investigation and decision procedures (European Union, 2006, fiche 960064; Japan 2002, p. 42; Japan, 2006, pp. 43–44).

2.1e Government procurement issues

Barriers to foreign participation in government procurement According to the EU, the US has placed a series of substantial barriers to foreign participation in domestic government procurement programs (European Union, 2006, fiche 960059). The government of Japan also considers the various Buy American provisions to be inconsistent with the spirit, if not the letter, of GATT. Japan has asked the US government to review the status of Buy American programs (European Union, 2006, fiche 960100; Japan, 2002, pp. 71–72).

Three basic statutes shape government procurement policies in the United States. The Buy America Act (United States, 1933) directs Federal agencies to purchase for public use only goods that have been "manufactured in the United States" (41 USC 10(a)-(d)). To be produced or manufactured in the United States, 50 per cent or more of the content must have been processed within the United States.

Most procurement by the Federal government is subject to the terms of the Executive Order 10582, which significantly expands the scope of the 1933 Buy American Act. Most states and local governments have also enacted some form of "Buy American" legislation. Many programs that are administered at the state and local levels have substantial funding from Federal government grant programs. These programs are usually subject to the procurement restrictions enacted at both the Federal and state or local levels. The terms of these restrictions differ from program to program.

The second factor is a federal system and the various Federal grants programs that create complexities in government procurement at the state and local levels that limit foreign bidding opportunities as a practical matter.

However, the US is also a signatory to the WTO *Agreement on Government Procurement* (GPA), which explicitly authorizes foreign access to government procurement markets. US ratification of the GPA was based on reservations for service contracts, construction contracts and national security items. This was consistent with established American policy (Nuttle, 1979).

The Trade Agreements Act of 1979 authorizes the US president to suspend enforcement of the Buy America Act against countries that have acceded to the 1994 Agreement on Government Procurement and have extended similar rights to US companies. This partial exception has been expanded for some programs in subsequent legislation. For example, the Department of Homeland Security appropriations bill for 2005 would enforce the Buy America Act for all procurement. Under the terms of the Surface Transportation Assistance Act of 1987, as amended by the Intermodal Surface Transportation Efficiency Act of 1991, mass transit rolling stock purchased with Federal funds must be made in the US. The definition of "made in the US" in the Act is raised to 60 per cent by value. All iron and steel used in projects funded by the Federal Highway Administration must be manufactured in the US. AMTRAK, the national passenger rail service, must apply the Buy America Act to all purchases over $1 million. Most states have "buy American" and/or "buy state" requirements for government procurement contracts.

Thirty-seven of the 50 states are participating in the GPA. However, local implementation is uneven and the Act does not include local governments or publicly owned utilities. Thus, foreign contractors are often shut out from the bidding, not because the terms are prohibitive, but because they are essentially indeterminate (European Union, 2006, fiche 960059).

US barriers to foreign participation in defense procurement contracts On one hand, the US has been opening up the defense procurement process to foreign companies through the negotiation of memoranda of understanding (MOU) with the foreign host governments that set forth the terms of participation. MOUs have been signed with most of the NATO countries.

However, the EU argues that the terms of participation have substantially lessened the effectiveness of the MOU program. Most of the requests for proposals are classified. Managers working for foreign companies are not eligible for security clearance unless they have a need to know, that is, unless they are already working on a classified contract. Some products have to be manufactured in facilities located on US soil. US export regulations limit the transfer of technology developed in the US to companies or countries outside the US. These requirements discourage foreign companies from bringing in technologies they have developed elsewhere for incorporation into a product to be sold to the US government (European Union, 2006, fiche 960056).

The Berry Amendment The US has been imposing country-of-origin restrictions on contracts issued by the US Department of Defense since 1941. These provisions apply primarily to government procurement of textiles, food and specialty metals. Under the terms of the Berry Amendment the Department of Defense is required to increase a bid involving products from non-qualifying countries by 50 per cent when comparing it against bids for the procurement of US-origin products. Foreign-sourced specialty metals must be smelted within the United States in order to quality for government procurement (European Union, 2006, fiche 960055).

Limits on using foreign satellite launchers The National Space Policy Directives of 1990 and 1994 prohibit US government agencies from using foreign launch vehicles. One exception, NASA, is authorized to use foreign launch vehicles on collaborative projects that do not involve the transfer of funds. The restrictions were originally justified as a means of strengthening US military capabilities. However, the policy has been extended to cover launching services for civilian satellites. The EU argues that these are discriminatory measures that favor US industry that can't be justified by national defense interests (European Union, 1006, fiche 960057).

Buy America requirement on transportation projects The US Department of Transportation Federal Highway Administration funds between 40 per cent and 80 per cent of the costs of most local transportation projects. State and/or local governments usually fund the balance. All goods and services bought for transportation projects involving Federal funds must meet Federal Buy American requirements. Domestic content requirements are usually set at 60 per cent. To be eligible to participate, the bids from non-conforming vendors must be increased by up to 25 per cent (European Union, 2007, fiche 960058).

Small business set-asides The Small Business Act of 1953 directs US Federal government agencies to place a fair portion of their purchase contracts with small businesses. All contracts involving payments of more than \$2500 and less than \$100 000 are automatically set aside for small businesses, unless minimum bid requirements are not met. The small business set-asides are specifically exempt from the provisions of the Government Procurement Agreement. To qualify as a small business, a company must have a place of business within the US and have fewer than a specified number of employees, usually 500.

Minority business set-aside programs These have been developed by a number of state governments. It is a Federal–state partnership: the national Small Business Administration certifies the eligibility of local businesses for minority status through the Small Disadvantaged Business Certification and Eligibility Program (European Union, 2007, fiche 960300). As a practical matter it would be very difficult for a foreign-owned business to participate in the small business set-asides.

In 1999, the small business set-aside program was expanded with the addition of a 1 per cent set-aside program for businesses located in "historically underutilized business zones". The HUBzone set asides grew gradually to 3 per cent of all Federal government procurement in 2003 (European Union, 2007, fiche 960300).

2.1f Safeguard issues

The Cuban Liberty and Democratic Solidarity Act of 1996 (Helms-Burton Act) This Act (United States, 1996 22 United States Code secs 5021–6091) authorized any US citizen who had property seized by the Cuban government to sue in US courts anyone who subsequently traffics in that property. The Secretary of State is directed to deny entry to anyone who has been involved in the confiscation of Cuban property previously owned by US nationals. The Act was passed over the objections of President Clinton, who delayed full implementation for several years.

Japan argues that this authorization for unilateral actions in US courts against foreign corporations is inconsistent with GATT/WTO obligations. The EU, Canada and Mexico have enacted laws barring their nationals from complying with Helms-Burton requirements. The EU asked for WTO consultations in 1996. No progress was made, so a dispute panel was established. Both the Clinton and Bush Administrations suspended the authorization for filing suits in US courts. The EU agreed to suspend the dispute resolution process if the US Congress would provide the president with the authority to also suspend the provisions governing authorization to enter the US. No progress has been made on this issue since then (European Union, 2006, fiche 960295; Japan, 2002, pp. 74–76: Japan, 2006, pp. 67–68; World Trade Organization, *DS 176*).

The Anti-Dumping Act of 1916 (ADA) This was a major source of contention. The basic tests for dumping were generally consistent with the provisions of the ADA, which was discussed in Chapter 2. The 1916 statute simply states that: "It shall be unlawful . . . to import . . . articles at a price substantially less than the actual market value . . . at the time of exportation to the United States . . . Provided that such act . . . be done with the intent of destroying or injuring an industry in the United States" (15 USC 72 *et seq.*).

The procedures and penalties of the 1916 Act are inconsistent with the requirements of the ADA in significant areas. The ADA agreement authorizes offended countries to impose "countervailing duties on imports from the dumping firm that are equal to the magnitude of the dumping margin". The 1916 Act authorizes the government to impose criminal sanctions, including a fine of up to $5000 and a year in jail. Any party that is injured by the dumping can sue the offending company for treble damages, including reasonable attorney's fees.

Both the EU and Japan have been seriously upset by both the provisions of the 1916 Act (Japan, 2002, pp. 11–16; Japan 2006 pp. 22–23). Intergovernmental discussions did not resolve the issue, and the EU asked for consultations under the DRU on 9 June 1988. Consultations failed to resolve the issue. The EU asked for the establishment of DRU panel on I November 1998. A panel was created I April 1999.

The panel report was circulated on 31 March 2000. It concluded that the provisions of the 1916 Anti-Dumping Law violated Articles VI:1 and VI:2 of GATT, Articles 1, 4 and 5.5 of the Anti-Dumping Agreement and Article XVI:4 of the WTO agreement. Basically, the US law was deficient because it provided for treble damages, it did not provide for exclusive remedies for injuries caused by dumping, and it did not include some of the procedural safeguards required by the international agreements (World Trade Organization, 2007, *DS 136*).

Japan asked for consultations over the failure of the US to repeal the Anti-Dumping Act of 1916 on 10 February 1999. The panel was organized on 26 July 1999. The Japanese panel came to the same conclusions as the EU panel (World Trade Organization, 1999, *DS 162*).

The US filed a notice to appeal the conclusions on 29 May 2000. The appeals panel upheld the original conclusions and the Appellate Body adopted the Report on 26 September 2000. On 21 December 2001, the US announced an intention to implement the findings of the Report by repealing the provisions of the 1916 Anti-Dumping Act.

On 7 January 2002, the EU and Japan asked for authorization to suspend tariff concessions on the grounds that the US had not, in fact, made any progress towards implementation of the panel recommendations. The US argued that the EU and Japan had not followed the appropriate procedures in making this request. The US also requested the appointment of an arbitrator to resolve the issue of damages. On 27 February 2002, the parties asked that the arbitration be suspended to give the US further opportunities to repeal the 1916 Act.

The Byrd Amendment (The Continued Dumping and Subsidy Act of 2000 (19 United States Code 1675c) This required any monies recovered through the imposition of anti-dumping duties to be distributed to the companies that filed or supported the petition against dumping. This rewards companies for prosecuting anti-dumping cases, which is inconsistent with the terms of the ADA. In the 2006 METI Report, Japan argues that this is illegal under the WTO Agreement (Japan 2002, pp.21–22, 26–27; Japan, 2006, pp.19–21; European Union, 2006, fiche 02004).

In 2000, Japan the EU, Australia, South Korea, Brazil, India, Thailand, Indonesia and Chile requested consultation with the US about the Byrd Amendment under the WTO dispute resolution process. Canada and Mexico joined in the process in 2001. The issue was not resolved through the consultation process and dispute resolution panels were organized in 2001. The report of the consolidated panel was circulated in 2002. The Panel found that the Byrd Amendment was in violation of the WTO agreement for multiple reasons. A repeal of the amendment was the recommended remedy (World Trade Organization, 2002, *DS 217*).

The US appealed the panel's decision in October 2002. The Appellate Body upheld the Panel's original findings. The WTO Dispute Resolution Body adopted the Appellate Panel's report. The US let the implementation deadline pass without taking any measures to implement the recommendations of the Panel.

In January 2004, Japan, the EU, Canada, the Republic of Korea, Mexico, Brazil, India and Chile requested WTO approval for the imposition of countermeasures. The US argued that the proposed countermeasures were inappropriate. This dispute was referred to arbitration. In August 2004, the arbitrator ruled that the authorized level of retaliation was 0.72 times the level of disbursements made under the Byrd Amendment. The countermeasures were implemented by Japan, the EU, Chile and Mexico in 2005. President Bush signed the Deficit Reduction Act of 2005 on 8 February 2006, which repealed the Byrd Amendment. However, the statute stated that disbursements under the Byrd Amendment would continue during a transition period. Japan extended the time for imposing countermeasures until August 2006. The

2007 METI Report called on the US to cease the enforcement of the Byrd Amendment during the transition period.

The US planned to continue using the existing rules for the pending cases. This, the complainants argued, was unacceptable. The arbitrator circulated recommendations on the countermeasures that the EU and Japan could impose on the US for its failure to comply with the Dispute Resolution conclusions.

The US asked for arbitration on the magnitude and timing of the penalty. The arbitrator's report was circulated on 24 February 2004. The penalty was to be based on damages imposed by US courts on European and Japanese companies under the 1916 Act. By 2007, the Act had been repealed, the Hyde amendment was enacted and the EU and Japan were threatening sanctions, eight years after the dispute was first referred to the WTO.

The Byrd Act was repealed for new claims in January 2006. However, the provisions of the Act continued to be applied for pending cases until 1 October 2007.

The use of the zeroing methodology Under the zeroing methodology, the US International Trade Commission would assign a value of zero to the difference between the foreign price and the US import price on an item whenever the US price was higher than the foreign price. However, these data are, in fact, evidence that dumping had not occurred. Since the use of the zeroing methodology essentially ignores important evidence against a finding of dumping, it can seriously skew investigations towards a finding that dumping had occurred.

On 12 June 2003, the EU asked for WTO consultations on the use of the zeroing methodology. The panel was created on 27 October 2004. Argentina, Brazil, China, Taipei, Hong Kong, India, Japan, Korea, Mexico, Norway and Turkey joined in as third parties to the dispute (World Trade Organization, 2006, *DS 294*).

The panel report was circulated for comment on 31 October 2006. The panel concluded that the use of the zeroing methodology was inconsistent with the requirements of the Anti-Dumping Agreement. The US appealed the decision. The report of the appellate panel was circulated on 18 April 2006. The findings of Panel 294 were upheld. On 24 April 2007, the US announced that it had implemented the conclusions of Panel 294. The EU argued that the US actions did not constitute a repeal of the zeroing methodology and asked for consultations over the US claim. Brazil and Korea asked to join in the discussions.

US retaliation against discrimination in foreign government procurement Under Title VII of the Federal Buy America Act (as amended by the

Omnibus Trade and Competitiveness Act of 1988), the USTR is directed to report annually to Congress on discrimination by foreign governments against US products and services. The USTR is also directed to enter into consultations with the named governments on the basis of the findings in the report. The US government is authorized to take unilateral measures if the discrimination is not resolved within a year. The one-year deadline was extended to 18 months in the US Uruguay Round Agreement Act.

The EU and Japan agree that the initial process of identifying countries that discriminate and entering into bilateral discussions is entirely within the scope and spirit of GATT/WTO. However, the subsequent authorization for unilateral measures is inconsistent with the Agreement on Government Procurement. In fact, the US identified the Japanese telecommunications market as one of the areas in which there was discrimination against US vendors. However a mutually satisfactory resolution was achieved through the US–Japan Economic Framework Talks and no unilateral measures were taken (European Union, 2006, fiche 990060; Japan, 2006, pp. 64–66).

Section 301 of the Trade Act of 1974 This authorizes the United States Trade Representative to take unilateral actions against unreasonable, unfair or discriminatory international practices or against foreign violations of international agreements. The USTR is required to take action in cases where the foreign government actions violate GATT or other trade agreements, or are unjustifiable and burden or restrict US commerce. USTR action is discretionary if the foreign offense is unreasonable or discriminatory and burdens US commerce. If there is a finding that the foreign government action violates the terms of Section 301, then the USTR may suspend the benefits of trade agreements that would otherwise be applicable, impose duties and other import restrictions or levy other restrictions on the sale of foreign services in the US. In effect, the USTR can take unilateral actions that bypass the WTO mechanisms for adjudicating international trade disputes.

The EU asked for WTO consultations on Section 301 in November 1998. The talks did not resolve the issue, so a dispute resolution panel was created in March 1999. Japan participated as a third party in support of the EU's position. The US president issued guidelines for administering Section 301 that included a pledge to maintain consistency with the WTO Agreement (European Union, 2006, fiches 960050 and 99003; Japan, 2002, pp. 63–71; Japan, 2006, pp. 58–62; World Trade Organization 1999, *DS 152*).

The carousel rule on amending items subject to retaliatory measures The Trade and Development Act of 2000 includes a "carousel provision" that requires the USTR to rotate the items on which the US can impose retaliatory measures under a WTO dispute resolution process every 180 days to ensure that all sanctions are enforced. This measure was taken in response to the failure of the EU to promptly implement corrective actions after losing WTO cases on beef hormones and bananas. Japan argues that this provision is inconsistent with the WTO Dispute Resolution Understanding (see Chapter 2). However, the carousel provision has never been utilized so the dispute is not particularly relevant (European Union, 2006, fiche 990090; Japan 2002, pp. 72–73).

The Iran and Libya Sanctions Act of 1996 The "Damato" Act authorizes the US president to take a series of unilateral actions against any company that does significant business in Iran and/or Libya. These measures include denying US Ex-Im export assistance, US export licenses and government procurement contracts, prohibiting US financial institutions from loaning more than $10 million per year and prohibiting their designation as primary dealers in US debt instruments (European Union, 2007, fiche 960061; Japan, 2002, pp. 76–78; Japan, 2006, pp. 68–71).

Japan argues that these sanctions are inconsistent with WTO/GATT obligations, especially since they may be applied extraterritorially, even though the law has never been applied. It officially expired in August 2001. US business consistently opposed reauthorization. However, President Bush signed a bill authorizing a five-year extension on 3 August 2001. The reauthorization included a requirement that the president report on the effectiveness of the law within 30 months. As a result of the efforts of Libya to normalize relations with the US, the provisions authorizing sanctions against companies doing business in Libya were suspended on 23 April 2004. However, the measures against Iran were strengthened and the provisions for expiry of the measures were eliminated.

Countervailing duties against steel products from Europe The US imposed countervailing duties in 1998 against a number of French, British and Spanish steel companies. Some of the firms covered by the countervailing duties had been owned by the British government and were later privatized. The US continued to impose duties on the ground that there had been a continuation in the identity of the privatized firms, even though their financial situation had changed substantially (European Union, 2007, fiche 060079). The EU asked for WTO consultations and a panel was organized in November 2001. In 2002, the panel found that the loss of state subsidies should have been grounds for reviewing the finding that there had been dumping and that the US was in violation of the Subsidies and Countervailing Measures Agreement. The US appealed the panel's finding. The appellate panel upheld the original finding.

In 2004, the EU asked for further WTO consultations because the US had failed to implement the appellate panel findings. A second panel was then organized in September 2004. The second panel only found for the EU on the issue of the continuation of countervailing duties against the privatized British firms. The US issued a report on implementation measures in November 2005 (World Trade Organization, 2005, *Dispute Resolution Panels DS 138, DS 212*).

The EU also complained that the US Department of Commerce had based a finding that dumping had occurred on inadequate evidence. The Department of Commerce had both refused to accept the data provided by a British firm, Firth Rixson Special Steels Limited, and had failed to develop an adequate evidentiary basis for the decision on its own (European Union, 2007, fiche 060117).

2.2 Domestic Regulations Affecting International Trade

2.2a Standards and technical requirements

The Passenger Motor Vehicle Content Information Disclosure Act of 1992 This states that all passenger cars and light trucks sold in the United States must carry labels that specify the content percentage of US and Canadian parts, the country, state and city of final assembly, the country of origin of the engine and transmission and the top two countries supplying the foreign-built components, if the percentage of foreign components exceeds 15 per cent.

The Japanese government regards this requirement as an implicit trade barrier. Foreign car manufacturers using a high percentage of non-US or Canadian components must engage in an enormous amount of clerical work to track component sources and values. The US argues that this information helps consumers make more informed decisions. In 2003, the US stated that this requirement would be hard to change since it was imposed by Congress. The US representative suggested that the US, Japanese and EU automakers might develop a joint strategy regarding content labeling requirements that could be adopted in all three regions (European Union 2006, fiche 060101; Japan, 2002, pp. 38–39; Japan 2006, pp. 39–41).

The Corporate Average Fuel Economy (CAFE) rules The Energy Policy and Conservation Act of 1975 set forth the CAFE regulations, which state that the autos sold in the US by a particular manufacturer must, on average, meet minimum mileage requirements. Furthermore, the CAFE fleet averages must be calculated separately for cars made in the US and cars made abroad.

Many foreign manufacturers concentrate on selling large, high-value, high-margin cars in US markets. As a result, the CAFE requirements tend to affect foreign exporters more than US manufacturers. Foreign manufacturers regularly pay between $1m and $20m annually in CAFE penalties (European Union, 2006, fiche 980072). Japan argued that these requirements were inconsistent with GATT commitments to national treatment for imported products (EU 2007, fiche 960073; Japan, 2002, pp. 39–41; Japan 2006, pp. 41–42).

The EU asked for WTO consultations before the GATT Council on the legality of the CAFE rules in May 1992. The discussions were fruitless and a dispute resolution panel was created in September 1994. The panel held that the CAFE rules discriminated against imported cars, both smaller and larger ones, and was inconsistent with GATT. The US rejected the findings on the grounds that the CAFE rules had no material effect on European commercial interests. In a January 2003 meeting of the Automotive Consultative Group, the US argued that the issue was difficult for the government to handle and that a resolution would require Congressional action.

The failure to use the metric system The US and Liberia are the only two countries that still rely primarily on the imperial system of metrology. Japan argues that the failure of the US to follow international practice in metrology hampers international trade and may be inconsistent with the requirements of the Agreement on Technical Barriers to Trade.

In the second Annual Report of Structural Impediments follow-up, the US made a commitment to use the metric system in federal procurement, subsidy programs and commercial activities and to implement a Department of Commerce study on ways to substantially expand the use of the metric system by the private sector. In the 2000 Report on the US–Japanese Enhanced Initiative on Deregulation and Competition Policy, the US made a commitment to coordinate the full implementation of the Uniform Packaging and Labeling Regulations between the National Institute of Standards and Technology (NIST) and the National Conference on Weights and Measures. The US also pledged to update the Fair Packaging and Labeling Act to permit metric-only labeling. However, little progress has been reported on the issue since 2000 (European Union, 2006, fiche 060144; Japan, 2002, pp. 41–42; Japan 2006, pp. 42–43).

2.2b Intellectual property policies

The "first to invent" doctrine In determining the relative validity of competing patent applications, the US follows the principle that the "first to invent" has priority. Outside the US, priority almost always goes to the "first to file". The EU argues that the "first to invent" principle often creates the opportunity for endless litigation in which the US applicants often have an advantage. In contrast, relative priorities under the "first to file" principle can be determined through reference to generally unambiguous public documents. The potential insecurity in IP rights that is created by the US system constitutes a significant barrier to EU–US trade (European Union, 2006, fiche 980141).

The Hillmer Doctrine on Intellectual property Foreign corporations often file for a US patent in order to protect their intellectual property within the United States. From time to time, these applications may be contested on the grounds that the foreign applicant does not have priority of invention. Outside the US, questions of priority are settled on the basis of priority of application. The foreign corporation would only have to show that it applied for a patent, either in its own country or abroad, before the protesting party. This is usually a simple process. In the US though, questions of priority are based on the Hillmer Doctrine, which bases decisions on priority according to who was first to file in the US.

Japan and the EU acknowledge that the Hillmer Doctrine may be valid under Article 2 of the TRIPS Agreement and/or the Patent Cooperation Agreement, depending on the interpretation of the text. A patent reform bill that would have abolished the Hillmer Doctrine was introduced in the US House of Representatives on 8 June 2003. It did not pass and no further actions were reported (European Union, 2006, fiche 060123; Japan 2002, pp. 52–54; Japan, 2006, pp. 48–50).

Videogame rentals under US copyright law Section 109(b)(1)(A) of the US Copyright Act authorizes rental rights for computer programs. Section (B) is the paragraph exempting videogames from granting rental rights. Japan argues that US law is inconsistent with Articles 9 and 13 of the TRIPS Agreement, and Articles 1–12 of the Berne Convention. These policies are also inconsistent with international practices. Videogames should be covered by US copyright laws.

The EU asked for consultations. These discussions failed to resolve the issues and a dispute resolution panel was established in May 1999. Japan, Australia, Canada and Switzerland participated as third parties. The panel decision in the year 2000 supported the EU position. In June 2003, the US and the EU agreed that the US would provide \$3.3 billion in compensation for damages. Thus far, the US has failed either to comply with this agreement or to conform national law to international requirements (World Trade Organization, 2007, *DS 160*).

Cuban trademarks under US trademark law Section 211 of the Omnibus Act of 1998 prohibits US courts from recognizing trademarks that have been claimed by Cuban nationals that are associated with property confiscated by the government of Cuba. Both the EU and Japan argue that this policy is fundamentally inconsistent with the terms of both the TRIPS Agreement and basic WTO principles (European Union, 2006, fiche 990079; Japan, 2006, p. 50).

The EU asked for bilateral consultations in 1999. A dispute resolution panel found for the EU. On 2 January 2002, the Appellate Panel upheld the most important findings of the Dispute Resolution Panel. On 1 February 2002, the US stated its intentions to adhere to its WTO obligations. The US has still not implemented the findings of the Appellate Panel (World Trade Organization, *DS 176*).

The "Barbershop" exemption Section 110(5) of the 1978 copyright law allows business proprietors to play broadcast music in public places, such as bars, restaurants and shops, without paying a royalty to the copyright holder. EU copyright holders have incurred substantial losses as a result of this provision. Both the EU and Japan have raised this issue with the US.

The EU asked for WTO consultations over the issue. A panel was organized in 2000. Both the original panel and the subsequent appellate panel concluded that the US law was inconsistent with the TRIPS Agreement in connection with the Berne Convention on the Protection of Literary and Artistic Works. An arbitrator decided that the penalty should be \$1 219 000 per year.

Since the US could not make a commitment that Congress would amend the law in the near future, a compromise was reached. For the penalty, the US agreed to financially contribute to EU performing societies with the goal of promoting the further development of authors' rights.

This was a three-year agreement that expired on 21 December 2004. No changes were made in the US law and there were no pending proposals for a change. The EU had reserved the right to suspend concessions to the US under WTO agreements in the event that this issue was not resolved in a satisfactory manner. The EU therefore proposed to levy a special fee on the importation of US goods that are subject to EU intellectual property claims. The US protested this measure and the matter was referred to arbitration. Arbitration proceedings were subsequently suspended (European Union, 2007, fiche 970191; Japan, 2002, pp. 55–57; Japan, 2006, pp. 51–52; World Trade Organization, *DS 160*).

Government use of patented materials Under Article 31 of the TRIPS Agreement, governments are obliged to promptly notify parties holding patent rights in the event that the government makes use of patented materials. The EU alleges that the US has, in many cases, failed to carry out this responsibility (European Union, 2006, fiche 980140).

Limits on authors' moral rights The Berne Convention recognizes the rights of artists to: prevent others from claiming authorship of their work; prevent others from modifying their work in prejudicial ways while keeping their name associated with it; and prevent the use of their name as author of works they did not create. The EU argues that the recognition of these moral rights is very limited under US law, even though the US acceded to the Berne Convention in 1989 (Japan, 2002, pp. 52–53; Japan 1996, p. 52–53; European Union, 2006, fiche 980142).

The handling of intellectual priority infringement cases Under Section 337 of the Tariff Act of 1930, companies in the US can file for "exclusion orders" that will bar the importation of products that would infringe on the applicants' intellectual property rights. These procedures are not available against domestic products that may infringe on IP rights. The EU charges that the International Trade Commission has instituted a series of Section 337 cases against European products on the basis of very weak claims. These seem to have no other purpose than to force European exporters to agree to terms imposed by their US competitors (European Union, 2006, fiche 980139).

2.2c Market regulation issues

Foreign corporation tax reporting requirements The US corporate tax code requires certain foreign-owned corporations to maintain a separate set of records documenting all transactions with related entities. This obligation is not imposed on US-owned corporations. The EU recognizes that there is a legitimate purpose for collecting this information. However, it argues that the actual burden outweighs the potential benefits (European Union, 2006, fiche 960069).

Fragmented markets for electrical products The EU argued that the existence of multiple, overlapping jurisdictions in the regulation of electrical equipment constitutes a barrier to trade. At the national level, the safety of electrical products is regulated by OSHA, the Occupational Safety and Health Administration, with the minor involvement of the Federal Communications Commission and the Consumer Products Safety Commission. Electrical products are also regulated by state and regional building codes. There are at least three basic models for these codes, each with many local variations. Finally, the courts impose a type of *ex post facto* regulation through product liability lawsuits. The complexity of this system makes it difficult for foreign manufacturers to identify the design and performance parameters for electrical products they would like to export to the US (European Union, 2006, fiche 960054).

2.3 US Policies Affecting Exports

2.3a Export restraints

Export Management Systems The International Economic Powers Act (IEPA) authorizes the US government to impose restrictions on agricultural exports for reasons of domestic shortages or foreign policy goals. The Act was used to restrict the sale of soybeans to Japan in 1973 and of wheat to the Soviet Union and Poland in 1974 and 1975.

Japan accepts the position that the Act is consistent with international law. Most of the GATT restrictions apply to import tariffs and procedures. There are relatively few restrictions in international law on export tariffs and quantitative restrictions. However, the Japanese argue that the IEPA distorts international markets and adversely affects the domestic food security of importing nations (Japan, 2002, pp. 8–10; Japan 2006, pp. 8–10).

Export restrictions on logs The US has restricted domestic logging operations in order to protect the habitats of the spotted owl and other endangered species. These restrictions have limited the domestic supply of logs, which led to the passage of the Foreign Conservation Shortage and Relief Act of 1990. Under the authority of this Act, the US has banned the export of logs taken from Federal lands west of longitude 100.

The US argues that this restriction is for the conservation of exhaustible natural resources and is therefore exempt from GATT under the provisions of Article XX(g) and therefore is not covered by Article XI. Japan argues that there are no restrictions on the harvesting and sale of logs for domestic commerce. The ban may therefore be in violation of GATT Article XI. Japan has pushed for discussions of this issue in both the Doha Round and in bilateral negotiations (Japan, 2002, pp. 7–8; Japan, 2006, pp. 15–16).

2.3b Export subsidies

Export subsidies in the 2002 Farm Bill Existing agricultural subsidies couldn't compensate farmers for losses due to the worldwide slump in grain prices that began in the late 1990s as a result of the strong dollar and an increase in EU agricultural subsidies. The US Congress enacted a series of emergency farm assistance programs between 1998 and 2001. Under the Export Enhancement Program, farmers could receive subsidy bonuses for chicken production that were equal to the value of any discounts they might provide to their export buyers. The Dairy Incentive Export Program provided similar subsidies for the export of dairy products. The Export Credit Guarantee Program provided government guarantees to banks issuing letters of credit to importers in developing countries to cover US agricultural imports. Loan guarantees were also available. The EU and Japan repeatedly complained about different aspects of these programs (European Union, 2006, fiches 960092, 960303 and 010050; Japan, 2002, pp. 27–30).

A new Farm Bill was passed in May 2002. It combined the features of both the old parity program and the newer production flexibility contract program. Additional subsidy payments were to kick in when the combined value of market income and production flexibility contract proceeds fell below a nominal ("parity") level. The program included soybeans for the first time. The 2002 Farm program also maintained the export incentive programs that were developed in the interim farm support measures.

Many countries have expressed concern over the provisions of the programs enacted with the passage of the 2002 Farm Bill. Export subsidies for agricultural products to specific countries, per se, do not violate the terms of the Agricultural Agreement that was negotiated in the Uruguay Round. However, the aggregate levels of farm subsidies must not exceed the commitments made by the US. In the Uruguay Round, the US agreed to limit the aggregate measure of support given to US farmers. Japan is monitoring US farm payments under the 2002 Program to ensure that the commitments made by the US to limit subsidies to US farmers are not exceeded (Japan, 2006, pp. 35–38).

Aircraft development subsidies The EU has challenged subsidies given to Boeing by the states of Washington and Kansas to encourage the company to build or expand plants in these regions. The subsidies have an estimated value of almost $5b. The EU argues that these subsidies constitute a breach of GATT obligations (European Union, 2007, fiche 970301).

Talks between the US and the EU failed to resolve the dispute and the EU asked for the organization of a dispute resolution panel (World Trade

Organization, 2007, Panel *DS 317*). The US refused to provide the panel with the necessary documentation, so a second panel was created in 2005. Australia, Brazil, Canada, China and Japan asked to join the dispute. This panel was expected to complete its work by July 2008 (World Trade Organization, 2007, *DS 353*).

Subsidies for US merchant ships operating in international trade The US government subsidized the construction, operation and financing of US flag ships built in US yards that were operated in international trade (The Merchant Marine Act of 1920). The level of subsidy was equal to the difference between foreign flag costs and US flag costs. As a result, the US became home to the most expensive national flag fleet in the world. The US refused to accept the 1994 OECD agreement on shipping subsidies. The US also prohibits foreign flag vessels from carrying cargo from one US port to another. The US is allowed to limit domestic shipments to domestic vessels under Article 3 of the 1994 GATT Agreement. However, the UK argues that the US definition of a "ship" is too broad (European Union, 2006, fiche 960098; Japan, 2006, pp. 12–13).

Foreign sales corporations Under the EU rules for VAT, exporters do not pay any VAT on exports. Instead, full VAT is paid to the importing country. This has the effect of eliminating the option for the EU member states to lower their VAT rates in order to promote exports to other EU states. However, it places US exporters at a significant disadvantage in comparison with their European colleagues. While EU corporations can export to the US, tax free, US exporters to the EU have to pay both US taxes and European VAT.

Sections 921–927 of the United States Internal Revenue Code authorized the creation of untaxed "foreign sales corporations", which could function as profit centers for major exporters. FSCs were the successors of DISCs, domestic international sales corporations. Their purpose was in part to offer some of the advantages that were available to European exporters under the VAT rules.

The European Union argued that the tax benefits available to FSCs were prohibited under the Subsidies and Countervailing Measures (SCM) Agreement and the Agreement on Agriculture. The dispute was referred to the WTO and a panel was formed in 1998. The panel report was circulated in October 1999. The EU had prevailed on all major points. The United States appealed. The Appellate Body report found that the United States was in violation of the SCM Agreement but not with parts of the the Agriculture Agreement. The appellate panel report was adopted by the Dispute Resolution Body in 2000.

The US enacted the FSC Repeal and Extraterritorial Income Exclusion Act in 2000. The EU argued that the repeal had not, in fact, brought the United States into compliance with its international obligations. A new panel was formed and the report was circulated in August 2001. It concluded that the United States was still out of compliance with international obligations. The appellate body generally agreed the dispute panel conclusions.

In 2005, the EU reported that the US had not complied with the requirements of the SCM Agreement and the Agricultural Agreement. A third panel was formed. The decision went against the United States, which filed an appeal. The appellate body report was issued in 2006, which was again against the United States. The dispute was then referred back to the original panel (World Trade Organization, 2007, DS 108).

3. ISSUES RAISED FOR THE FIRST TIME IN 2007

The list of 27 emerging issues is set forth in Table 4.2.

3.1 Import-related Issues

3.1a Trade administration

Cotton import fee The US collects a fee equal to 0.03 per cent of the value of imported cotton. Initially the fee was imposed on cotton producers to provide funding for advertising purposes. However, the fee is now imposed on all imported cotton goods (European Union, 2006, fiches 060081, 060082 and 060140).

The container security initiative There are four major elements to the 2002 Container Security Initiative (CSI); the identification of high-risk containers, pre-screening containers before they arrive in the US, using technology to screen high-risk containers, and developing and using smart and secure containers. In order to mitigate any effects on trade, the US and the EU concluded an agreement that expands customs cooperation to include the CSI. In 2005, the US agreed to have EU ports that met CSI requirements participate in the program on a cooperative basis. This agreement has yet to be implemented. Absent this agreement, the requirements of the CSI are creating major delays and new costs for EU companies exporting to the US. Some European engineering companies, which often ship high-technology equipment, have dropped out of US markets because of the costs and delays created by the CSI (European Union, 2006, fiche 060106).

Table 4.2 Issues raised in 2007 but not in 2002

Issue	Complainant		WTO
	EU	Japan	
1. Import-related			
a. Trade administration issues			
Cotton import fee	x		
Container security requirements	x		
Port Security Act	x		
b. Sanitary and phytosanitary restrictions			
Inspection requirements on fresh fruit	x		
Limits on the importation of foreign milk	x		
Registration of food handling facilities	x	x	
c. Access to service markets			
Cargo reservation for food aid program	x		
Restrictions on foreign fishing in US waters	x		
Telecommunications market restrictions		x	
Capital equivalency deposits	x		
d. Safeguard issues			
Continued penalties for hormone-treated beef	x		
2. Domestic issues			
a. Standards and technical requirements			
Government-mandated HDTV format	x		
Cruise ship equipment standards	x		
b. The regulation of medical products			
Standards defining organics	x		
Approvals of OTC pharmaceuticals	x		
Payment of medical device user fees	x		
c. Intellectual property rights			
Limits on patents for novelty plants	x		
Brand comparisons in cosmetics	x		
d. Market regulation issues			
Sarbanes-Oxley Act	x		
Taxation of foreign ship repairs	x		
Regulation of pressure equipment	x		
3. Export-related			
a. Export barriers			
Extraterritorial export restrictions		x	
b. Subsidies			
Airline service subsidies	x		
Engine development subsidies	x		

The Port Security Initiative This is an expansion of the CSI to include foreign businesses in the security assurance system. This is also creating barriers to trade (European Union, 2006, fiche 060107).

In 2006, the US enacted the Safe Port Act, which mandates the foreign use of integrated non-intrusive imaging and radiation detection equipment on all US-bound containers. This approach runs counter to the modern practices of basing security assurances on effective intelligence and targeting, limiting the use of direct scanning to higher probability targets. It could seriously slow down the passage of traffic from the EU to the US (European Union, 2006, fiche 060141).

3.1b Sanitary and phytosanitary restrictions

Inspection requirements for fresh fruit The EU also argues that the US inspection requirements for fresh fruit are excessive (European Union, 2006, fiche 040059).

Barriers against the importation of fresh milk In the US, "grade A" milk products are regulated jointly by the states and the Federal Food and Drug Administration (FDA) through the National Conference on Interstate Milk Shipments (NCIMS). In order for a foreign firm to sell grade A products in the US, it would have to sign a contract with a state, which then would agree to exercise regulatory oversight. Alternatively, the country of origin could agree to follow US milk control regulations and become a member of NCIMS. Finally, the exporting company could register with the FDA, which could then certify the adequacy of the country of origin regulations. None of these options are particularly easy to achieve (European Union, 2006, fiche 060104).

Registration requirements for foreign-food handling facilities The US Bioterrorism Act imposes a requirement for the registration of all foreign food-handling facilities supplying foodstuffs to the US, prior notification of all food shipments to the US, traceability in the handling of all shipments, and procedures for the administrative detention of suspect food shipments. The EU argues that these provisions have an unwarranted extraterritorial effect and that they impose a significant administrative burden on EU companies exporting food to the US. These types of programs should only be developed in partnership with the US major trading allies (European Union, 2007, fiche 040003; Japan, 2006, pp.18–19).

3.1c Access to service markets

US cargo reservation policies for the food aid program Food aid exported by the US government under Public Law 480 or donated by the Commodity

Credit Corporation under Public Law 416-b must be shipped on US flag vessels. At least 75 per cent of US food aid exports under the World Food Program (WFP) must be shipped on US flag vessels. The WFP includes the difference between US and foreign flag freight rates as an operational cost. This has the effect of limiting the funding that can be used to provide food aid. (European Union, 2006, fiche 060115).

Restrictions on foreign fishing in US waters Title 46, US Code section 12108 prohibits awarding fishing licenses to people using foreign-built fishing boats. The American Fisheries Act of 1998 raised the percentage of the shares that must be held by US citizens for a ship to be considered American from 50 per cent to 75 per cent (European Union, 2006, fiche 060108).

US unilateral actions in telecommunications services The US emphasizes reciprocity as well as traditional non-discrimination policies in opening up US telecommunications markets to foreign participants. The USTR's office is directed to identify "priority foreign countries" that deny "mutually advantageous market opportunities" for US telecommunications equipment and services. The president is then directed to enter into bilateral negotiations to assure equitable market access. It this goal isn't achieved in 18 months, then the president has authority to limit the access of the relevant countries to US telecommunications markets. The USTR is also charged with reviewing foreign government compliance with the terms of any telecommunications agreements. A finding of non-compliance must be treated as equivalent to a failure to provide mutually advantageous market access (Japan, 2006, pp. 62–64).

Capital equivalency deposits The EU complains that the US Office of the Comptroller of the Currency imposes "asset pledges" on foreign banks doing business in the United States even though these banks are also subject to minimum reserve requirements through their home country regulations (EU, 2006, fiche 060126).

3.1d Safeguard issues

Continued penalties for hormone-treated beef The EU had banned the importation of beef treated with growth hormones and the US had initiated WTO consultations on the issue. In 1998, the WTO panel found in favor of the US on the grounds that the EU decision had not been based on scientific evidence and so violated the SPS agreement. When the EU refused to lift the ban, the US imposed penalties on EU imports. The EU now argues that the ban on hormone-treated beef has been justified on the basis of subsequent scientific research so the continued imposition of penalties by the US is not justified (European Union, 2007, fiche 060080).

3.2 Domestic Legislation Affecting International Trade

3.2a Standards and technical requirements

High definition TV format In 1996, the FCC ordered the exclusive use of ATSC standards and technology for high-definition TV signals in the US. The DVB-T standard is used instead in the EU and the two systems are not compatible. The EU argues that the FCC should have authorized the use of either standard and let the market decide. By imposing a standard that is not compatible with the system in use in the EU, the FCC has created an unnecessary trade barrier (European Union, 2007, fiche 060083).

Cruise ship standards Although most cruise ships are constructed in Europe, the major cruise market is in the US. Ships serving these markets must comply with US regulations. Coast Guard regulations prohibit the use of some equipment that is widely used in the EU. This imposes unnecessary trade barriers and raises costs (European Union, 2006, fiche 060192).

3.2b Medical products regulations

Standards defining "organic" Under the terms of the 2001 National Organic Program, there is a provision authorizing the recognition of foreign production as organic if it complies with US requirements. The US and the EU entered into bilateral discussions that would hopefully lead to a mutual recognition agreement. Substantial progress was made in the initial talks. However, the discussions stalled in 2004 and there is no new roadmap for progress in the discussions (European Union, 2006, fiche 060105).

Approvals of pharmaceutical and herbal products for over-the-counter use The Food and Drug Administration must give prior approval before a new medical product can be commercialized. Many new products must go through a lengthy and expensive series of clinical trials before approval. However, new products that are based on materials and chemicals that have already been approved and have been shown to be safe in the marketplace can avoid the need for clinical trials.

This distinction places a significant burden on EU exporters who want to introduce new products into the US over-the-counter (OTC) market. In many cases, these products are based on herbal remedies that are new to the US market. Since the ingredients are, in many cases, new to US markets, these products have to go through a long and expensive process of developing clinical trial information. The EU is calling for better coordination between US and EU OTC regulation (European Union, 2006, fiche 060039).

Payment to US corporations of medical device user fees Companies that want to place their medical devices on the US market must first have their products approved by the Food and Drug Administration. This can be a long and expensive process. Under the Medical Device User Fee and Modernization Act of 2002 (United States, 2002), the FDA can reduce and/or provide reimbursement for part of the fees. Applicant companies must provide their US income tax forms to prove eligibility for the program. This effectively prevents foreign companies from participating in the program (European Union, 2007, fiche 060130).

3.2c Intellectual property policies

Limits on patents for novelty plants Under US law, breeders of new plant types have one year in which to file for a US patent after the plant has initially been placed on the market. International practice codified in the International Convention for Protection of New Varieties is to allow a four-year period. Because of the abbreviated US grace period, European companies have to decide almost immediately after commercializing a new product if they want to export to the US. This imposes an unnecessary burden on international trade (European Union, 2007, fiche 070001).

Toleration of brand comparisons in perfume The US permits companies selling low-cost perfumes to advertise comparisons between their products and other high-price, high-prestige perfume products. The EU argues that this practice may violate the prohibition in the Paris Convention against promoting confusion and unfair competition (European Union, 2006, fiche 060122).

3.2d Market regulation

The Sarbanes-Oxley Act This has imposed significant costs on European firms listed on the New York Stock Exchange. European auditing firms may also be faced with new inconsistencies between US and EU auditing requirements (United States, 2002).

Taxation of foreign ship repairs The US imposes a 50 per cent *ad valorem* tax on the value of ship repairs made outside the US and on foreign equipment used on US flag ships. There is no similar tax on repairs carried out in the US. These provisions may not apply to repairs made to LASH (lighter aboard ship) barges. However LASH technology is rarely used outside the US, so this exception has little value (European Union, 2006, fiche 060111).

Fragmented regulation for pressure equipment The EU argues that a similar situation exists in the US with respect to the regulation of equipment containing fluids or gasses under pressure or high vacuum. OSHA has the lead responsibility at the Federal level. State government agencies with jurisdiction over workplace safety also play an important role in pressure equipment regulation. All agencies tend to draw on the basic provisions of the Boiler and Pressure Vessel Code that is published by the American Society of Mechanical Engineering (ASME). However, the local deviations from the ASME Code create difficulties for US companies that want to export pressure equipment to the US (European Union, 2006, fiche 060041).

3.3 US Policies Affecting Exports

3.3a Export restrictions

Extraterritorial enforcement of US export control regulations The US bans the export of a selected number of critical products, generally as anti-nuclear proliferation or anti-terrorist measures. These measures potentially have an extraterritorial effect, since the prohibitions can include a ban on the diversion of legitimately exported materials to third countries after they have left the US.

Japan is concerned that the provisions for extraterritorial limits to further trade in exported materials could violate the GATT/WTO obligations. From a practical perspective, situations could arise where the US exporter did not inform the (Japanese) importer about trade restrictions until the deal was essentially done. Although the export control system regulations include a "code of good conduct" that includes an importer notification requirement, these aspects of the regulations are not legally binding on exporters (Japan, 2006, pp. 71–72).

3.3b Export promotion

Airline service subsidies The tragedy of 11 September 2001 created major financial problems for US commercial air carriers. In response to these problems, the US government provided $5b in direct assistance, $10b in loan guarantees, and subsidies for the cost of war risk insurance. The EU argues that these measures are excessive and constitute significant relief from international competitive pressures (European Union, 2006, fiche 060128).

Table 4.3 Issues raised about US trade policies in 2002 but not in 2007

Policy	Complainant		WTO
	EU	Japan	
1. Import policies			
a. Restrictions on access to service markets			
Restrictions on foreign legal services		x	
b. Safeguard issues			
Sunset provisions on anti-dumping cases		x	
Anti-dumping duties on steel	x	x	x
2. Export related			
a. Subsidies			
Foreign sales corporations	x	x	x

Aircraft engine subsidies The EU argues that the manufacturers of large jet engines for civilian aircraft benefit from research carried out with government funding for the development of military jet engines (European Union, 2006, fiche 060121).

4. TRADE ISSUES RAISED IN 2002 BUT NOT IN 2007

An issue raised by the EU is considered to have been "settled" if it is set forth on a fiche that has been withdrawn or if the analysis on the fiche indicates that a resolution was achieved before 2004. A trade issue raised by Japan is considered to have been resolved if was raised in 2002 and then omitted from the 2006 or 2007 reports. The list of four settled issues is set forth in Table 4.3.

4.1 Import Issues

4.1a Restrictions on access to service markets

Restrictions on foreign legal services Japan pressed the US through the US–Japan Regulatory Reform and Competition Policy Initiative to expand opportunities for Japanese lawyers to practice in the US. Only 24 states and the District of Colombia allowed foreign attorneys to practice. Many states required foreign applicants to have five years work experience as a lawyer, and limited the experience to the five years before the application to join the bar. Japan wanted the work experience requirement to be shortened and relaxed (Japan, 2002, p 52).

4.1b Safeguard issues

Sunset provisions on anti-dumping cases According to Article 11.3 of the Anti-Dumping Agreement, countervailing duties should expire within five years unless there has been a determination that dumping has continued beyond that date. Japan argued that the sunset provisions in US Anti-dumping laws set an unreasonably high termination standard and promoted the unjustifiable prolongation of countervailing duties in the US (Japan, 2002, pp. 23–24).

Disputes over the anti-dumping duties imposed on imported steel products The US imposed anti-dumping duties on a wide range of imported steel products in early 2000. There was some evidence that these actions were intended by the US administration to shore up a lagging US steel industry. These actions were taken shortly after the passage of the Byrd Amendment.

The imposition of these anti-dumping duties triggered a flurry of complaints to the WTO about the US actions. In this work, we are only considering cases filed before the World Trade Organization by the EU and Japan. The long list of other countries that asked to participate in these cases on the side of the complainants indicates the high level of global concern about the US actions (Japan, 2002, pp. 17–21; 32–35).

Japan asked for consultations over a preliminary finding by the US Department of Commerce and the US International Trade Commission that hot-rolled steel products from Japan had been dumped on the US markets. A panel was created on 11 February 2000. Brazil, Canada, Chile, the EU and Korea also participated in the panel (World Trade Organization, 2005, *DS 184*).

On 10 November 2000, the EU asked for consultations with the US over the imposition of anti-dumping duties on certain steel products imported from Germany. A panel was created on 10 September 2001 (World Trade Organization, 2007, *DS 213*).

In January 2002, Japan again requested consultations with the US over the decision by the US to continue anti-dumping duties on steel imported from Japan. A panel was organized on 17 July 2002 (World Trade Organization, 2003, *DS 244*). Japan filed a third request for consultations on US anti-dumping duties on 20 March 2002 (World Trade Organization, 2002, *DS 249*). The work of panel 249 was subsequently merged with panel 248.

The EU filed another complaint about US anti-dumping duties on imported steel products on 7 March 2002. Japan, Korea, Switzerland, Canada, Venezuela, Norway, China, Mexico, Brazil and New Zealand asked to participate in the litigation. A total of seven separate requests for consultations were brought together in one panel (World Trade Organization, 2003, *DS 248*).

The EU filed a final request for consultations over anti-dumping duties on steel on 25 July 2002. Canada and Japan asked to participate (World Trade Organization, 2007, *DS 262*). Italy also asked for consultations with the US over the imposition of anti-dumping duties (World Trade Organization, 2007, *DS 225*). No panel was created for either request.

Key US assertions were rejected both at the trial and appellate levels in every panel that was actively prosecuted. The issues of law raised by the US varied somewhat from panel to panel. The US had failed to show domestic injury or to take unforeseen developments into account in making a dumping determination (Word Trade Organization, 2007, *DS 248*). The US unreasonably refused to accept information on home-market sales that was presented by the defendant after the administrative deadline but within a reasonable period of time (World Trade Organization, 2007, *DS 184*). The US had unreasonably concluded that dumping would probably continue if the tariffs were removed, even though it had no firm information to support that position (World Trade Organization, 2007, *DS 213*).

On 10 December 2003, the US president announced that all safeguard measures on steel had been terminated on 4 December in accordance with Section 204 of the US Trade Act of 1974. This action effectively ended the countervailing duty cases that had been filed with the World Trade Organization.

4.2 Issues Concerning US Exports

4.2a Subsidies

Foreign Sales Corporations The creation of Foreign Sales Corporations (FSCs) was intended to lower the rate of taxation on exports from the US. A portion of the revenues from FSCs that sell or lease US products outside the US was exempt from US taxation. Dividends paid by an FSC to the parent corporation could also be treated as non-taxable income. The system was generally used by US corporations conducting business through foreign subsidiaries.

Both the EU and Japan argued that the FSC system constituted an illegal export subsidy. It also offered a different treatment to domestic goods than to foreign goods, in violation of the GATT principle of non-discrimination (Japan, 2002, pp. 24–26). The EU asked for WTO consultations on the legality of the FSC system in November 1997 and Japan participated in the consultations as a third party. No resolution was achieved on the issue and a dispute resolution panel was convened in September 1998 (World Trade Organization, 2007, *DS 108*).

The dispute resolution panel report was issued in October 1999. The Panel concluded that the FSC system was inconsistent with the GATT/WTO principles. The US appealed the ruling. In February 2000, the Appellate Body held that the original panel ruling was proper. The US declared that it would repeal the FSC provisions by 1 November 2000.

Congress repealed the FSC provisions and replaced them with the Extraterritorial Income Exclusion Act of 2000 (ETI). The EU argued that the goods and services covered by the ETI rules must still have a 50 per cent US content, that the tax benefits only applied to revenues from sales outside the US, and that the transition rules in effect maintained the FSC rules beyond the promised 1 November 2000 deadline.

The EU, with Japan participating as a third party, asked that the issue be referred to a Dispute Resolution Panel. The issue was referred back to the original DS108 panel. On 1 August 2001, the panel ruled that the ETI rules constituted an export subsidy in violation of the GATT Agreement on Subsidies and Countervailing Measures (ASCM). The US referred the decision to an Appellate Body on 1 October 2001. In January 2002, the Appellate Body upheld the Dispute Resolution Panel decision in favor of the EU and Japan. On August 2002, a WTO arbitrator ruled that the $4 billion tariff concessions proposed by the EU represented an appropriate countermeasure.

The provisions of the ETI were repealed with the passage of the American Jobs Creation Act of 2004 on 22 October 2004. Under the terms of the Act, the provisions of the ETI were to be phased out gradually, with total termination at the end of 2006. Furthermore, the provisions of the ETI were to remain in effect beyond the end of 2006 for any contracts signed before 17 September 2003.

The EU and Japan are arguing that these transition provisions are inconsistent with both the ASCM rules and the findings of the WTO dispute settlement panels. The EU requested the establishment of a DRU panel to hear the dispute over US responses to the original panel decisions. On 17 January 2006, the issue was again referred back to the original panel (Japan, 2002, pp. 24–26; World Trade Organization, 2007, *Dispute Settlement Body DS 108*).

REFERENCES

Note: the European Union and Japan references are ordered by date then fiche number: *the World Trade Organization references are ordered by Dispute Resolution Panel number*.

European Union, Directorate General Trade (2006), "Merchandising Processing Fee", Fiche 960048, *Market Access Database*.

European Union, Directorate General Trade (2006), "Harbour Maintenance Tax and Harbour Maintenance Fee", Fiche 960049, *Market Access Database.*
European Union, Directorate General Trade (2006), "Section 232 of the 1962 Trade Expansion Act", Fiche 960050, *Market Access Database.*
European Union, Directorate General Trade (2006), "Electrical and Electronic Equipment Barriers", Fiche 960054, *Market Access Database.*
European Union: Directorate General Trade (2006), "Berry Amendment to the 1941 Defense Appropriations Act", Fiche 960055, *Market Access Database.*
European Union, Directorate General Trade (2006), "Memoranda of Understanding (Defense Acquisitions)", Fiche 960056, *Market Access Database.*
European Union, Directorate General Trade (2006), "Space Launching Services", Fiche 960057, *Market Access Database.*
European Union, Directorate General Trade (2006), "Buy America Act and Buy American Provisions", Fiche 960059, *Market Access Database.*
European Union, Directorate General Trade (2006), "The Exon-Florio Amendment", Fiche 960064, *Market Access Database.*
European Union, Directorate General Trade (2006), "Energy Acts", Fiche 960066, *Market Access Database.*
European Union, Directorate General Trade (2006), "Tax Code Reporting Requirements", Fiche 960069, *Market Access Database.*
European Union, Directorate General Trade (2006), "United States: Bovine Animals and Products", Fiche 960083, *Market Access Database.*
European Union, Directorate General Trade (2006), "Agricultural Export Subsidies and Promotion", Fiche 960092, *Market Access Database.*
European Union, Directorate General Trade (2006), "The Jones Act and Shipbuilding Subsidies", Fiche 960098, *Market Access Database.*
European Union, Directorate General Trade (2006), "Steel Local Content Requirements", Fiche 960100, *Market Access Database.*
European Union, Directorate General Trade (2006), "Textile Rules of Origin", Fiche 960179, *Market Access Database.*
European Union, Directorate General Trade (2006), "Helms Burton Act", Fiche 960295, *Market Access Database.*
European Union, Directorate General Trade (2006), "Conditional National Treatment for Investments", Fiche 960301, *Market Access Database.*
European Union, Directorate General Trade (2006), "Export Credit Guarantee Program", Fiche 960303, *Market Access Database.*
European Union, Directorate General Trade (2006), "US Customs Refusal of EU Origin", Fiche 970144, *Market Access Database.*
European Union, Directorate General Trade (2006) "Corporate Average Fuel Economy (CAFE), Fiche 980072, *Market Access Database.*
European Union, Directorate General Trade (2006), "IPR Infringement Cases (Section 337 of 1930 Tariff Act)", Fiche 980139, *Market Access Database.*
European Union, Directorate General Trade (2006), "Government Use of Patents", Fiche 980140, *Market Access Database.*
European Union, Directorate General Trade (2006), "Principle of First to Invent", Fiche 980141, *Market Access Database.*
European Union, Directorate General Trade (2006), "Author's Moral Rights", Fiche 980142, *Market Access Database.*
European Union, Directorate General Trade (2006), "Sections 301–310 of the Trade Act", Fiche 990003, *Market Access Database.*

European Union, Directorate General Trade (2006), "US Dual-Use Export Controls", Fiche 990060, *Market Access Database*.
European Union, Directorate General Trade (2006), "Section 211 of Omnibus Appropriations Act (Havana Club)", Fiche 990079, *Market Access Database*.
European Union, Directorate General Trade (2006), "Section 407 of the Trade and Development Act (Carousel Law)", Fiche 990090, *Market Access Database*.
European Union, Directorate General Trade (2006), "Agricultural Marketing Loans", Fiche 010050, *Market Access Database*.
European Union, Directorate General Trade (2006), "Byrd Amendment (Continued Dumping and Subsidy Offset Act)", Fiche 020004, *Market Access Database*.
European Union, Directorate General Trade (2006). "United States: Fresh Fruit", Fiche 040059, *Market Access Database*.
European Union, Directorate General Trade (2006), "Sarbanes-Oxley Act", Fiche 060018, *Market Access Database*.
European Union, Directorate General Trade (2006), "Pharmaceutical and Herbal Products (FDA Approval)", Fiche 060039, *Market Access Database*.
European Union, Directorate General Trade (2006), "Pressure Equipment Regulations", Fiche 060041, *Market Access Database*.
European Union, Directorate General Trade (2006), "Textile Documentation and Labeling Requirements", Fiche 060081, *Market Access Database*.
European Union, Directorate General Trade (2006), "Textile Tariffs", Fiche 060082, *Market Access Database*.
European Union, Directorate General Trade (2006), "Jewelry Tariff Levels", Fiche 060100, *Market Access Database*.
European Union, Directorate General Trade (2006), "American Automobile Labeling Act", Fiche 060101, *Market Access Database*.
European Union, Directorate General Trade (2006), "Marine Recreational Craft", Fiche 060103, *Market Access Database*.
European Union, Directorate General Trade (2006), "Milk Products (Grade A)", Fiche 060104, *Market Access Database*.
European Union, Directorate General Trade (2006), "Organic Products", Fiche 060105, *Market Access Database*.
European Union, Directorate General Trade (2006), "Container Security Initiative (CSI)", Fiche 060106, *Market Access Database*.
European Union, Directorate General Trade (2006), "Customs–Trade Partnership Against Terrorism (C-PAT) Scheme", Fiche 060107, *Market Access Database*.
European Union, Directorate General Trade (2006), "Shipping Code Restrictions for EU Fishermen", Fiche 060108, *Market Access Database*.
European Union, Directorate General Trade (2006), "Ship Repairs Outside U.S.", Fiche 060111, *Market Access Database*.
European Union, Directorate General Trade (2006), "Food Aid Program", Fiche 060115, *Market Access Database*.
European Union, Directorate General Trade (2006), "Aircraft Engine Manufacturers", Fiche 060121, *Market Access Database*.
European Union, Directorate General Trade (2006), "Perfume Imitations", Fiche 060122, *Market Access Database*.
European Union, Directorate General Trade (2006), "Hillmer Doctrine", Fiche 060123, *Market Access Database*.
European Union, Directorate General Trade (2006), "Capital Equivalency Deposits", Fiche 060126, *Market Access Database*.

European Union, Directorate General Trade (2006), "Aircraft State Aid", Fiche 060128, *Market Access Database*.
European Union, Directorate General Trade (2006), "Shipping on US Flagged Vessels", Fiche 060129, *Market Access Database*.
European Union, Directorate General Trade (2006), "Cotton Import Fee", Fiche 060140, *Market Access Database*.
European Union, Directorate General Trade (2006), "Safe Port Act", Fiche 060141, *Market Access Database*.
European Union, Directorate General Trade (2006), "Footwear and Leather Tariffs", Fiche 060143, *Market Access Database*.
European Union, Directorate General Trade (2006), "Non-use of International Standards", Fiche 060144, *Market Access Database*.
European Union, Directorate General Trade (2006), "Coast Guard Regulations", Fiche 060192, *Market Access Database*.
European Union, Directorate General Trade (2007), "Transport-Related Buy American Provisions", Fiche 960058, *Market Access Database*.
European Union, Directorate General Trade (2007), "Iran–Libya Sanctions Act and Iran Freedom Support Act", Fiche 960061, *Market Access Database*.
European Union, Directorate General Trade (2007), "Gas Guzzler Tax", Fiche 960073, *Market Access Database*.
European Union, Directorate General Trade (2007), "Ceramics and Glass Tariffs", Fiche 960074, *Market Access Database*.
European Union, Directorate General Trade (2007). "Ornamental Plants Established in Growing Media", Fiche 960081, *Market Access Database*.
European Union, Directorate General Trade (2007), "Hardy Nurse Stock Media", Fiche 960082, *Market Access Database*.
European Union, Directorate General Trade (2007), "Maturate meat products", Fiche 960088, *Market Access Database*.
European Union, Directorate General Trade (2007), "Small Business Act", Fiche 960300, *Market Access Database*.
European Union, Directorate General Trade (2007), "Section 110(5) of 1976 Copyright Act (Irish Music)", Fiche 970191, *Market Access Database*.
European Union, Directorate General Trade (2007), "Boeing Subsidies", Fiche 970301, *Market Access Database*.
European Union, Directorate General Trade (2007), "Farm Bill", Fiche 020074, *Market Access Database*.
European Union, Directorate General Trade (2007), "Bioterrorism Act", Fiche 040003, *Market Access Database*.
European Union, Directorate General Trade (2007), "Jewelry Tariff Levels", Fiche 060040, *Market Access Database*.
European Union, Directorate General Trade (2007), "CVD Measures Against Privatized EU Firms (DS 212)", Fiche 060079, *Market Access Database*.
European Union, Directorate General Trade (2007), "Hormones Dispute (Continued Suspension of Obligations)", Fiche 60080, *Market Access Database*.
European Union, Directorate General Trade (2007), "Digital Terrestrial Television", Fiche 060083, *Market Access Database*.
European Union, Directorate General Trade (2007), "Firth Rixon Case", Fiche 060117, *Market Access Database*.
European Union, Directorate General Trade (2007), "Steel Sunset Reviews", Fiche 060125, *Market Access Database*.

European Union, Directorate General Trade (2007), "Medical Device User Fee", Fiche 060130, *Market Access Database*.

European Union, Directorate General Trade (2007), "Plant Patents", Fiche 070001, *Market Access Database*.

Japan, Ministry of Economy, Trade and Industry (2002), "Harbor Maintenance Tax 'HMT' (Harbor Services Fee)", *Report on Compliance by Major Trading Partners with Trade Agreements*, pp. 4–6.

Japan, Ministry of Economy, Trade and Industry (2002), "Merchant Shipping Act of 1920 (Jones Act)", *Report on the Compliance by Major Trading Partners with Trade Agreements*, p. 6.

Japan, Ministry of Economy, Trade and Industry (2002), "Export restrictions on logs", *Report on the Compliance by Major Trading Partners with Trade Agreements*, pp. 7–8.

Japan, Ministry of Economy, Trade and Industry (2002), "Export management system", *Report on the Compliance by Major Trading Partners with Trade Agreements*, pp. 8–10.

Japan, Ministry of Economy, Trade and Industry (2002), "Method of calculating tariffs on clocks and wristwatches", *Report on the Compliance by Major Trading Partners with Trade Agreements*, pp. 10–11.

Japan, Ministry of Economy, Trade and Industry (2002), "Anti-dumping measures", *Report on the Compliance by Major Trading Partners with Trade Agreements*, pp. 11–16.

Japan, Ministry of Economy, Trade and Industry (2002), "US Anti-Dumping Act of 1916 (WT/DS162/R)", *Report on the Compliance by Major Trading Partners with Trade Agreements*, pp. 16–17.

Japan, Ministry of Economy, Trade and Industry (2002), "US Anti-dumping measures on certain hot-rolled steel products from Japan (WT/DS184/R)", *Report on the Compliance by Major Trading Partners with Trade Agreements*, pp. 17–21.

Japan, Ministry of Economy, Trade and Industry (2002), "Anti-Dumping Measures: The Byrd Amendment (The Fiscal Year 2001 Agricultural Appropriations Bill)", *Report on the Compliance by Major Trading Partners with Trade Agreements*, pp. 21–22.

Japan, Ministry of Economy, Trade and Industry (2002), "Sunset provisions", *Report on the Compliance by Major Trading Partners with Trade Agreements*, pp. 23–24.

Japan, Ministry of Economy, Trade and Industry (2002), "Tax treatment for export companies (ETI, formerly FSC regimes)", *Report on the Compliance by Major Trading Partners with Trade Agreements*, pp. 24–26.

Japan, Ministry of Economy, Trade and Industry (2002), "Byrd Amendment (Agricultural Appropriations Act of 2001)", *Report on the Compliance by Major Trading Partners with Trade Agreements*, pp. 26–27.

Japan, Ministry of Economy, Trade and Industry (2002), "The United States: subsidies and countervailing measures: export promotion of agricultural products", *Report on the Compliance by Major Trading Partners with Trade Agreements*, pp. 27–30.

Japan, Ministry of Economy, Trade and Industry (2002), "Welded carbon quality pipe lines", *Report on Compliance by Major Trading Partners with Trade Agreements*, pp. 32–35.

Japan, Ministry of Economy, Trade and Industry (2002), "Standards and conformity assessment systems: American Automobile Labeling Act", *Report on the Compliance by Major Trading Partners with Trade Agreements*, pp. 38–39.

Japan, Ministry of Economy, Trade and Industry (2002), "Regulation on corporate average fuel economy (CAFE)", *Report on the Compliance by Major Trading Partners with Trade Agreements*, pp. 39–41.

Japan, Ministry of Economy, Trade and Industry (2002), "Adoption of the metric system", *Report on the Compliance by Major Trading Partners with Trade Agreements*, pp. 41–42.

Japan, Ministry of Economy, Trade and Industry (2002), "Cross-sectional regulations", *Report on the Compliance by Major Trading Partners with Trade Agreements*, p. 42.

Japan, Ministry of Economy, Trade and Industry (2002), "Financial services", *Report on the Compliance by Major Trading Partners with Trade Agreements*, pp. 43–45.

Japan, Ministry of Economy, Trade and Industry (2002), "Telecommunications", *Report on the Compliance by Major Trading Partners with Trade Agreements*, pp. 45–47.

Japan, Ministry of Economy, Trade and Industry (2002), "Maritime Transport", *Report on the Compliance by Major Trading Partners with Trade Agreements*, 48–52.

Japan, Ministry of Economy, Trade and Industry (2002), "Professional services (legal services)", *Report on the Compliance by Major Trading Partners with Trade Agreements*, p. 52.

Japan, Ministry of Economy, Trade and Industry (2002), "Patent system", *Report on the Compliance by Major Trading Partners with Trade Agreements*, pp. 52–54.

Japan, Ministry of Economy, Trade and Industry (2002), "Copyright and related rights", *Report on the Compliance by Major Trading Partners with Trade Agreements*, pp. 55–57.

Japan, Ministry of Economy, Trade and Industry (2002), "Expansion of the subjects protected by performance", *Report on the Compliance by Major Trading Partners with Trade Agreements*, p. 57.

Japan, Ministry of Economy, Trade and Industry (2002), "Section 301 of the Trade Act of 1974", *Report on the Compliance by Major Trading Partners with Trade Agreements*, pp. 63–71.

Japan, Ministry of Economy, Trade and Industry (2002), "Provisions involving government procurement: Title VII", *Report on the Compliance by Major Trading Partners with Trade Agreements*, pp. 71–72.

Japan, Ministry of Economy, Trade and Industry (2002), "The carousel rule on amending items subject to retaliatory measures", *Report on the Compliance by Major Trading Partners with Trade Agreements*, pp. 72–73.

Japan, Ministry of Economy, Trade and Industry (2002), "Unilateral measures: the Helms-Burton Act", *Report on the Compliance by Major Trading Partners with Trade Agreements*, pp. 74–76.

Japan, Ministry of Economy, Trade and Industry (2002), "Iran and Libya Sanctions Act", *Report on the Compliance by Major Trading Partners with Trade Agreements*, pp. 76–78.

Japan, Ministry of Economy, Trade and Industry (2006), "The United States: quantitative measures: export management system", *Report on the Compliance by Major Trading Partners with Trade Agreements*, pp. 8–10.

Japan, Ministry of Economy, Trade and Industry (2006), "Harbor Maintenance Tax 'HM1'", *Report on Compliance by Major Trading Partners with Trade Agreements*, pp. 11–12.

Japan, Ministry of Economy, Trade and Industry (2006), "Merchant Shipping Act of 1920 (Jones Act)", *Report on Compliance by Major Trading Partners with Trade Agreements*, pp. 12–13.

Japan, Ministry of Economy, Trade and Industry (2006), "Export management systems", *Report on the Compliance by Major Trading Partners with Trade Agreements*, pp. 14–15.

Japan, Ministry of Economy, Trade and Industry (2006), "Export restrictions on logs", *Report on the Compliance by Major Trading Partners with Trade Agreements*, pp. 15–16.

Japan, Ministry of Economy, Trade and Industry (2006), "The United States", *Report on Compliance by Major Trading Partners with Trade Agreements*, p. 17.

Japan, Ministry of Economy, Trade and Industry (2006), "Public Health Security and Bioterrorism Preparedness and Response Act of 2002 (The Bioterrorism Act)", *Report on Compliance by Major Trading Partners with Trade Agreements*, pp. 18–19.

Japan, Ministry of Economy, Trade and Industry (2006), "Anti-dumping measures: the Byrd Amendment" (Amendment to the Tariff Act of 1930 DS 217/DS 234)", *Report on Compliance by Major Trading Partners with Trade Agreements*, pp. 19–21.

Japan, Ministry of Economy, Trade and Industry (2006), "Calculation of dumping margin via the zeroing procedure (WT/DS194) and delay in implementing the WTO recommendation", *Report on the Compliance by Major Trading Partners with Trade Agreements*, pp. 22–23.

Japan, Ministry of Economy, Trade and Industry (2006), "The United States: subsidies and countervailing measures: export promotion of agricultural products", *Report on the Compliance by Major Trading Partners with Trade Agreements*, pp. 35–38.

Japan, Ministry of Economy, Trade and Industry (2006), "Rules of origin on watches and clocks", *Report on the Compliance by Major Trading Partners with Trade Agreements*, p. 39.

Japan, Ministry of Economy, Trade and Industry (2006), "American Automobile Labeling Act", *Report on the Compliance by Major Trading Partners with Trade Agreements*, pp. 39–41.

Japan, Ministry of Economy, Trade and Industry (2006), "Regulation on corporate average fuel economy", *Report on the Compliance by Major Trading Partners with Trade Agreements*, pp. 41–42.

Japan, Ministry of Economy, Trade and Industry (2006), "Adoption of the metric system", *Report on the Compliance by Major Trading Partners with Trade Agreements*, pp. 42–43.

Japan, Ministry of Economy, Trade and Industry (2006), "Trade in services: the Exon-Florio Amendment", *Report on the Compliance by Major Trading Partners with Trade Agreements*, pp. 43–44.

Japan, Ministry of Economy, Trade and Industry (2006), "Financial services", pp. 44–45.

Japan, Ministry of Economy, Trade and Industry (2006), "Financial Services: the United States", pp. 45–46.

Japan, Ministry of Economy, Trade and Industry (2006), "Maritime transport",

Report on the Compliance by Major Trading Partners with Trade Agreements, pp. 46–47.
Japan, Ministry of Economy, Trade and Industry (2006), "Patent system (Hillmer Doctrine)", *Report on the Compliance by Major Trading Partners with Trade Agreements*, pp. 48–50.
Japan, Ministry of Economy, Trade and Industry (2006), "Trademark systems (WT/DS176: US Omnibus Act 211)", *Report on the Compliance by Major Trading Partners with Trade Agreements*, p. 50.
Japan, Ministry of Economy, Trade and Industry (2006), "Copyright exceptions (WT/DS160), US Copyright Act 110(5)", *Report on the Compliance by Major Trading Partners with Trade Agreements*, pp. 51–52.
Japan, Ministry of Economy, Trade and Industry (2006), "Expansion of the subjects protected by performer rights", *Report on the Compliance by Major Trading Partners with Trade Agreements*, pp. 52–53.
Japan, Ministry of Economy, Trade and Industry (2006), "US Buy American legislation", *Report on the Compliance by Major Trading Partners with Trade Agreements*, p. 55.
Japan, Ministry of Economy, Trade and Industry (2006), "The United States: unilateral measures related to Section 301 of the Trade Act of 1974", *Report on the Compliance by Major Trading Partners with Trade Agreements*, pp. 58–62.
Japan, Ministry of Economy, Trade and Industry (2006), "The United States: unilateral measures: telecommunications provisions", *Report on the Compliance by Major Trading Partners with Trade Agreements*, pp. 62–64.
Japan, Ministry of Economy, Trade and Industry (2006), "The United States: provisions involving government procurement", *Report on the Compliance by Major Trading Partners with Trade Agreements*, pp. 64–66.
Japan, Ministry of Economy, Trade and Industry (2006), "Unilateral measures: The Helms-Burton Act", *Report on the Compliance by Major Trading Partners with Trade Agreements*, pp. 67–68.
Japan, Ministry of Economy, Trade and Industry (2006), *Myanmar Sanctions Act*, pp. 68–71.
Japan, Ministry of Economy, Trade and Industry (2006), "The United States: unilateral measures; use-export control regimes", *Report on the Compliance by Major Trading Partners with Trade Agreements*, pp. 71–72.
Nuttle, F. (1979), *Trade Act of 1979 (S. 1376 – H. 4537)*, Washington DC, The Heritage Foundation.
United States (1968), *The Exon-Florio Amendment*, codified at 50 United States Code 2170 *et seq.*
United States (1996), *Cuban Liberty and Solidarity Act* (The Helms-Burton Act) Public Law 104-114, codified at 22 United States Code, 6021–6091.
United States (1974), *Trade Act of 1974* (Section 301), codified at 19 United States Code 2411, *et seq.*
United States (2002), *Medical Device User Free and Modernization Act of 2002*, codified at 116 Stat. 1588–1620.
World Trade Organization (2007), "United States: tax treatment for 'Foreign Sales Corporations'", *Dispute Settlement Panel DS 108*.
World Trade Organization (2009), "US Harbour Maintenance Tax", *Dispute Resolution Panel DS 118*.
World Trade Organization (2007), "Anti-Dumping Act of 1916", *Dispute Resolution Panel DS 136*.

World Trade Organization (2009), "Imposition of countervailing duties on products originating in the UK", *Dispute Resolution Panel DS 138*.
World Trade Organization (1999), "United States: Sections 301–310 of the Trade Act of 1974", *Dispute Resolution Panel DS 152*.
World Trade Organization (2007), "Section 110(5) of US Copyright Act", *Dispute Resolution Panel DS 160*.
World Trade Organization (1999), "United States: Anti-Dumping Act of 1916", *Dispute Resolution Panel DS 162*.
World Trade Organization (2009), "Definitive safeguard on imports of wheat gluten", *Dispute Resolution Panel DS 166*.
World Trade Organization (2007), "Sec. 211 Omnibus Appropriations Act", *Dispute Resolution Panel DS 176*.
World Trade Organization (2005), "United States: anti-dumping measures", *Dispute Resolution Panel DS 184*.
World Trade Organization, "Countervailing measures on . . . products from the EU", *Dispute Resolution Panel DS 212*.
World Trade Organization (2007), "United States: countervailing on certain corrosion-resistant carbon steel plan products from Germany", *Dispute Resolution Panel DS 213*.
World Trade Organization (2002), "United States: Continued Dumping and Subsidy Act of 2000", *Dispute Resolution Panel DS 217*.
World Trade Organization (2007), "United States: anti-dumping duties on seamless pipe from Italy", *Dispute Resolution Panel DS 225*.
World Trade Organization (2007), "Sunset review of anti-dumping measures (Japan)", *Dispute Resolution Panel DS 244*.
Word Trade Organization (2007), "United States: definitive safeguard measures on imports of certain steel products", *Dispute Resolution Panel DS 248*.
World Trade Organization (2002), "United States: definitive safeguard measures on imports of certain steel products", Dispute Resolution Panel 249.
World Trade Organization (2007), "Sunset reviews of anti-dumping and countervailing duties", *Dispute Resolution Panel DS 262*.
World Trade Organization (2006), "United States: law, regulations and methodologies for calculating dumping margins (zeroing)", *Dispute Resolution Panel DS 294*.
World Trade Organization (2007), "United States: measures affecting trade in large civil aircraft", *Dispute Resolution Panel DS 317*.
World Trade Organization (2006), "United States: measures affecting trade in large civil aircraft – second complaint", *Dispute Resolution Panel DS 353*.

5. Background to trade policy in the European Union

1. INTRODUCTION

Three themes emerge from the following analyses. The first is the broad acceptance of the premise that the government of the European Union has a comprehensive responsibility to safeguard the welfare of the population. The second theme is the expertise and leadership provided by government bureaucrats in the planning process, with relatively little input from business and other social groups. The third theme is the relative weakness of the mechanisms for coordinating across policy areas, especially with respect to international trade policy.

2. THE CONTEXT OF GOVERNANCE IN THE EUROPEAN UNION

2.1 A Cultural Perspective

Twenty-seven very different countries constitute the membership of the EU. Although the EU member states have very different histories and paths to development, they almost all share a common characteristic: the path of development led from a tradition of monarchy and the claims of strongly centralized government to the current realities of democracy and decentralized government. Furthermore, the social battles for political liberalization were often dominated by groups that offered comprehensive visions of the future. This included, for example, socialists, communists, anarchists and Christian democrats.

This is in sharp contrast with the pattern of American development. In the US, the struggle has been to create a viable national government from a collection of largely independent colonies. The subsequent political battles generally focused on current crises rather than comprehensive social visions. These issues included, for example, anti-slavery, states' rights, anti-immigration and prohibition.

The differences in the two historical tasks have left imprints on present expectations about the proper functions of government. In the EU, the culture of governance emphasizes the need for a government that is strong enough to implement comprehensive programs that will shield its population from the slings and arrow of outrageous fortune (Hix, 1999). The efforts of business to lobby for particular advantages are generally regarded as selfish efforts by narrow interests to subvert the commonweal. In the US, in contrast, governments are expected to offer small-step solutions to immediate problems. The efforts of business to influence the policy process are more widely accepted. After all, shouldn't everyone have an opportunity to have their voices heard in the democratic process (Milner, 1993)?

The history of the European Union has promoted the acceptance of a comprehensive, paternalistic vision of governance. There has been a continuing debate over whether the EU should be viewed as a new sovereign government. If so, then the "democratic deficit" at the EU level is a serious issue (Hix, 2008). Alternatively, the EU could be viewed as a coordinating committee in service to the sovereign member states. Given this view, there is no democratic deficit. The reality of the EU has been far closer to the "coordinating committee" vision than the "sovereign government" view. Given this view, there is nothing wrong with the EU as the source of integrated planning in pursuit of comprehensive visions, as long as the execution is firmly under the control of the elected member state governments.

The development of the EU was consistent with the "coordinating committee" vision. World War II was a disaster for virtually all western European nations. It was clear that the endless cycle of European wars had to come to an end. A safe place had to be found for an often belligerent Germany. It was increasingly clear by 1948 that the conflicts in Europe were, in fact, not over. A shattered Europe was facing an expansionary Russian empire. The threat was not just external. Unless development came rapidly, the Marxist revolutionaries could come to power through the democratic process. A successful customs union could spark economic development and provide the political glue that would keep Germany peaceful and NATO together (Fischer, 2000).

Leadership in the EU for the first 20 years was largely provided by the government of France. During the early days when membership in the EU was limited to the "inner six", only the French were in a position to provide leadership. The politics of Italy were too chaotic for it to challenge French leadership. Germany had entered into a long-term period of political defensiveness about the atrocities of the Third Reich. The Benelux countries were too small to lead. The EU bureaucracy therefore became the implementation arm for ambitious French political leadership.

The domination of French leadership was not challenged until the accession of the British to EU membership. Although this strengthened the extent of bargaining among the leadership of European governments in setting EU policies, it did not change the overall pattern of top-down political leadership for the European Union (Hix, 2008).

2.2 A Governmental Perspective

There are four major institutions in the EU. The Council consists of the representatives from the member states, and it has to review and approve all major decisions. It is not formally involved in either planning for new proposals or managing their implementation once passed.

Although every country has representation on the Council, the votes they control are weighted according to population. This is "qualified majority voting". The goal, in general, is to make sure that passage of any controversial measure will require a majority of the member states representing a majority of the overall EU population.

The representation from the member states will vary according to the issue under discussion. The Council of Europe discusses any major constitutional issues. Membership consists of the heads of state for the 27 EU member countries. For the discussion and approval of more specialized issues, membership of the relevant council will be drawn from the appropriate national ministers. Thus the labour council will consist of the national labor ministers and will be convened to discuss labor legislation and so on.

The chair of the Council is passed among the various EU countries every six months in a regular sequence of rotation. The government of the country presiding over the Council has some control over the agendas and memberships in council meetings. Continuity in Council administration and deliberations is provided by COREPER, the Committee on Permanent Representation. COREPER is organized by Council subject areas.

The Commission is the bureaucratic arm of the European Union. It is responsible for both the planning and initiation of new policy proposals and for supervising their implementation once they have been enacted as an EU decision, directive or regulation.

The Commission works closely with the Council. The Commission is divided into 26 directorates general (DG). Each DG has jurisdiction over a different area of EU policy. The directors general are named by the EU member state governments. Although the directors general are required to take an oath of office forswearing national allegiance, the system has been set up to ensure that each national government will have an opportunity to name at least one director general.

There are machineries in place for the coordination of the Commission. The Secretariat reports to the president of the Commission. Decisions on Commission issues are made by a majority vote of the directors general during their weekly meetings.

However, the internal decision-making processes of the directorates general has largely been based on the development of working alliances with their counterpart ministries at the national government levels, and the relevant authorities in COREPER. The organization of advisory committees has provided an institutional basis for these alliances.

Directorate General Enterprise, for example, has jurisdiction over the CE marking system for regulating product safety. The legal basis for this system is set forth in 23 "new approach" directives. A lot of the meat in these directives is contained in the appendices. DG Enterprise has organized advisory committees for each of the directives. The members of these committees are appointed by the ministries of commerce or industry in the member states. In turn, the leaders of these ministries name the members of the Council when it is discussing business-related issues. The assumption has been that a directive advisory committee has the authority to amend the contents of the directive appendices as long as the measure was passed in the committee by qualified majoring voting (Hix, 1999; George and Bache, 2001).

This system has encouraged comprehensive planning for a particular issue with only limited pressure to balance competing concerns advanced by other interests. It gives subject experts in the Commission and national governments opportunities to plan policies in their narrow areas without the necessity for compromises with competing considerations. There is some evidence that policy advocates at the national level rely on the EU to implement policies that might not be accepted at the national level, especially if implemented in only one country (Lenschow, 2006).

The mechanisms for coordination among the various directorates general are weak. There is a presidency of the Commission, but the powers of the office are limited. In some cases, two or more directorates general share jurisdiction over a common policy or project. Even so, coordination has generally been weak. As long as DG Enterprise has the support of the relevant ministries of the national governments and the appropriate section of COREPER, there is limited incentive to coordinate closely with the other directorates general.

There are two limitations to the scope and effectiveness of Commission planning. One is the growing role of the European Parliament. This has 785 members who are directly elected by the citizens of the EU for five-year terms. It was thought that they would line up by country. Instead, the parliamentary coalitions have been organized by ideology and areas of policy concerns. This has contributed to the scope and cohesion of policy development in the European Parliament.

The European Parliament had only a limited role in the policy process for the first 30 to 40 years of the EU. Parliament was entitled to vote on policy initiatives. However, the Council could easily override a parliamentary vote. In effect, the European Parliament was an advisory body (George and Bache, 2001).

This pattern began to change after 1992 and the Treaty of Maastricht. At present, Parliament has essentially the power to amend, accept or reject Commission proposals. Now, the Council has to share the rights of final approval with the Parliament. The reconciliation procedures which are invoked when Parliament and Council pass different versions of the same basic legislation have become far more important. Parliament is also questioning the right of the directorates general to use the committee process as a back door route to avoid parliamentary oversight.

The member states pose a second set of limitations on the powers of the directorates general. There are two forms of legislation. A "directive" is an order from the EU to the member states to conform their laws to EU requirements. A regulation is a policy statement that is to be implemented by the Commission directly. In reality, both routes to legislation are largely implemented by the member states. The legal term for this is "subsidiarity", a policy of implementing policies at the lowest feasible administrative level. Legally, a directive has no legal effect until it is "transposed" into national law by the member states. Even regulations are largely implemented at the state level. The governing institutions of the EU simply do not have the resources to implement programs such as customs clearance and the common agricultural policy.

EU participation in international trade regulation is divided among many levels. Directorate General Trade has lead responsibility for representing the EU in international negotiations. However, the member states are also active in international negotiations as representatives of their sovereign countries. Several directorates general participate in specialized international agencies on behalf of the EU. Directorate General Trade has primary responsibility for trade-related issues. Directorate General Health is involved with the Food and Agriculture Organization, the International Organization for Epizootics, the International Plant Protection Convention and the Codex Commission on sanitary and phytosanitary issues. Directorate General Enterprise is involved with business and product regulation. As we have seen, the political structures involved in these processes encourage comprehensive planning in narrow policy areas.

2.3 A Business Perspective

A theme is clear. Under the rules of the EU, business input into the policy process is limited to areas and avenues defined by the political leadership (George and Bache, 2001). For example, under the rules of the Commission, the directorates general are obliged to solicit input from the community, including business interests, on new proposals. There are several stages to the process of developing new policies and draft legislation. A general discussion of an issue is published as a "green paper". The relevant directorate general will often solicit comments in writing and/or through a series of regional conferences. The next step is the publication of a ""white paper", which sets forth a legislative proposal and supporting materials. Public comments are again solicited. The last step is the development of a draft directive or regulation. The directorate general will usually contract for the development of a "business impact statement" that assesses the probable effect of implementation on the European economy.

In reality, business access to the policy process in the EU has been restricted. Business and professional trade associations are generally well represented at the national level. However, the organized representation of business at the EU level has been limited. Lobbying is widely considered as a selfish and slightly illegitimate act under the prevailing ideology of governance. Given the limited opportunities for independent influence, there has been little motivation to develop an American-style system of lobbying.

To a significant extent, a lot of the "business input" that the Commission receives has been solicited by the Commission. The business impact statements are generally developed under contract to the Commission, which will often commission trade associations to submit comments and to participate in the conferences. The pressures towards orthodoxy are apparent.

Other areas of business–government cooperation in the EU are generally influenced by government policies. The European process of standards development illustrates the limits on business input into the policy process.

EU national governments designate one or two agencies as the sole standards development organizations (SDOs) for their countries. In many cases, the sponsoring governments fund a substantial portion of the SDOs' budgets. In some cases, the national standards committees are regarded as *de facto* arms of the relevant ministries. The British Standards Institute is one of the few standards development agencies that is largely free of government support and influence.

The "harmonized" standards that are often used to implement EU initiatives are developed by three regional standards development organizations. CENELEC (the European Electrotechnical Standardization Committee) is responsible for electrotechnical standards. ETSI (the European Telecommuncations Standards Institute) handles telecommunications standards and CEN (the European Standard Committee) is responsible for developing standards in all other areas. The memberships of CEN, CENELEC and ETSI consist of the EU national standards development organizations.

Most of the work carried out by CEN and CENELEC is under contract with DG Enterprise, which must approve the standards before they can be considered for use in implementing EU legislation.

The national experts working on CEN, CENELEC and ETSI are nominated by the national SDOs. They generally vote in accordance with instructions from the national "mirror committees". Standards developed by CEN, CENELEC and ETSI must be transposed into national standards sets and all conflicting national standards must be withdrawn. In this system, the autonomy of the industry experts who develop the draft standards is constrained by the national standards associations, the member governments and the directorates general that are providing the funding. The system is in sharp contrast to the US system for standards development, which has minimal government input (Hanson, 2005).

Until relatively recently, the members of the EU Parliament have largely resisted business lobbying efforts. In recent years though, parliamentarians have come to appreciate the availability of independent sources of information, which can often be provided by business.

There are three other channels for business influence in the EU policy process. Many EU governments have adopted informal policies of protecting "national champions" in business. The directorates general, as we have seen, want very much to keep the state governments happy. Many members of the directorate staff are very aware that the EU is not held in high regard by the voters of Europe. The Commission is therefore unlikely to propose anything that would seriously upset regional businesses or the EU economy. Finally, business participates in the development of the product standards that are used to implement EU policies even if under tight state constraints.

2.4 A Voter Perspective

A starting point is the acceptance of the fact that there are limits to the popularity of the European Union. There is widespread support for the values of peace, prosperity and unity. However, popular support for

Table 5.1 Changing support for the EU

Percentage agree: "Do you favor membership in the EU?" "Is membership in the EU a good thing?"					
	Belgium	Germany	France	Ireland	Italy
1979	69	81	75	68	85
1989	76	69	70	81	83
1999	54	59	48	82	60
2008	74	67	60	74	55

Source: *Eurobarometer*, 1980, 1990, 2000, 2008.

specific institutions, initiatives and programs is overall far lower. Table 5.1 sets forth some of the data.

We can speculate as to the reasons why a venture as successful as the EU should not be more warmly received. For one, It is hard to see any concrete evidence of the EU in daily life. The major function of the Union is to coordinate national policies. The execution of these policies is left to the national governments.

Furthermore, the unifying policies of the Union can often be regarded as eroding national identities. Early on, the EU was concerned with the ways in which national governments would use product standards to protect national markets. The results were seen in decisions against the German Beer Purity Law, Italian pasta regulations and French bottling requirements for the mineral water industry. These policies provide fertile ground for jibes against "silly eurocrats".

In reality, some of the basic policies of the EU do offer potential challenges to the cultural identities of the member states. One of the cornerstones of EU policy is freedom of movement. This is perhaps best embodied in the Schengen Agreement, which is an agreement among the major EU members in continental Europe to abolish all border controls for EU citizens. The practical effect can be seen in the continental train stations where the lanes for "EU passport holders" bypass all immigration checks.

These policies have contributed to the widespread European anxiety about the loss of cultural identity (Medrano, 2003). Most of the horror stories involve immigrants from outside the EU, such as the Turkish communities in Germany and North Africans in France and Denmark. However, the potency of these issues contributes to unease about the EU as well. This was particularly true when EU membership was extended to a number of countries that had been generally regarded as outside the

Table 5.2 Changing EU unemployment rates

	National unemployment rates (%)				
	1970	1980	1990	2000	2007
France	2.5	6.5	8.6	9.1	8.6
Germany	0.5	2.0	5.0	7.8	8.7
Italy	3.2	4.4	7.0	9.2	6.2
UK	3.1	6.9	7.1	5.5	5.4

Source: United States (2008), table 1319.

western European political orbit, such as Spain, Poland, Hungary and Estonia.

Other factors have contributed to the limited weak public commitment to the EU as an institution. The first 30-odd years after the Treaty of Rome were generally characterized by strong political recovery and almost explosive economic growth. Growth rates after 1990 fell substantially throughout much of Europe. Falling growth rates make it easier to question the benefits of EU membership. However, the pains of economic dislocation were not felt equally in all areas.

Rising unemployment has been a particularly sensitive issue. EU welfare programs usually provided cushions for people who lost their jobs. However, the changing economic conditions have made the search for the first new job far more difficult. Changing economic conditions in the EU have created the risk of developing a class of people who are permanently unemployed. National estimates for unemployment rates are set forth in Table 5.2.

The power and sensitivity of these cultural and economic issues have created a strong incentive for EU managers to emphasize the importance of protecting community values in the development of EU programs. As a result, EU trade policy is rather inconsistent. On one hand, the EU pushes for a general policy of trade liberalization. The European multinationals have been aggressively pushing for trade liberalization through agencies such as the Trans-Atlantic Business Dialog, particularly in the Uruguay Round. On the other hand, the EU has consistently defended the economic interests of domestic producers and former colonies (Hix, 1999; Gavin, 2001; Messerlin, 2001).

Several other recent issues have left an imprint on EU trade policy priorities. Food safety has been a major issue. Bovine spongiform encephalopathy (BSE or "mad cow disease") is caused by eating neural materials from infected animals. It can be spread across herds by the common practice of including brain and spinal cord remnants in animal feed. It can spread to humans by the consumption of beef products that include neural material from infected cows. Mad cow disease is progressive, incurable and inevitably fatal. The latency period of the disease is up to four years. There is no test for the disease until the symptoms appear.

Mad cow disease killed 163 people in the UK during the 1980s and 37 people in the rest of Europe. The major cause was found to be infected British beef; 179 000 infected cows were found in the UK. It was estimated that 450 000 potentially infected cattle were slaughtered for food in Britain before the source of the infection was discovered. A total of 4.4 million cattle were slaughtered to contain the epidemic.

These events raised public sensitivity to food safety issues. European concerns have extended to the proliferation of genetically modified organisms, the use of growth hormones and the techniques for sanitizing newly killed chickens. All of these initiatives are likely to be supported by the Green parties that are influential in EU politics.

Climate change is another major issue. Europe is a peninsula on the Asian land mass that sticks out into the North Atlantic. The Gulf Stream has usually served to keep the European peninsula warm in the winter and cool in the summer. As a result of global warming, the volume of the Gulf Stream has declined by approximately 30 per cent. The result has been a series of unseasonably warm summers and cold winters. The human costs have been substantial (*New York Times*, 2006; *Philadelphia Inquirer*, 2006, Brown, 2007). These events have strengthened the position of the Greens in EU politics. Any EU initiative in the environmental arena is likely to be well received.

3. CONCLUSIONS

The EU policy system seems to be well organized to support comprehensive planning in relatively narrow areas. There are strong incentives for emphasizing policies that are seen as directly supporting community integrity.

REFERENCES

Brown, D. (2007), "As temperatures rise, health could decline", *Washington Post*, 17 December, p. A7.

Fischer, T. (2000), *The United States, The European Union and the "Globalization" of World Trade: Allies or Adversaries?* Westport, Conn., Quorum Books.

Gavin, B. (2001), *The European Union and Globalization: Towards Global Democratic Governance*, Cheltenham, UK, Edward Elgar.
George, S. and I. Bache (2001), *Politics in the European Union*, Oxford, Oxford University Press.
Hanson, D. (2005), *CE Marking, Product Standards and World Trade*, Cheltenham, UK, Edward Elgar.
Hix, S. (1999), *The Political System of the European Union*, New York, St. Martin's Press.
Hix, S. (2008), *What's Wrong with the European Union and How to Fix It,* Cambridge, Polity Press.
Lenschow, A. (2006), "Environmental policy in the European Union: politics and polity dimensions" in K. Jorgensen, M. Pollack and B. Rosamond (eds), *Handbook of European Union Politics*, London, Sage.
Medrano, J. (2003), *Framing Europe: Attitudes to European Integration in Germany, Spain and the United Kingdom*, Princeton, Princeton University Press.
Messerlin, P. (2001), *Measuring the Costs of Protection in Europe: European Commercial Policy in the 2000s*, Washington: Institute for International Economics.
Milner, H. (1993), "Maintaining international commitments in trade policy" in Kent Wearer and Bert Rockman (eds), *Do Institutions Matter? Government Capabilities in the United States and Abr*oad, Washington, Brookings Institution, pp. 345–69.
New York Times (25 January 2006), "World Briefing Europe: freeze grips Europe", p. A12.
Philadelphia Inquirer (29 July 2006), "Heat wave frazzles Europe too", p. A4.
United States, Department of Commerce (2008), Statistical Abstract of the United States, at www/census.gov.copmpendia/statab/2008/2008edition.html, accessed 30 May 2009.

6. Issues concerning EU trade practices

1. INTRODUCTION

Forty-trade issues were raised against the EU by the United States and Japan between 2002 and 2006/2007. A theme of "social protection" seems to run through many of these issues. The major problems were caused by EU environmental initiatives, as well as protection of foodstuffs and cultural traditions.

2. ISSUES RAISED IN 2002 AND 2006/2007

The list of 18 issues raised against the EU in both 2002 and 2007 is set forth in Table 6.1.

2.1 Import-related Issues

2.1a Trade administration

Tariff classifications for computer peripherals EU tariffs on electronic products, absent special agreements, are relatively high. Computers and computer peripherals are covered by the Information Technology Agreement and should be admitted into the country tariff free. Instead, the EU is classifying several categories of computer-related equipment as "general electronics" and assessing a duty of 6 per cent *ad valorem.*

Japan argues that these machines are designed to be used as digital computer peripherals, which gives them their "essential character". Alternatively, they should be classified under the heading which occurs last in numerical order. Under either rule, digital multi-purpose machines should receive a 0 per cent EU tariff rate (Japan, 2002, p. 80; Japan, 2006, p. 175; Japan, 2007, p. 11; United States 2007, p. 206).

The banana wars The EU has a longstanding policy of favoring ex-colonies in trade arrangements. Under the "general system of preferences",

Table 6.1 Issues raised concerning EU trade practices in 2002 and 2007

Cases against the EU	United States		Japan		WTO
	2007	2002	2006	2002	
1. Import-related					
a. Trade administration					
Computer peripherals	x		x	x	
The banana wars	x	x			x
b. Sanitary and phytosanitary measures					
Growth hormones	x	x			x
Poultry sterilization	x	x			
Wine production	x	x			
Animal by-products regulations	x	x			
c. Government procurement					
Telecommunications markets	x	x			
d. Access to service markets					
Investment barriers	x	x			
e. Safeguard measures					
Anti-dumping rules			x	x	
2. Domestic-related					
a. Standards and technical requirements					
REACH	x	x	x		
WEEED and RoHS	x	x	x	x	
b. Pharma and medical device regulation					
Pharma price controls	x	x			
c. Intellectual property					
Biotechnology patents	x	x			
Wine labeling restrictions	x	x			
Geographic indicators	x	x			
Limits on media services	x	x	x	x	
3. Export-related					
a. Export subsidies					
Airbus subsidies	x	x			x
Canned fruit subsidies	x	x			

all countries can give special tariff benefits to the poorest countries. However, the EU provided additional benefits for its impoverished former colonies by setting quotas for imported bananas. US fruit distributors buy from or produce most of their bananas in Latin America, and could not compete for the EU banana markets.

Successive WTO dispute resolution panels ruled against the EU. The EU agreed to end the quota system and go to a tariff-only system for regulating banana imports on 1 January 2006. The 2002 USTR report expressed optimism that the longstanding US–EU dispute over bananas was coming to a close (United States, 2002, pp. 109–110).

Instead, the EU proposed a new arrangement in the fall of 2005. Most-favored nation (MFN) tariffs on imported bananas were set at 176 euros/ton while bananas imported from former colonies in Africa, the Pacific and the Caribbean would continue to benefit from a zero tariff rate quota. Ecuador asked for WTO consultations on this proposal. The US joined in as a third party (United States, 2002, pp. 109–110; United States 2007, pp. 206–207; World Trade Organization, 2006, *DS 16*; World Trade Organization, 2006, *DS 27*).

There were some real moral concerns underlying the banana wars. On one side was the US, upholding the principle of free trade and trying to enforce the commitments to open markets. From the perspective of the EU though, bananas were virtually the only export crop for many smaller Caribbean and African producers. They were also relatively high-cost producers. Free trade had the effect of killing their export markets.

2.1b Sanitary and phytosanitary requirements

The Hormones Directive (European Union, 1996) The EU has banned the importation of beef from cattle that have been treated with growth-promoting hormones since the early 1990's. The US referred the dispute to the WTO dispute settlement procedure in May 1996. The Panel ruled in favor of the US in 1999 on the grounds that the EU could not show any health risks associated with the consumption of hormone-treated beef. The US was authorized to impose sanctions on EU imports with a value of $116.8 million per year. Negotiations over a resolution of the dispute were continuing (United States, 2002, pp. 112–113; United States 2007, pp. 219–220; World Trade Organization, 2006, *DS 26*). The EU subsequently protested the continued imposition of countervailing duties by the US. See the comments in Chapter 4 on Dispute Panel 320 (World Trade Organization, 2007).

Poultry sterilization Techniques The EU has prohibited the importation of poultry from the US that have been dipped in chlorinated water to prevent the spread of salmonella (European Union, 1975). The EU approved the use of lactic acid and tri-sodium phosphate as an antibiotic dip for poultry. Audits of European sanitary practices showed that some member states were allowing domestic producers to use chlorinated water as an antibacterial. The US was seeking EU approvals for a range of disinfecting measures and for a more consistent enforcement of EU internal regulations (United States 2002, p. 113; United States 2007, p. 220).

Wine production techniques The EU has insisted since the mid-1980s that only all wines sold in the EU must have been produced in accordance with approved oenological practices. Not all US wines conform to these requirements. The US and the EU were in unsuccessful negotiations for a proposed bilateral wine agreement from 1999 to 2001. The EU has been allowing the importation of US wines under a "derogation" from these requirements; this was scheduled to lapse on 31 December 2003. The US was afraid that the derogation would lapse and future US wine exports to the EU would be limited. The US also argued that the Europeans should, like the Americans, allow free trade in all wines unless a health or safety concern could be shown (United States 2002, pp. 106–107; United States, 2007, p. 206).

Animal by-products regulations EC regulation 1774/2002 (European Union, 2002c) regulates the importation of animal by-products that are not fit for human consumption. Discussions were held on how to mitigate the potentially adverse impact on US exports of meat by-products to the European Union. Nevertheless, the regulation cut US exports to the European Union by approximately $100 million, especially in the areas of dry dog food and other animal protein. The Commission organized an international conference on animal by-products in 2006, and the United States participated widely. Nevertheless, the regulation has not been amended and it continues to be interpreted in different ways by different member states (United States, 2002, p. 114; United States, 2007, pp. 219–220).

2.1c Government procurement

Telecommunications The EU Commission has adopted a policy of applying neither the Government Procurement Agreement nor the EU–US memorandum of understanding on procurement (European Union, 1995a) to the EU telecommunications market as long as there is sufficient competition among EU suppliers. In 1999, the EU issued a finding that there was, in fact, sufficient competition so the provisions of neither the GPA nor the MOU would be enforced.

Both the USTR and Japan protested this decision. The Japanese government argued that the EU had failed to enforce the Interconnection Directive (97/33/EC) and that state regulators were still creating barriers to foreign participation in European telecommunications markets (Japan, 2002, p. 90; United States, 2002, pp. 120–122, 130–135; United States, 2007, p. 241).

2.1d Access to service markets

Investment barriers Under European Union law, only firms that are controlled by EU nationals and have majority EU ownership can offer aviation services. Similar restrictions apply to foreign participation in the maritime trades. Foreign participation in banking, insurance and investment services are subject to reciprocal national treatment clauses. Similar restrictions apply to oil exploration and development under the 1994 Hydrocarbons Directive (European Union, 1994). These requirements may be inconsistent with the GATS Agreement (United States, 2002, p. 135; United States, 2007, pp. 244–245).

2.1e Safeguard measures

Anti-dumping policies Under the EU Anti-Dumping Regulation (European Union, 1995b), the Commission is to deduct only the direct selling costs from the domestic price while both the direct and indirect selling costs are to be deducted from the price of imported goods. The result would be an artificially large gap between the estimates of imported prices and domestic costs, leading to an overestimate of the dumping margins. Under the EU rules, any anti-dumping duties that have already been paid are to be deducted from the landed price of the goods. In other words, payment of assessed countervailing duties has the effect of increasing the estimated magnitude of the dumping margin on future transactions. Furthermore, products that are not included in the original complaint may be covered in the imposition of anti-dumping duties without justification. The EU's accession rules have led to the extension of anti-dumping findings to new states without any findings of dumping or damage. Japan argues that these policies are inconsistent with the Anti-Dumping Agreement (Japan, 2002, pp. 81–82, 95–95: Japan, 2006, pp. 178–180, 187–188).

2.2 Domestic Regulations

2.2a Standards and technical requirements

The REACH regulation (European Union, 2006b) The EU has developed a comprehensive set of environmental policies that are based on three principles. First, regulatory policies should be based on the "precautionary principle". The government should assume responsibility for regulation unless a product, process or situation can be shown to be safe. Second, the environmental costs of a product should be reflected in the price. In other words, the polluter should pay. Third, the emphasis should be on avoiding environmental harm not on remediation after the fact.

The new REACH regulations reflect these priorities. Companies selling or using chemicals within the EU will be required to develop a chemical dossier for their products that will include information on chemical and mechanical characteristics, irritability, toxicity, mutagenicity, bioaccumulation and biodegradation. The level of the testing required to develop these data depends on the tonnages handled per year. The manufacturer will have to define use parameters for its product on the basis of the information set forth in the dossier. The REACH regulations will not apply to polymers, or to the monomers that are used to make polymers, as long as the polymerization takes place within the EU.

The Japanese government argues that this exemption unfairly favors European polymer manufacturers (Japan, 2007, pp. 11–12). Japan subsequently has opened discussions with EU on this issue (Japan, 2006, pp. 182–184).

When commenting on an early draft of the regulation, the United States argued that the proposal would be a "costly, complex and burdensome regulatory system which could prove unworkable in its implementation" (United States, 2002, p. 115). As an alternative, the United States urged the European Union to adopt a risk-based system which could pose less of a challenge to international trade (United States 2007, pp. 221–222).

The WEEED and RoHS directives RoHS, the EU Restrictions on the Use of Hazardous Substances in Electrical and Electronic Equipment Directive (European Union 2002a) severely limits the use of mercury, lead, cadmium, hexavalent chromium, PDCC and BPCC in electrical and electronic equipment. WEEED, the Waste from Electrical and Electronic Equipment Directive, imposes recovery/recycling requirements (European Union, 2002b). The EU Directive on Batteries and Accumulators (European Union 2006a) imposes similar requirements on battery manufacturers.

The US and Japan have argued that the ban on "useful" nickel-cadmium batteries is overbroad. The costs of recycling disposable alkaline and manganese batteries may be excessive. The processes for implementing these measures are far from transparent (Japan, 2002, pp. 88–90; Japan 2006, 180–181; United States, 2002, pp. 116–117; United States, 2007, pp. 222–223).

2.2b Pharmaceutical and medical device regulation

Price controls on pharmaceuticals US companies exporting pharmaceuticals to the EU faced a number of issues. EU laws governing the internal free market provided assurances that pharmaceuticals, like other goods, could move freely within the EU (United States, 2002, p. 107). However, the EU member states imposed their own strict price controls over drugs sold within their national territories. In part, these conditions resulted from the policies of the various national health services. Prices varied from country to country. This often led to the emergence of "grey market" transactions, where domestic intermediaries would buy up drugs in low-price market for resale in higher-price markets.

It was also common for governments to offer a higher rate of reimbursement for drugs that were on a list of approved pharmaceuticals. US companies complained that the procedure for having new drugs added to the approved list was onerous, arbitrary and far from transparent (United States, 2002, pp. 107–109; United States 2007, pp. 207–212).

2.2c Intellectual property

Biotechnology patents The EU adopted directive 98/44 (European Union, 1998) authorizing legal protection for biotechnology inventions. All member states were to be in compliance with the directive by 30 July 2000. Some of the member states, especially Austria, were not in compliance by 2002. Furthermore, the directive was not binding on the European Patent Office (United States, 2002, p.125). A number of member states were still out of compliance with the biotechnology patent directive in 2007 and the European Commission had started legal proceedings against them (United States, 2007, pp. 214, 232).

Trademarks and geographic indicators Council Regulation 510/2006 limits the use of geographic indicators in wines, spirits and other foods. The EU bars the use of semi-generic place names, such as burgundy, chablis or champagne, on wines that do not come from those regions.

The US has been critical of EU wine labeling requirements. These restrictions include limits to the use of "traditional expressions" indicating types of wines, such as "ruby" or "tawny", even though they do not reference a specific region. In some cases, the enforcement of these regulations requires companies to abandon trademarks that had previously been recognized by the EU, in violation with the terms of the TRIPS agreement (United States, 2002, p. 125).

The US position was that negotiations over the issue of wine labeling would be welcome, but that they would seek reciprocal recognition for US place names and traditional expressions (United States, 2002, pp. 106–107). In 2006, The US and the EU concluded a new agreement on some aspects of the wine trade as a prelude to the negotiation of a broader agreement that would cover most or all of the issues under discussion (United States, 2007, p. 206).

EU restrictions on trade in media services Under the terms of the 1989 Broadcast Directive (European Union, 1989) the EU member states were obliged to ensure that a majority of TV transmission time be reserved for materials of European origin, "where practicable". The directive had been transposed into national law in all EU countries by the end of 1993. In several cases, the national legislation was more restrictive than the EU directive. France imposed a 60 per cent European and 40 per cent French content requirements. The German Youth Protection Authority had the power to designate media as unsuitable for minors and to impose viewing restrictions. These requirements were creating problems for the emerging DVD market (Japan, 2002, p. 93; Japan, 2006, pp. 184–185; United States, 2002, pp. 127–128: United States, 2007, pp. 236–237).

2.3 Export Regulation Issues

2.3a Subsidies

Aircraft and aircraft engine development subsidies The USTR Report also alleged that EU member states were subsidizing the Airbus Company and Airbus engine manufacturers. Alleged benefits included equity infusions, debt forgiveness, marketing assistance and economic pressure on purchasing governments. The EU argued that the assistance was in compliance with the 1992 US–EU Agreement on Large Civil Aircraft. The US argued that the assistance was in violation of the WTO Agreement on Subsidies and Countervailing Measures. The US requested further discussions (United States, 2002, pp. 122–124; United States 2007, pp. 228–229; World Trade Organization, 2006, *DS 316*, World Trade Organization, 2009, *DS 347*).

Agricultural subsidies: canned peaches The US and the EU have been arguing over the EU rules governing the sale of canned fruit for many years. The terms of accession for Greece to the EU included a subsidy for Greek production of canned peaches. US exporters have lost a substantial portion of the EU market as a result. GATT ruled in favor of the US. The 1985 US–EU Canned Fruit Agreement was to have ended the dispute. Unfortunately, the Agreement seems to be administered in a distorted and discriminatory manner (United States, 2002, pp. 139–140: United States, 2007, p. 230).

3. ISSUES RAISED ONLY IN 2006/2007

Nine issues were raised only in 2006/2007. The are listed in Table 6.2.

3.1 Import-related Issues

3.1a Trade administration

New member accession rules Ten countries joined the EU in 2004. They were Cyprus, the Czech Republic, Estonia, Hungary, Latvia, Lithuania, Malta, Poland, Slovakia and Slovenia. On accession, their foreign trade was covered by the EU tariff policies. In many cases, the EU tariffs were higher than the pre-existing tariffs. Under GATT rules, tariff increases are to be negotiated with the countries affected. Countries that are affected by unilateral tariff increases are entitled to compensation, often through reductions in other tariffs. Japan has argued that no discussions were held about the tariffs that increased on accession. Japan has asked for compensation through tariff reductions on three items: camcorders, digital cameras and photoengraving film.

METI noted that Poland increased tariffs on imported cars to 35 per cent two months before the EU–Poland accession agreement went into effect. Under the terms of the Agreement (p. 187), the Polish tariff was gradually reduced to the EU level by 2004 and accession. Japan argues that the tariff increase right before the agreement went into effect was intended to take advantage of the phase-in provisions, thus allowing Poland to impose an abnormally high tariff on cars imported from Japan during this period. India raised a similar complaint with the WTO and was given a special country tariff rate quota under the generalized system of preferences. Japan would like similar consideration. Similar issues arose with the admission of Bulgaria and Romania into the EU on January 1 2007 (Japan, 2006, pp. 187–188; United States, 2007, p. 205).

Table 6.2 Cases raised only in 2006/2007

Cases against the EU	United States		Japan		WTO
	2007	2002	2006	2002	
1. Import-related					
a. Trade administration					
New member accession rules	x		x		
Consistency in customs administration					
b. Sanitary and phytosanitary requirements					
Genetically modified organisms	x				x
Wood packing material directive	x				
c. Access to service markets					
Postal services	x				
2. Domestic-related					
a. Standards and technical requirements					
Precautionary principle	x				
Metric directive	x				
b. Intellectual property					
Patent fees	x				
Geographic indicators	x				

Consistency in customs administration The EU is responsible for developing and enforcing customs policies for all common market members. However, the policies set down by Brussels are administered locally by the national governments. The US has argued that the EU is unable to assure community-wide uniformity in the administration of EU customs law.

The United States asked for consultations on this issue before the World Trade Organization. No agreement could be reached so a dispute resolution panel was organized in 2005. The panel basically found for the European Union and the United States appealed. In 2006, the Appellate Body found that the trial panel had erred and that the complaints by the United States were valid. However, the EU has not implemented the requirements of the Appellate Panel Report (United States, 2007, pp. 204–205; World Trade Organization, 2008, *DS* 315).

3.1b Sanitary and phytosanitary issues

Genetically modified organisms Directive 01/18 set the terms of biotechnology approvals in the EU. According to the US, the terms of the directive were vague and potentially onerous. The length of time needed to review and approve new biotechnology products at the EU level was approaching two years. Furthermore, the Commission was proposing new legislation that would require mandatory labeling and product traceability of all genetically engineered materials. The proposed threshold for traceability was 0.1 per cent. This could pose serious problems for US agricultural exporters interested in European markets.

Several European member states had been using their domestic authority over agricultural management to ban the importation and/or use of genetically engineered materials within their national borders. Austria imposed a national ban on several biotechnology products that had already received EU approval. The European Commission was not initiating the steps needed to force Austrian recognition of the EU approval.

Germany postponed the initial national approval of the first biotechnology product "for further study of legal issues". Greece refused to respond to requests to authorize field tests for bioengineered seeds. Italy maintained its ban on the use of four bioengineered corn varietals; the Italian Agricultural minister stated that Italian policy called for a biotech-free food chain (United States, 2007, pp. 213, 214–219; World Trade Organization, 2006, *DS 291*).

Wood Packaging Material Directive In February 2005, the European Union enacted a directive regulating the use of wood as a packaging material (European Union, 2004). The directive is more stringent than the Guideline for Regulating Wood Packaging Material (IPSM-15) which was approved by the members of the International Plant Protection Council, including the European Union (United States Trade Representative, 2007, p. 221).

3.1c Access to service markets

Postal services The 2007 USTR report argued that the postal service rules in some EU countries limited US access to European express and package markets. In Belgium, the state railroad was allegedly able to use its monopoly position and exemption from VAT to subsidize domestic package and express services. In Germany, the government had successfully delayed complying with an EU order banning predatory pricing and the use of loyalty rebates in postal services (United States, 2007, pp. 237–238).

3.2 Domestic Regulation

3.2a Standards and technical requirements

The precautionary principle A common threshold issue in regulation is how to respond to the inevitable gaps in the available information. The polar opposites might be an insistence on certainty before acting or an insistence that the government should step in if there is a hint of a problem. By adopting the precautionary principle, the EU has come down on the side of aggressive regulation (European Union, 2000a). The precautionary principle can be summarized as a preference for regulation unless the *laissez faire* proponents can show that regulation is not needed. The US has argued that this bias in favor of regulation will tend to clog the channels of commerce (United States Trade Representative, 2007, p. 213).

The Metric directive When the Metric Directive (80/181/EEC) comes into force in 2010, it will prohibit the use of non-metric measurements on or for any product sold in the EU. Virtually all products sold in the US would have to be relabeled before they could be exported to the EU. Enforcing the Metric Directive will be particularly harmful for US exporters since only two countries in the world still use imperial measurements: the United States and Liberia. The date for implementing the Metric Directive has been postponed many times under US pressure. The USTR would like to have it derogated all together (United States, 2007, p. 224).

3.2b Intellectual property issues

Patent fees The US has argued that the fees charged by the EU and some member states for filing patent applications are excessive (United States, 2007, p, 231).

Geographic indicators The USTR report recognized that the EU was committed to strong protection for intellectual property rights within the framework of the TRIPS Agreement, the WTO Agreement on Trade Related Aspects of Intellectual Property Rights. However, Community Regulations 1493/99 and 2081/92 limit the use of geographic indications in the descriptions of alcoholic and other agricultural products to European companies. EU recognition of foreign uses of these indications must be based on the ratification of specific bilateral agreements. The US and the EU have not entered into any such agreement. The USTR argued that this requirement was a violation of the TRIPS Agreement (United States 2007, pp. 232–233).

4. ISSUES RAISED ONLY IN 2002

Issues that were raised in 2002 that were not included in the 2006 and 2007 reports are considered to have been resolved. There are 18 of them. The resolved issues are listed in Table 6.3.

4.1 Import Issues

4.1a Trade administration

Rules of origin for photocopiers In July 1989, the EU published a list of the activities that would not confer national origin for photocopiers. However, the EU has failed to publish a list of the criteria that should be used to determine national origin. The Japanese have argued that this discrepancy is inconsistent with Article 2(f) of the Agreement on Rules of Origin (Japan, 2002, p. 87).

Justification for a common market Article XXIV:8 of GATT authorizes the formation of a common market on condition that substantially all the trade in the region is covered by the trade liberalization measures. Japan has argued that the EU maintains many restrictions on agricultural trade within the EU and in the free trade agreements they maintain with a number of allied countries. Japan has therefore argued that the EU may not meet the legal requirements for establishing a common market (Japan, 2002, pp. 94–95).

4.1b Sanitary and phytosanitary requirements

BSE quarantine measures In June 2000, the European Commission adopted Commission Decision 2000/418/EC, intended to prevent the spread of bovine spongiform encephalopathy. This policy extended the provisions of the earlier policy to materials such as the skull, spinal cord, tonsils and ileum. The same prohibitions were applied to imported cattle, sheep and goats, regardless of whether or not BSE had ever been found in the exporting countries. Provisions were made to classify herds in the countries of origin according to the probabilities of hosting BSE-contaminated flocks. The prohibitions would not be applied to livestock coming from areas in which there was no evidence of BSE-infected livestock in the domestic herds.

The US was not granted the safe flock exemption and meat exports to the EU have been significantly compromised. The US Department of Agriculture has submitted evidence of no infection in US herds, but the EU continued to impose the BSE restrictions on meat imported from the US (United States, 2002, pp. 113–114).

Table 6.3 Issues raised only in 2002

Cases against the EU	United States	Japan	WTO
1. Import-related			
a. Trade administration			
Rules of origin: photocopiers		x	
Justification for the common market		x	
b. Sanitary and phytosanitary restrictions			
BSE quarantine measures	x		
National SPS inconsistences	x		
Gelatin regulation	x		
Excessive plant quarantine		x	
c. Access to service markets			
Legal services	x		
Postal services	x		
Accounting and auditing services	x		
Tourism services		x	
2. Domestic-related			
a. Standards and technical requirements			
Fertilizer standards	x		
Aircraft engine hush kits	x		
Gas connector standards	x		
Roofing shingle standards	x		
Anchor bolt standards	x		
Certification procedures	x		
b. Intellectual property			
Biotechnology patents	x		
c. Market regulation			
Taxation of electronic commerce	x		

The EU has also proposed legislation that would limit the sources of animal by-products not intended for human consumption to animals that have been certified for human consumption. This includes, for example, the use of animal by-products as animal feed and pet food.

National inconsistencies in SPS measures US companies interested in exporting bovine semen and embryos to France must first obtain a license from the French Customs Service and approvals from the French Ministry of Agriculture. French law prohibits the importation of any product containing vitamin-enriched flour since vitamins can only be added to dietetic food supplements. The Italian government interprets the EU sanitary and phytosanitary requirements in ways that are significantly different from other EU countries. This has created problems for US companies interested in exporting processed meats, wood products, poultry products, game meats, animal feeds and seafood to Italy. US exports of bull semen are restricted by Italian "qualitative" regulations that impose high costs and favor domestic producers (United States, 2002, pp. 119–120).

Gelatin manufacture EU legislation adopted in 2000 substantially strengthened the regulation of factories that manufactured gelatin for human consumption. The regulations required the testing of the animal products that were used for manufacturing gelatin as well as the gelatin that was produced. Compliance with these requirements would be very difficult for US gelatin manufacturers that were interested in exporting to the EU. The US and the EU were negotiating over an agreement that would allow US exports to the EU to continue (United States, 2002, pp. 114–115).

Excessive plant quarantine requirements The EU has required a two-year inspection period for bonsai plants imported from Japan. The inspected plants can only be imported from Japan for a period of three years after the inspection has been completed. Japan argued that these requirements were excessively rigid and not supported by any scientific rationale (Japan, 2002, p. 88).

4.1c Access to service markets

Trade in legal services Both France and Germany impose restrictions on the ability of foreign nationals to offer legal advice in these countries (Japan 2002, p. 94; US, 2002, p. 129).

Accounting and auditing services The EU is a signatory to the General Agreement on Trade in Services. Nevertheless, EU member states, including Austria, Denmark, France and Greece, have imposed restrictions on foreign firms offering accounting and auditing services that may be inconsistent with GATS (United States, 2002, p. 130).

Tourism services Japanese tour companies in Italy and Spain must hire local guides, few of whom are fluent in Japanese (Japan, 2002, p. 94).

4.2 Domestic issues

4.2a Standards and technical requirements

Fertilizer standards EC Directive 76/116 states that triple phosphate fertilizer must be 93 per cent soluble to qualify for the designation of "EC type fertilizer". Fertilizers from the US are, in general, 90 per cent soluble and were barred from this market (United States, 2002, pp. 117–118).

Aircraft hush kits EU Council Regulation 925/99 took effect in May 2000. It potentially limited registration and use in Europe of jet-powered civil aircraft that had an engine bypass ratio below a set level. Engines made in Europe met this requirement while engines made in the US did not. The ostensible justification for the regulation was to limit aircraft noise around airports. However, there were no significant differences between the US and EU engines in the level of radiated noise. Both the US and the EU engines passed the most stringent noise standards developed by the International Civil Aviation Organization (United States, 2002, p.118).

Gas hose connector standards The EU passed the Gas Fired Appliances Directive (European Union, 1990) in 1990. An American company had developed a system for connecting gas-fired appliances to the fuel source that allowed for the use of flexible woven steel pipes with a quick disconnect coupling to link the gas source with the gas-powered appliance. This system is far more flexible and easier to install than the customary use of brazed black iron piping to link a gas-fired appliance with a gas source. French workers refused to install the US gas piping system. Initial discussions revolved around the issue of whether the gas line connection system was properly covered by the Gas Fired Appliances Directive. The issue was subsequently resolved on the EU side in favor of the French position when CEN adopted a standard implementing the Gas Fired Appliances Directive that prohibited the use of the US system. The US protested that this outcome was an unjustified exclusion of a US product from the EU market (United States, 2002, p. 119).

Roof shingles The Construction Product Directive (European Union, 1988) covers construction products that have been placed on the market or put into service in the EU. CEN was developing a standard governing bitumen roof shingles as of the 2002 USTR report. If enacted, the draft standard would have excluded most US-made bitumen shingles from EU markets on the grounds that they were too heavy. The US protested that there was no factual support for this expected exclusion (USTR, 2002, p. 119).

Anchor bolts A draft CEN standard (ETAG 001) defined the performance requirements for anchor bolts used in all concrete structures according to norms that are widely accepted for use in cracked concrete structures, which is a higher risk and more demanding application. Anchor bolt manufacturers in the US and the EU asked the Commission to require amendments to the draft standard so it would better reflect accepted international requirements regarding concrete anchor bolts for use in uncracked concrete structures. The Commission said it was willing to ask for these changes in the draft standard. However, the European Organization for Testing and Acceptances, which certifies EU test houses, continued to insist that the standard based on the cracked concrete requirements should be used as the basis for testing and certification of all concrete anchor bolts. The US was protesting this lack of progress (United States, 2002, p. 119).

CE mark product certification process rules The CE marking system was developed with the twin goals of assuring product safety and promoting the viability of the internal free market in the EU. Under the CE marking rules, companies making higher-risk products have to hire "notified bodies", private organizations that are authorized to certify product compliance with the CE mark requirements. Notified bodies can be located anywhere in the EU.

It could take many months for an organization to meet the qualifications for designation as a notified body. This posed a potential barrier for candidate notified bodies in the accession countries. Normally they would have to start the notification process after their country formally joined the EU. By the time this process was completed, notified bodies from other EU countries would have dominated their national markets.

The EU therefore invited the accession countries to participate in a Pre-Accession Evaluation of Conformity Assessment, or PECA process. Candidate organizations that had successfully completed the PECA process would be designated as notified bodies as soon as their countries formally joined the EU. In the EU, American organizations can, and are, designated as notified bodies. However, only accession country national organizations were eligible to participate in the PECA process. The USTR argued that this was discriminatory (United States, 2002, p. 111).

4.2b Intellectual property rules

Biotechnological patents The US also had several reservations about EU member state practices. Austria, for example, was resisting the transposition of the EU Directive on the Legal Protection of Biotechnological Inventions into national law. The USTR also argued that Belgium,

France, Germany and Italy had not been doing enough to stamp out retail sales of counterfeit goods. Swedish law does not allow copyright holders to be compensated for reproductions done for purely private use (United States, 2002, pp. 111–112).

4.2c Market regulation

Taxation of electronic commerce The Council of Ministers has also approved the principle of a proposed EU Directive on the taxation of electronic commerce. Broadly speaking, VAT would apply to all electronic transactions. The tax rate would be set by the rules in the country of the buyer, not the seller. Electronic service suppliers located outside the EU would have to register with a VAT authority in a single European state. VAT revenues generated in transactions with other EU countries would be paid to the country of registration and transferred to the buyer's country. Implementation of these rules would favor EU electronic service providers, which would only have to charge VAT at their national level. Foreign internet service providers would have to base the charges for VAT on the country of the customer, which is a far more complex task (United States, 2002, p. 139).

REFERENCES

Note: The references under Japan and the United States are ordered by date then page numbers. World Trade Organization references are ordered by Dispute Resolution Panel Number.

European Union (1975), *Council Directive 75/431/EEC of 10 July 1975 Amending Directive No 71/118/EEC on Health Problems Affecting Trade in Fresh Poultry Meat.*

European Union (1988), *Council Directive 89/106/EEC of 21 December 1988 on the Approximation of the Laws, Regulations and Administrative Provisions of the Member States Relating to Construction Products.*

European Union (1989), *Council Directive 89/552/EEC of 3 October 1989 on the Coordination of Certain Provisions Laid Down by Law, Regulation or Administrative Action in Member States Concerning the Provision of Television Broadcast Activities.*

European Union (1990), *Council Directive 90/396/EEC of 29 July 1990 on the Approximation of the Laws of the Member States Relating to Appliances Burning Gaseous Fuels.*

European Union (1992), *Council Regulation (EEC) No 2081/92 on the Protection of Geographical Indicators of Origin for Agricultural Products and Foodstuffs.*

European Union (1994), *Directive 94/22/EC of the European Parliament and of the Council of 30 May 1994 on the Conditions for Granting and Using Authorizations for the Prospection, Exploration and Production of Hydrocarbons.*

European Union (1995a), "Agreement in the form of an exchange of letters between the European Community and the United States of America on government procurement", *Official Journal* L 134, 20 June 1995, pp. 0026–0036.
European Union (1995b), *Council Regulation (EC) No 384/96 of December 1995 on Protection against Dumped Imports from Countries not Members of the European Community*.
European Union (1996), *Council Directive 96/22/EC of 29 April 1996 on the Use in Stockfarming of Certain Substances Having a Hormonal Or Thyrostatic Action and Beta-agonists and Repealing Directives 81/602/EEC, 88/146/EEC and 88/99/EEC*.
European Union (1997), *Council Directive 97/47 of 28 July 1987 Amending the Annexes to Council Directives 77/101/EEC, 79/737/EEC and 91/357/EEC (text with EEA relevance)*.
European Union (1998), *Directive 98/44/EC of the European Parliament and of the Council of 6 July 1998 on the Legal Protection of Biotechnological Inventions*.
European Union (2000a) "Commission adopts communication on precautionary principle", *Press Release*, IP/00/96.
European Union (2000b), *Commission Decision of 29 June 2000 Regulating the Use of Materials Presenting Risks as Regards to Transmissible Spongiform Encephalopathies and Amending Decision 94/474/EC (notified under document number C(2000) 1735) (text with EEA relevance)*.
European Union (2002a), *Directive 2002/95/EEC on the Restriction of Use of Certain Hazardous Substances in Electrical and Electronic Equipment*.
European Union (2002b), *Directive 2002/96/EC of the European Parliament and of the Council of 27 January 2002 on Waste Electrical and Electronic Equipment (WEEE)*.
European Union (2002c), *Regulation (EC) No 1774/2002 of the European Parliament and of the Council of 3 October 2002 Laying Down Health Rules Concerning Animal Byproducts not Intended for Human Consumption*.
European Union (2004), *Commission Directive 2004/102/ED of 5 October 2004 amending annexes II, IV and V to council Directive 2000/29/EC on Productive Measures Against the Introduction Into the Community of Organism Harmful to Plants or Plant Products and Against Their Spread Within the Community*.
European Union (2006a), *Regulation 510/2006 of March 2006 on the Protection of Geographical Indicators and Designations of Origin for Agricultural Products and foodstuffs*, as amended.
European Union (2006b), *Directive 2006/66/EC of the European Parliament and of the Council of 6 September 2006 on Batteries and Accumulators and Waste Batteries and Accumulators and Repealing Directive 91/157/EEC*.
European Union (2006c), *Regulation (EC) No 1907/2006 of the European Parliament and of the Council of 18 December 2006 concerning the Registration, Evaluation, Authorization and Restriction of Chemicals (REACH), establishing a European Chemicals Agency, amending Directive 1999/45/EC and repealing Council Regulation (EEC) No 793/93 and Commission Directive 91/155/EEC and 93/67/EEC and 2000/21/EC*.
Japan, Ministry of Economy, Trade and Industry (2002), "Arbitrarily imposed high tariffs", *Report on Compliance by Major Trading Partners with Trade Agreements*, p. 80.
Japan, Ministry of Economy, Trade and Industry (2002), "Problems involved in Determining the Existence of Dumping", *Report on the Compliance by Major Trading Partners with Trade Agreements*, pp. 81–82.

Japan, Ministry of Economy, Trade and Industry (2002), "Rules of origin", *Report on the Compliance by Major Trading Partners with Trade Agreements*, p. 87.
Japan, Ministry of Economy, Trade and Industry (2002), "Phytosanitary measures", *Report on the Compliance by Major Trading Partners with Trade Agreements*, p. 88.
Japan, Ministry of Economy, Trade and Industry (2002), "Draft Directives on Waste Electric and Electronic Equipment ordinance (WEEE), Draft Directives on the Restrictions of the Use of Certain Hazardous Substances in WEEE (RoS), Draft Directives on Batteries and Accumulators (with a view to replacing Directive 9/157/EEC and 93/86/EEC", *Report on the Compliance by Major Trading Partners with Trade Agreements*, pp. 88–90.
Japan, Ministry of Economy, Trade and Industry (2002), "Trade in services: telecommunications", *Report on the Compliance by Major Trading Partners with Trade Agreements*, p. 90.
Japan, Ministry of Economy, Trade and Industry (2002), "Audio-visual", *Report on the Compliance by Major Trading Partners with Trade Agreements*, p. 93.
Japan, Ministry of Economy, Trade and Industry (2002), "Professional services (legal services)," *Report on the Compliance by Major Trading Partners with Trade Agreements* p. 94.
Japan, Ministry of Economy, Trade and Industry (2002), "Tourism and travel related services", *Report on the Compliance by Major Trading Partners with Trade Agreements*, p. 94.
Japan, Ministry of Economy, Trade and Industry (2002), "Meeting the condition of 'substantially all the trade' under Article XXIV:8 of GATT", *Report on the Compliance by Major Trading Partners with Trade Agreements*, pp. 94–95.
Japan, Ministry of Economy, Trade and Industry (2002), "'Automatic' extension of anti-dumping measures to new members of the EU, 'selective' non-application of anti-dumping measures imports from EU members", *Report on the Compliance by Major Trading Partners with Trade Agreements*, pp. 95–96.
Japan, Ministry of Economy, Trade and Industry (2006), "Regional Integration" Members' *Report on the Compliance by Major Trading Partners with Trade Agreements*, pp. 185–186.
Japan, Ministry of Economy, Trade and Industry (2006), "High tariff products: the classification issue", *Report on the Compliance by Major Trading Partners with Trade Agreements*, p. 175.
Japan, Ministry of Economy, Trade and Industry (2006), "Anti-Dumping", *Report on the Compliance by Major Trading Partners with Trade Agreements*, pp. 178–180.
Japan, Ministry of Economy, Trade and Industry (2006), "Directives on Waste Electrical and Electronic Equipment (WEEE), Directives on the Restriction of the Use of Certain Hazardous Substances in Electrical and Electronic Equipment (RoHS) and Draft Directive on Batteries and Accumulators", *Report on the Compliance by Major Trading Partners with Trade Agreements*, pp. 180–181.
Japan, Ministry of Economy, Trade and Industry (2006), "Framework Directive on Eco-Design Requirements on Energy Using Products (EuP)", *Report on the Compliance by Major Trading Partners with Trade Agreements*, pp. 181–182.
Japan, Ministry of Economy, Trade and Industry (2006), "Draft Regulations on Registration, Evaluation and Authorization of Chemicals (REACH)",

Report on the Compliance by Major Trading Partners with Trade Agreements, p. 182–184.
Japan, Ministry of Economy, Trade and Industry (2006), "Trade in services: audio-visual services", *Report on the Compliance by Major Trading Partners with Trade Agreements*, pp. 184–185.
Japan, Ministry of Economy, Trade and Industry (2006), "Automatic extension of anti-dumping measures to new members of the EU", *Report on the Compliance by Major Trading Partners with Trade Agreements*, pp. 187–188.
Japan, Ministry of Economy, Trade and Industry (2007), "Correction of tariffs on products covered by information technology agreements", *Report on the Compliance by Major Trading Partners with Trade Agreements*, p. 11.
Japan, Ministry of Economy, Trade and industry (2007), "Registration, Authorization and Evaluation of Chemicals (REACH)", *Report on the Compliance by Major Trading Partners with Trade Agreements*, pp. 11–12.
United States Trade Representative (2002), "Arbitrarily high tariffs", *Report on Foreign Trade Barriers*, p. 80.
United States Trade Representative (2002), "Restrictions Affecting U.S. Wine Exports", *Report on Foreign Trade Barriers*, pp. 106–107.
United States Trade Representative (2002), "Spanish and Portuguese corn tariff-rate quotas", *Report on Foreign Trade Barriers*, p. 107.
United States Trade Representative (2002), "Market access restrictions for U.S. pharmaceuticals", *Report on Foreign Trade Barriers*, pp. 107–109.
United States Trade Representative (2002), "Import and distribution of bananas, *Report on Foreign Trade Barriers*, pp. 109–110.
United States Trade Representative (2002), "Protocols to the Europe Agreement on Conformity Assessment (PECAs)", *Report on Foreign Trade Barriers*, p. 111.
United States Trade Representative (2002), "Biotechnology", *Report on Foreign Trade Barriers*, pp. 111–112.
United States Trade Representative (2002), "Ban on beef from cattle treated with growth promoting hormones", *Report on Foreign Trade Barriers*, pp. 112–113.
United States Trade Representative (2002), "Poultry regulations", *Report on Foreign Trade Barriers*, p. 113.
United States Trade Representative (2002), "Transmissible Spongiform Encephalopathies (BSE) Regulations", *Report on Foreign Trade Barriers*, pp. 113–114.
United States Trade Representative (2002), "Animal byproduct legislation", *Report on Foreign Trade Barriers*, p. 114.
United States Trade Representative (2002), "Gelatin regulation", *Report on Foreign Trade Barriers*, pp. 114–115.
United States Trade Representative (2002), "Electrical and electronic equipment (EEE)", *Report on Foreign Trade Barriers*, p. 115.
United States Trade Representative (2002), "Electrical and electronic equipment (EEE)", *Report on Foreign Trade Barriers*, pp. 116–17.
United States Trade Representative (2002), "Triple phosphate fertilizer", *Report on Foreign Trade Barriers*, pp. 117–118.
United States Trade Representative (2002), "Hushkitted or new engine modified and recertified aircraft", *Report on Foreign Trade Barriers*, p. 118.
United States Trade Representative (2002), "Anchor bolts", *Report on Foreign Trade Barriers*, p. 119.

United States Trade Representative (2002), "Gas connector hose standard", *Report on Foreign Trade Barriers*, p. 119.
United States Trade Representative (2002), "Roofing shingles", *Report on Foreign Trade Barriers*, p. 119.
United States Trade Representative (2002), "Member state practices", *Report on Foreign Trade Barriers*, pp. 119–120.
United States Trade Representative (2002), "Government procurement: discrimination in the utilities sector", *Report on Foreign Trade Barriers*, pp. 120–122.
United States Trade Representative (2002), "Export subsidies: government support for airbus", *Report on Foreign Trade Barriers*, pp. 122–124.
United States Trade Representative (2002), "Patenting of biotechnological inventions", *Report on Foreign Trade Barriers*, p. 125.
United States Trade Representative (2002), "Trademarks", *Report on Foreign Trade Barriers*, p. 125.
United States Trade Representative (2002), "Service barriers: television broadcast directive", *Report on Foreign Trade Barriers*, pp. 127–28.
United States Trade Representative (2002), "Legal services", *Report on Foreign Trade Barriers*, p. 129.
United States Trade Representative (2002), "Accounting and auditing services", *Report on Foreign Trade Barriers*, p. 130.
United States Trade Representative (2002), "Telecommunications market access", *Report on Foreign Trade Barriers*, pp. 130–135.
United States Trade Representative (2002), "Investment barriers", *Report on Foreign Trade Barriers*, p. 135.
United States Trade Representative (2002), "Taxation of electronic commerce", *Report on Foreign Trade Barriers*, p. 139.
United States Trade Representative (2002), "Other barriers: canned fruits", *Report on Foreign Trade Barriers*, pp. 139–140.
United States Trade Representative (2007), "Customs administration", *Report on Foreign Trade Barriers*, pp. 204–205.
United States Trade Representative, (2007), "EU enlargement", *Report on Foreign Trade Barriers*, p. 205.
United States Trade Representative (2007), "Restrictions affecting U.S. wine exports", *Report on Foreign Trade Barriers*, p. 206.
United States Trade Representative (2007), "WTO Information Technology Agreement", *Report on Foreign Trade Barriers*, p. 206.
United States Trade Representative (2007), "Bananas", *Report on Foreign Trade Barriers*, pp. 206–207.
United States Trade Representative (2007), "Market access restrictions for U.S. pharmaceuticals", *Report on Foreign Trade Barriers*, pp. 207–212.
United States Trade Representative (2007), "Standards, testing, labeling and certification", *Report on Foreign Trade Barriers*, p. 213.
United States Trade Representative (2007), "Standards, testing, labeling and Certification; overview", *Report on Foreign Trade Barriers*, p. 213.
United States Trade Representative (2007), "Agricultural biotechnology products", *Report on Foreign Trade Barriers*, pp. 214–219.
United States Trade Representative (2007), "Pressure equipment", *Report on Foreign Trade Barriers*, p. 214.
United States Trade Representative (2007), "EU hormone directive", *Report on Foreign Trade Barriers*, p. 219.

United States Trade Representative (2007), "Barriers affecting trade in cattle, beef, poultry and animal by-products", *Report on Foreign Trade Barriers*, pp. 219–220.
United States Trade Representative (2007), "Poultry meat restrictions", *Report on Foreign Trade Barriers*, p. 220.
United States Trade Representative (2007), "EU directive on wood packaging material (WPM)", *Report on Foreign Trade Barriers*, p. 221.
United States Trade Representative (2007), "Emerging regulatory barriers: chemicals", *Report on Foreign Trade Barriers*, pp. 221–222.
United States Trade Representative (2007), "Waste management (WEEE and RoHS Directives)", *Report on Foreign Trade Barriers*, pp. 222–223.
United States Trade Representative (2007), "Battery directive", *Report on Foreign Trade Barriers*, p. 223.
United States Trade Representative (2007), "Energy using products (EUP)", *Report on Foreign Trade Barriers*, pp. 223–224.
United States Trade Representative (2007), "Metric directive", *Report on Foreign Trade Barriers*, p. 224.
United States Trade Representative (2007), "Subsidies policies: government support for airbus", *Report on Foreign Trade Barriers*, pp. 228–229.
United States Trade Representative (2007), "Government support for aircraft engines", *Report on Foreign Trade Barriers*, p. 229.
United States Trade Representative (2007), "Canned fruit subsidies", *Report on Foreign Trade Barriers*, p. 230.
United States Trade Representative (2007), "Patents", *Report on Foreign Trade Barriers*, p. 231.
United States Trade Representative (2007), "Patenting of Biotechnological Inventions", *Report on Foreign Trade Barriers*, p. 232.
United States Trade Representative (2007), "Geographical indicators", *Report on Foreign Trade Barriers*, pp. 232–233.
United States Trade Representative (2007), "Television broadcast directive (Television without Frontiers Directive)", *Report on Foreign Trade Barriers*, pp. 236–237.
United States Trade Representative (2007), "Postal services", *Report on Foreign Trade Barriers*, pp. 237–238.
United States Trade Representative (2007), "Telecommunications market access", *Report on Foreign Trade Barriers*, p. 241.
United States Trade Representative (2007), "Ownership restrictions and reciprocity provisions", *Report on Foreign Trade Barriers*, pp. 244–245.
World Trade Organization (2006), "European Communities: regime for the importation, sale and distribution of bananas", *Dispute Resolution Panel DS 16*.
World Trade Organization (2006), "European Communities: measures concerning meat and meat products (hormones)", *Dispute Resolution Panel DS 26*.
World Trade Organization (2006), "European Communities: regime for the importation, sale and distribution of bananas", *Dispute Resolution Panel DS 27)*.
World Trade Organization (2009), "European Communities: provisional safeguard measures on certain steel products", *Dispute Resolution Panel, DS 260*.
World Trade Organization (2006), "European Communities: measures affecting the approval and marketing of biotech products", *Dispute Resolution Panel DS 291)*.
World Trade Organization (2006), "European Communities: selected customs matters", *Dispute Resolution Panel DS 315*.

World Trade Organization (2006), "European Communities: measures affecting trade in large civilian aircraft", *Dispute Resolution Panel DS 316*.
World Trade Organization (2007), "Continued Suspension of obligations in the EC–Hormones Dispute", *Dispute Resolution Panel DS 320*.
World Trade Organization (2009), "European Communities: measures affecting trade in large civilian aircraft (second complaint)", *Dispute Resolution Panel DS 347*).

7. Background to trade policy in Japan

1. THE CONTEXT OF GOVERNANCE IN JAPAN

1.1 A Cultural Perspective

The national territory of Japan consists of a chain of islands that stretch for roughly 1200 miles along the coast of China. The climate in the north is sub-Arctic, in the south it is sub-tropical. A central mountain chain dominates most islands. Urbanization is largely confined to the coastal plains in the central and southern islands. The coastal coves are separated by the geography of water and mountains.

The pressure of population density on the land has been substantial. It is commonly stated that Japan, with a population of 125 million, has almost half the population of the US in a territory the size of California. In reality, the population is jammed into an area that is, at best, half the size of California (Meyer, 1993).

China became a major cultural influence on the development of Japan during the 6th century. It left a legacy of similarities in culture and written language but a very different spoken language.

An important factor in the evolution of Japan was the thousand-year period of almost endless warfare that ran from 600 to 1600 AD. The feudal lords dominated each coastal strip and cove. These wars gradually led to the unification of Japan into a series of regional states. Tokugawa Ieyasu finally unified all of Japan into one feudal state in 1603 (Meyer, 1993).

The culture that emerged reflected the values of the feudal warrior, as summarized in the "Code of Bushido". Hierarchy was fundamental to the organization of the society and state. Status positions determined behaviors towards superiors and subordinates. The Code of Bushido summarized the values of the samurai: loyalty towards superiors was the fundamental virtue; individual morality was subordinate to the interests of the larger group; discipline, training and a respect for craftsmanship were highly valued. The goal was to benefit society as a whole (Vogel, 1987).

The Tokugawa Dynasty lasted from 1603 until 1867. Peace was imposed by a strong military presence and reverence for the emperor legitimated the government. The shogun was the supreme military commander. The *daimyos* or regional warlords, owed their loyalty to the shogun. The samurai, or knights, provided local control for their *daimyos*. The culture of feudal obligation was emphasized. Guns were outlawed; the *daimyos* knew all too well that a peasant with a gun could kill a samurai with a sword.

Caste distinctions were rigidly observed in this society. The shogun, *daimyos* and samurai were on the top. Artisans came next since they manufactured weapons. The peasants were below the artisans, but above the merchants, since they produced the food that was needed for the military caste. The merchants were at the very bottom, since they did not seem to contribute to the strength of the army in any appreciable way.

This system began to crumble towards the end of the Tokugawa period. The Tokugawa shogun had direct rule over only about a third of the country; the rest of Japan was governed by other clans that were subordinate to the Tokugawas. The Tokugawa dynasty was centered in Edo, or present-day Tokyo. Foreign trade began to develop in the southern parts of the country that had achieved a degree of independence from direct Tokugawa rule.

The *daimyos* usually moved the samurai to their castles, where they could serve as personal retainers. This took the samurai out of the villages, which became largely self-governing. The villagers were obliged to provide their samurai with a fixed quantity of rice or the equivalent every year. To give any less would lead to disaster. However, anything additional that was raised could be kept in the village.

This situation created ferocious pressures for entrepreneurial achievement. Successful innovation meant prosperity, shortfalls meant disaster. Villagers often teamed up with the despised merchants in their mutual search for new ways to make money.

The changes in the system affected the samurai as well. Many samurai living in court society found that they were expected to maintain a more lavish public state. They would buy the clothes and other items needed to honor their *daimyo* from the merchants. Since their incomes were fixed, they often had to borrow from the merchants to pay for their purchases. Thus the lowly merchants began to emerge as a more prosperous and powerful group (Vogel, 1987).

The system collapsed after 1853 when Admiral Perry's squadron blasted open the fortifications of Nagasaki fortress and demanded trading rights. The rape of China by the western powers gave a clear warning where "free trade" would lead. However, the shogun was not able to defend the integrity of Japan. The regime had failed in its most basic task, to protect the interests of those serving them. By keeping Japan isolated, the Tokugawa had allowed Japan to fall behind the West at a time of rapid industrialization and innovation in the tools of war (Griffis, 1895).

The junior samurai, in alliance with the merchants and peasants, revolted in 1867. The "Meiji Restoration", which led to the modernization of Japan, was firmly tied to the political symbols of the past. Their slogan was to "revere the emperor and expel the barbarian". Caste distinctions were abolished. The new ruling classes combined the inquisitiveness and managerial skills of the merchants with the military commitments of the samurai. They wanted not only to build a strong military force but also to develop the technology and economy needed to support it. Leadership was provided by the government. Educated samurai were recruited to the ministries.

The period between 1868 and 1912 could be characterized as an extended debate between the advocates of westernization, with its emphasis on constitutions, law and individual rights, and those who wanted only to strengthen the existing system through industrialization.

The military faction received a major boost when the Japanese navy destroyed the Russian fleet in the Russo-Japanese war. The ascendancy of the military was sealed after 1931 when Japan invaded Manchuria and China. Military rule would last until the final defeat in 1945, again at the hands of the Americans.

Post-mortems of Japanese military performance highlighted some of the characteristic strengths and weaknesses of Japanese society. Japan was well prepared for the beginning of the war; military technology was excellent. Japanese fighter aircraft, radars, battleships, aircraft carriers, submarines and torpedoes were among the best in the world. Japanese military personnel were well trained and highly motivated.

On the other hand, Japanese military operations were hampered by the combination of rigidity and high levels of rivalry among different services and different cliques. Once a military plan had been adopted by the members of a faction, all of the participants were pledged to execute it without change, even if it would clearly result in failure and death. Coordination across groups was very weak. The army, navy and air force commanders could only coordinate operations with difficulty. Assassination was used, from time to time, as a tool for settling inter-service conflicts (Harries and Harries, 1991).

Elements of the neo-feudal and constitutionalist approaches have essentially been combined in post-war Japan. Society is organized hierarchically. All relations are unequal. The *kohai*, or the subordinate party, owes total loyalty to his *senpai* or senior party. Above them all might be a *sensei* or leader. This is a very personal relationship. As Ruth Benedict pointed out, Japan is a culture of "shame". The greatest transgression that can be committed by a kohai is to break some obligation to the sensei (Benedict, 1954). The western concept of "guilt", which is based on a transgression of some universal, abstract rule, is not a major element in Japanese culture.

The *sensei*, in turn, has an obligation to seriously consider the interests of the *kohai*. The status of the person in a superior position depends in large part on the accomplishments and resources controlled by the subordinates who are dependent on him. In a military environment, seniors also have strong incentives to evaluate, train and support their subordinates. It is not that they are intrinsic equals; rather, they may be irreplaceable resources. The *kohai* may be able to take a high level of emotional support from the relationship. The Japanese term *amae* refers to subordinates' feelings that they are nurtured, protected and valued by their superiors.

Again, this is a very personal relationship. This exclusivity promotes rivalry among competing *sensei/kohai* hierarchies. Even today, Marubeni men will rarely talk to Mitsubishi men. In comparison with the outside world though, the participants in Japanese status hierarchies are likely to find more in common with each other than with *gaijin* (outsiders).

This relationship is an odd mixture of ascription and achievement. On one hand, the *kohai*'s identity is totally bound up in the status of the *sensei*. The strengths and weaknesses of the superior are attributed to the subordinate. A *sensei* would not be likely to seriously consider the interests of anyone who had not been proven to be a worthy *kohai*. The incentive for achievement comes from the fact that the *sensei* is not obliged to treat all *kohai* equally. Honor and rewards can be given to the subordinate who has proven himself to be the most worthy in the support of his superior.

These networks of reciprocal obligation stretch from the lowest levels to the most exalted. This chain of obligation pops up in some odd places. Many southern families refuse to live in the rural northern islands in part because there are no recognized schools for their children. Parents have to get their children into prestigious elementary schools if they are to have a chance of being considered for a good high school. Students who do not graduate from a good high school have no chance of being admitted to a prestigious university. Graduation from a good university is a necessary, if not sufficient, condition for landing a good job in business. Ascription is reflected in the importance of attending the right schools. There is no way to prove yourself outside of these narrow channels. Achievement comes in because only the people who excel in the lower schools will be accepted in the higher schools.

1.2 A Business Perspective

The unique features of post-war Japanese business organization have been influenced by the cultural patterns developed in the late Tokugawa period and the period of military expansion.

Senior government officials sit at the top of the status/power hierarchy.

Most major businesses are organized into *keiretsu*. These are diversified conglomerates linked by ties of reciprocal stock ownership, interlocking directorates and banking. There are six major *keiretsu*. The three largest, Mitsubishi, Mitsui and Sumitomo, can trace their development back to the *zaibatsu* that were organized during the earliest stages of Japan's modernization (Goto and Suzumura, 1997). An international trading house, a major bank and major steel and/or automobile companies usually form the core of each *keiretsu*. Policies and priorities for the *keiretsu* are set by the leaders of the core corporations. Execution is generally left to the management of the peripheral companies. The subordinate members of the *keiretsu* are expected to support the prosperity of the core corporations. Each company is expected to rely primarily on other companies in the *keiretsu* for its customer and supplier base.

In general, workers are expected to support the company and the company is expected to support its workers. Japanese companies invest very heavily in worker training. In return, Japanese workers are world-renowned for the extent to which they work in their own time to improve company processes. The employees of companies that are more central in the *keiretsu* have expectations of lifetime employment. Employees that are involved in the more useful initiatives have opportunities to move up to managerial ranks. Companies that are peripheral in the *keiretsu* are often under heavy short-term cost pressures from their superiors. They are less likely to offer the same level of security and opportunity to their workers.

Life in the more important Japanese companies is somewhat different. New hires are usually recruited from the graduates of the leading universities. New recruits are usually organized into groups that will essentially stay together for the first 20 years of their careers with the company. They start by spending six months or so in "boot camp", where they are humiliated, torn down and reconstituted as company men. There is a strong emphasis on learning at least the basics of all major functions in the company.

The groups are given problems or tasks which they are expected to address collectively. They are expected to recommend solutions to their seniors. Groups are evaluated collectively according to the usefulness of their proposals. Individuals are evaluated according to their contributions to the group. "Lifetime employment" means that the members of a group can never leave. No other group would have them.

The pressures for loyalty and conformity are substantial. On the other hand, these groups are unparalleled in their ability to make incremental improvements to existing products and processes. The Americans may have invented the video tape recorder. However, it took a Japanese company to take a machine the size of a large desk and reduce it to the size of two packs of cigarettes.

Competition in the Japanese economy is often muted. Although the supply chain operations of the major Japanese companies are world-renowned for efficiency, operations in other areas can be amazingly inefficient. The goal of most entrepreneurs is to develop personal relations with powerful people that would allow the exploitation of local pockets of advantage.

New initiatives in Japan usually involve the search for personal advantage by developing new alliances with useful people. Car salesmen, for example, may cultivate future sales by giving little gifts to families on the birthdays of their children. When the children grow up, they will have no choice but to buy from the person who has honored them so often.

Both senior and subordinates often benefit from market-limiting arrangements. Subordinates might enjoy opportunities and margins that would not otherwise be available to them. For the superior, subordinates who were previously in competition would now be dependent on him for his leadership in arranging mutually beneficial arrangements. This usually occurs in areas in which the core interests of the *keiretsu* are not involved. For example, the retail distribution system in Japan is enormously complex and very expensive. Every layer of added cost usually represents another instance where someone was able to gain a local advantage by developing a personal tie to someone in a position to protect their arrangements. These arrangements often benefited both subordinates and superiors in the status chain.

The Japanese economy grew at a phenomenal rate from 1950 to roughly 1990. Before 1990, Japanese industrial policy was simple: promote export expansion. The major manufacturing corporations enjoyed high margins on their domestic sales as a result of managed competition. The government kept interest rates artificially low so that companies could finance export expansion through debt. Companies could use real estate and stocks as collateral. With the economy booming and the stock market soaring, there was always enough on paper to cover the next set of loans. Even so, most companies were so highly leveraged that they were close to bankruptcy by western standards. However, industry leaders could use the cheap capital to finance growth back to solvency.

The system began to fail by 1990. The costs of doing business in Japan had been rising with the proliferation of market sharing arrangements. The nature of the *sensai/kohai* relationship made it difficult for superiors to let their *kohai* go out of business. The result was a prolonged period of muddling through that delayed the eventual corrections. Japan has been labeled the "disintegrating tiger" (Fischer, 2000). The magnitude of the decline is presented in Table 7.1.

There are several related reasons for the crash. The real-estate bubble

Table 7.1 Bursting the Japanese bubble

Year	Manufacturing index	5-year change (%)
1980	66.8	
1985	79.2	+ 18.6
1990	98.5	+ 24.3
1995	95.5	− 03.1
2000	100	+ 05.0
2004	101.7	+ 01.7

Source: United States (2008) table 1319.

popped, the stock market stalled and collateral values plummeted. Prosperity had bid up the cost of manufacturing in Japan and most major corporations had been moving factories off shore. The major corporations were no longer able to grow their way back into solvency. Auto manufacturers such as Nissan and Mazda stayed in the black only because they had been aggressively squeezing their suppliers. This too, came to an end (Tett, 2003).

Japanese banks were in a particularly difficult position. Because the government had kept interest rates very low, banking margins were very thin. Commercial banks could not write off their bad loans without going into bankruptcy themselves. The alternative was to loan their major clients the money they needed to make the payments on old loans. Culturally, this was an approved practice since the bankers were looking out for the interests of the companies that depended on them. Financially, of course, this practice was a disaster that postponed a resolution and made the problems much worse.

One solution was to bring in the barbarians, who could smash the way through to a resolution. Nissan, for example, brought in Renault, Mazda brought in Ford and the Long Term Credit Bank brought in a Wall Street venture fund (Tett, 2003).

1.3 A Government Perspective

The government, as the most powerful agency, sits on the top of the *sensei/kohai* hierarchy. Within the national government though, power is centered in the bureaucratic agencies not in the parliament. Most legislators are primarily interested in developing alliances with wealthy emerging groups for personal gain. The major power base for the members of the diet is their control over the "pork barrel", national appropriations for local projects (Nagata, 1996). Thus, the leading members of the Diet tend to have close relations with the larger construction companies and major landowners.

The bureaucratic agencies of the Japanese government are generally organized by business sector as well as by business function. The agencies are in a far better position to work with the same people in the private sector over a long period, thus facilitating the development of close working relations between senior bureaucrats and the senior *keiretsu* executives.

Most legislation is very general, leaving the details to be filled in through regulations or, more commonly, through "administrative guidance'. In Japan, the enactment of laws, cabinet orders and ministerial orders is carried out through specific procedures and the associated documentation is available publicly. Ministerial orders, communication notes and government–business consultations are generally not published or otherwise available to outsiders.

Government guidance is often exercised through "consultations" with business "advisory councils". This process is usually dominated by the senior government bureaucrats, who chair the meetings, set the agendas and keep the minutes. In turn, the development and enforcement of technical requirements is often delegated to trade associations. As the senior party in the relationship, the government bureaucrats are expected to provide guidance to the business participants in the process. In return, they are expected to be attentive to business interests, especially in the limitation of competition (Organisation for Economic Co-operation and Development, 1999).

Coordination across government ministries and offices is generally weak. Government agencies often compete for power and programs (OECD, 1999). Their shared partnerships with the same business interests provide a major source of coordination and continuity in government decision making (Jun and Wright, 1996).

The private sector relationships available to senior bureaucratic officials depend in large part on the subject matter jurisdiction of their departments. The Ministry of Economy, Trade and Investment (formerly the Ministry of International Trade and Industry) is, overall, the most important. The power of the other agencies depends on the subject matters under discussion. Relations among different agencies can be, in Japanese style, distant and contentious. Power grabs and squabbles over jurisdiction are not uncommon. This has an impact on international trade negotiations (Naka, 1996).

1.4 A Voter Perspective

Electoral districts in Japan have been drawn so as to greatly over-represent rural interests. Rural constituencies tend to be the most conservative and unchanging. Furthermore, the rural areas tend to be the regions with the highest level of investment in public construction. The results are seen in the dominance of the conservative Liberal Democratic Party in Japanese electoral politics.

For urban voters, party affiliation is a way to help resolve problems with the government with licenses, permits and so on. A useful politician is therefore less one who best represents your views on government policy; instead, the most useful political loyalties would be extended to politicians who can get things done in your favor. Again, voting tends to be less of a momentary choice, and more of a reflection of a long-term personal alliance. As a result, the ballot box has not been a strong vehicle for promoting change in the Japanese system of business.

2. DECISION MAKING IN JAPAN ON TRADE-RELATED ISSUES

There is very little coordination across Japanese ministries and agencies. The coordination of domestic decisions with overall government trade policies is weak. There is no central process for reviewing or assessing the impact of agency policies. There are no explicit requirements on the ministries to minimize the trade impacts of administrative decisions. The Japan Fair Trade Commission is very weak; it does not consider how domestic regulated monopolies could use their positions to gain unfair advantages in unregulated domestic markets.

According to conventional criteria, the Japanese market should be remarkably open to foreign trade. In 1999, tariffs averaged around 4.8 per cent, and tariffs on industrial goods were as low as 2.5 per cent. There were few formal trade barriers impeding access to Japanese markets. Nevertheless, Japan has generally been viewed as a very difficult market to enter, largely because of the dense web of business-to-business and government-to-business understandings on non-competitive practices and market allocation (Huntington, 1996; OECD, 1999; Ostry, 1997).

The Japanese government responded to foreign pressures to open domestic markets for foreign trade in 1990 with the initiation of the Japan–United States Structural Impediments Initiative talks. This led to the Japan–United States Framework for a New Economic Partnership.

In 1995, Japan launched a Deregulation Action Programme with the intent of implementing some of the initiatives that were discussed in the Talks. An Office of Trade and Investment Ombudsman (OTO) was created in 1994 to address the difficulties encountered by individual exporters. Unfortunately, the OTO has, in general, only addressed minor problems. It generally only looks at border issues and not at internal practices, and it cannot provide long-term solutions to endemic problems.

The fight over deregulation and transparency is largely between outsiders who are convinced of the need for reform and entrenched bureaucrats who want to keep the old ways. Given the weakness of the mechanisms for coordinating overall policies, power is generally in the hands of the bureaucrats. It is very difficult for any political leader to develop an effective government-wide reform initiative.

REFERENCES

Benedict, Ruth (1954), *The Chrysanthemum and the Sword: Patterns of Japanese Culture*, Rutland VT, Tuttle.

Fischer, T. (2000), *The United States, The European Union and the "Globalization" of World Trade: Allies or Adversaries?* Westport, Conn., Quorum Books.

Goto, A. and K. Suzumura (1997), "Keiretsu: interfirm relations in Japan" in Leonard Waverman, William S. Comanor and Akira Goto (eds), *Competition Policy in the Global Economy: Modalities for Cooperatio*n, London, Routledge, pp. 361–380.

Griffis, William Elliot (1895, reprint 2006), *The Mikado's Empire: A History of Japan from the Age of the Gods to the Meiji Era (660 BC – AD 1872*). Berkeley, Stone Bridge Press.

Harries, Meiron and Suzie Harries (1991), *Soldiers of the Sun: The Rise and Fall of the Imperial Japanese Army*, New York, Random House.

Huntington, Samuel (1996), *The Clash of Civilizations and the Remaking of the World Order*, New York, Simon and Schuster.

Jun, J. and D. Wright (eds) (1996), *Globalization and Decentralization: International contexts, Policy Issues and Intergovernmental Relations in Japan and the United States*, Washington, DC: Georgetown University Press.

Meyer, Milton (1993), *Japan: A Concise History* (3rd edn), Lanham MD, Littlefield Adams.

Nagata, Nadohisa (1996), "The role of central government and local government in Japan's regional development policies" in Jong Jun and Deil Wright (eds), *Globalization and Decentralization: Institutional Contests, Policy Issues and Intergovernmental Relations in Japan and the United States*, Washington, Georgetown University Press.

Naka, N. (1996), *Predicting Outcomes in United States–Japan Trade Negotiations*, Westport, Conn., Quorum Books.

Organisation for Economic Co-operation and Development (1999), *Regulatory Reform in Japan: Enhancing Market Openness Through Regulatory Reform*, Paris, OECD.

Ostry, Sylvia (1997), "Globalization, domestic policies and the need for harmonization" in Leonard Waverman, William S. Comanor and Akira Goto (eds), *Competition Policy in the Global Economy: Modalities for Cooperatio*n, London, Routledge, pp. 29–39.

Tett, Gillian (2003), *Saving the Sun: How Wall Street Mavericks Shook Up Japan's Financial World and Made Billions*, New York, HarperBusiness.

United States, Department of Commerce (2008), Statistical Abstract of the United States, at www.census.gov/compendia/statab

Vogel, Ezra (1987), "Japan: adaptive communitarianism" in George Lodge and Ezra Vogel (eds), *Ideology and National Competitiveness: An Analysis of Nine Countries*, Boston, Harvard Business School Press.

8. Issues concerning Japanese trade practices

1. INTRODUCTION

Trade barriers attributed to Japan fall into yet another pattern. The overriding interests can best be characterized as "relationship protective". The Japanese government does not impose many formal trade barriers, which are more common in the European Union. There is no particular emphasis on unilateral trade remedies and no exceptional mechanisms in place to defend domestic industries against foreign competition, as is common in the United States. Rather, the Japanese government is accused, primarily by the United States, of permitting and even supporting the emergence of collusive, anti-competitive activities in the private sector. This pattern seems to be most prevalent in agriculture, construction, telecommunications and business services.

2. ISSUES RAISED IN 2002 AND 2007

A summary of this pattern is set forth in Table 8.1, which lists the issues that were raised in both 2002 and 2007.

2.1 Import-related Issues

2.1a Trade administration issues

Rice Japan has imposed a quota tariff on imported rice. Up to 682000 metric tons of rice can be imported each year at a nominal tariff. Import quantities exceeding the quota are subject to a tariff of 341 yen per kg, for an effective rate of around 400 per cent *ad valorem*. Most of the rice imported under the quota is of medium quality and is purchased by the Ministry of Agriculture, Forestry and Fisheries (MAFF) for blending and industrial use. Most of the other 100000 tons or so of rice imported is handled by a non-transparent system for rice distribution. As a result, US rice sold to consumers in Japan costs around three times the prevailing market price (United States, 2002, pp. 219–220).

Table 8.1 Trade issues about Japan raised in 2002 and 2007

Complainant	US		EU		WTO
	2002	2007	2002	2007	
1. Import-related issues					
a. Trade administration					
Rice quota tariffs	x	x			
Tariffs on beef, citrus and cheeses	x	x			
Restrictive pork tariff rate system	x	x	x	x	
Restrictive wheat and corn import system	x	x			x
Fish quota rate tariffs	x	x			
Tariffs on wood and wood products	x	x			
Leather and footwear tariffs	x	x		x	x
Complex customs clearance procedures	x	x			
b. Sanitary and phytosanitary requirements					
Ban on livestock due to BSE	x	x	x	x	
Slow approvals for biotechnology strains	x	x			
Inspection, fumigation of cut flowers			x	x	
Slow approvals for new varietals			x	x	
Ban on US poultry	x	x			
Excessive fumigation	x	x	x	x	
Measures against swine fever			x	x	x
Restrictive residual standards	x	x	x	x	
Fire blight on tomatoes and cucumbers			x	x	
Refusal to recognize single SPS system				x	x
c. Service access barriers					
Telecommunications services	x	x	x	x	
Information technologies	x	x			
Entry limits to the electrical energy market	x	x			
Restrictive approvals for insurance	x	x	x		
Limited access to accounting services	x	x			
Limited access to Japanese legal services	x	x			
Limited access to landing rights	x	x			
Limited access to Japanese port system	x	x			
Limited access to construction markets	x	x			
Restrictions on foreign investments	x	x			
2. Domestic regulation issues					
a. Standards and technical requirements					
Definitions of alcoholic liquors			x	x	
Marine recreational craft	x	x			
b. Pharmaceuticals and medical products					
Arbitrary pharmaceutical price controls	x	x			

Table 8.1 (continued)

Complainant	US 2002	US 2007	EU 2002	EU 2007	WTO
Restrictions on dietary supplements	x	x			
Restrictions on energy drinks			x	x	
Cumbersome cosmetics regulations		x	x	x	
Restrictions on foreign medical technology		x	x	x	
Restrictions on food additives	x	x	x	x	
c. Intellectual property issues					
Limited scope of patent rights	x	x			
Internet copyright protection	x	x			
Arbitrary trade mark recognition	x	x			
Open trade secrets trials	x	x			
Weak border enforcement of IP rights	x	x			
Geographic indicators	x	x			
d. Toleration of restrictive business practices					
Antiquated corporate codes	x	x			
Regulation of anti-competitive practices	x	x			
Lack of transparency in government	x	x			
Anti-competitive practices in auto industry	x	x			

Although Japan has generally met the rice import commitments made during the Uruguay Round, an arbitrary and non-transparent distribution system limits US exports of high-quality rice to Japan. Virtually all the US rice imported under the quota is used for government stocks or re-exported as Japanese food aid. The relatively small fraction of rice imported from the US that enters Japanese domestic markets still goes for industrial uses and blending, rather than for sale as high-quality table rice form the US (United States, 2007, pp. 316–317).

Tariffs on beef, oranges and cheeses According to the US, Japan maintains high tariffs on a number of agricultural items that are important for US exporters. Japanese tariffs for beef are set at 38 per cent, 32 per cent on oranges, 40 per cent on processed cheeses, and 30 per cent on natural cheeses (United States, 2002, p. 219; United States, 2007, p. 318). The USTR argued that these tariffs are part of a general policy in favor of protecting domestic agriculture.

Pork import requirements US pork exports to Japan are subject to a gate pricing and safeguard system. Pork shipped in any month where the value of pork imports exceeds the average of the last three years by 19 per cent is subject to a steep tariff. As a result, import patterns are driven more by the goal of avoiding the gate pricing system than by the domestic demand for foreign pork (United States, 2002, p. 221; United States, 2007, p. 317). The European Union also raised this issue. Tariffs rose first by 16 per cent and then by 24 per cent in 2003 and 2004 (European Union, 2005, fiche 960109).

Quota rate tariffs for wheat and corn Most of the wheat exported to Japan from the US is also handled through the MAFF and released to Japanese flour millers at prices that are substantially higher than the market average. Japanese corn starch manufacturers must blend in at least one part of potato starch for every thirteen parts of corn starch. If a lesser amount of domestic potato starch is used, then the imported corn is subject to a 50 per cent *ad valorem* tariff. Otherwise, it can be imported tariff free (United States, 2002, p. 220; United States, 2007, p. 317).

Fish quotas Japan has imposed import quotas on, among other species pollock, herring, Pacific cod, mackerel, whiting, squid and sardines. These quotas include fish imported from the US (United States, 2002, p. 221: United States, 2007, p. 318).

Discriminatory standards for wood and wood products The Japanese lumber import system discourages the importation of processed wood. Japanese tariffs are lowest on raw lumber. In effect, the *ad valorem* rates increase in proportion to the amount of processing that has occurred in the exporting country. Restrictive product standards and building codes limit the use of imported lumber in Japanese construction. US lumber exporters can't certify compliance with Japanese standards because of the difficulties encountered in accrediting US inspection agencies to the Japanese requirements. The US government has been involved in a protracted effort to demonstrate that US standards and conformity assessment systems are equivalent to the Japanese requirements (United States, 2002, p. 221; United States, 2007, p. 319).

Tariffs and quotas on imported shoes and leather The Japanese have established a system of quotas governing the importation of leather from the US. The Japanese quota for imported footwear was raised from 2.4 million pairs to 12 million pairs during the 1990s. The process for setting and allocating quota rights lacks transparency. The size of the quotas is not related to patterns of domestic need and the quotas are not awarded according to the needs or probable uses of the importing entities.

Furthermore, the tariffs on shoe imports over quota imports remain very high, generally at 4300 yen per pair (European Union, 2005, fiche 050015; United States, 2002, p. 223; United States, 2007, p. 319).

The European Union asked for consultations with Japan on the issue through the WTO in 1998. However, the case is still pending. No panel was ever established nor settlement notified (World Trade Organization, 1998, *Dispute DS 147*).

Complex customs clearance procedures Customs processing costs and delays were another source of complaints about Japanese commercial policies. This has become a particularly sensitive area for the rapidly growing express carrier industry. The US has been urging Japan to change the customs regulations to make the simplified customs procedures that are already in place applicable to a wider range of import transactions. The US has also asked Japan to introduce a more equitable fee structure for the Air Nippon Automatic Cargo Clearance System. The threshold for the *de minimum* customs clearance process should be raised from 10000 yen to at least 30000 yen (United States, 2002, pp. 218–219). Although some progress was made in resolving these issues between 2002 and 2007, the basic problems remained (United States, 2007, pp. 315–316).

2.1b Sanitary and phytosanitary issues

Ban on livestock products due to BSE Japan imposed a broad ban on imported livestock products because of a fear of BSE. One cow was found in Washington State that had BSE. The ban covered imports of products such as meat, bone meal and tallow from the US, even though the US meets the criteria set by the OIE (International Organization for Epizootics) as "free from BSE" (United States, 2002, p. 224).

The ban was partially lifted in 2006. However, only beef from animals aged 20 months or younger was allowed in. This has greatly limited US beef exports to Japan, which used to be a $1.4 billion export (United States, 2007, p. 320). The Europeans have also argued that the Japanese policies concerning imported milk that are based on BSE concerns are inconsistent with the recommendations of the OIE Terrestrial Animal Health Code (European Union, 2004, fiche 040064). Japan has pledged to conduct a risk assessment on the issue. However, the ban has not been lifted (European Union, 2006, fiche 040045; United States, 2002, p. 224; United States, 2007, p. 320).

Approvals for biotechnology strains According to the USTR, Japan has adopted a scientifically valid process for reviewing and approving genetically modified foodstuffs. However, the time required for a review seems excessive. The US is also concerned about mandatory labeling of biotechnology products, even where no biotech modified materials can be found in the product (United States, 2002, pp. 225–226; United States, 2007, pp. 3211–322).

Inspection and fumigation of cut flowers In 1985, Japan and the Netherlands agreed on a pre-inspection system for cut flowers exported to Japan. In 1997, the Netherlands asked Japan to modify the agreement to recognize the results of the Dutch inspection system. Japan could monitor the Dutch system. So far, no action has been taken (European Union, 2005, fiche 960107).

Slow approvals for new varietals It can take up to two or three years for Japanese authorities to recognize new varietals and to authorize their importation. Japan does not recognize the EU as a single market for regulatory purposes. Each EU member state must negotiate separately for rights to export new varietals to Japan. Furthermore, Japan has a zero tolerance policy for plant pests that are not included on its list of no-quarantine organisms. This list is incomplete and importers often have to certify that their varietals are free of organisms that are already common in Japan (European Union, 2007, fiche 070244).

Ban on importing US poultry Japan has banned the importation of poultry from the US as a measure for controlling avian influenza. The US argues that this ban is not supported by scientific evidence and is not consistent with the recommendations of the Office of International Epizootics (United States, 2002, pp. 223–224; United States, 2007, p. 323).

Excessive use of fumigation Japan imposes excessive fumigation requirements. These are damaging to trade in fresh fruits and vegetables, which often do not survive the fumigation process. The fumigation requirements are often justified as necessary to control pests which are already present in Japan. This is contrary to accepted international practices, especially when domestic product from infested areas is not also subject to fumigation requirements (European Union, 2005, fiche 000002; United States, 2002, p. 225; United States, 2007, p. 321).

Restrictive measures against swine fever Japanese restrictions on the importation of pig meat from France go beyond what is recommended by the OIE to prevent the spread of classical swine fever (European Union, 2005, fiche 020069). The EU requested consultations with Japan through the WTO dispute resolution system in 1997. It argued that the Japanese rules violate GATT 1994 Articles I, X:3 and XIII and impair trade benefits that the EU should have enjoyed under the GATT 1994 agreements. However, no panel was ever established nor settlement notified (World Trade Organization, 2007, *Dispute DS 66*).

Restrictive residual standards Under Japanese regulations governing the maximum residue limits for pesticides in foodstuffs, foreign infractions are treated more severely than domestic infractions. The response to an infraction by a Japanese company is handled on a company-by-company basis. The responses to foreign infractions usually ban the importation of the product from the originating country, regardless of the company involvement (United States, 2007, pp. 320–321). This issue was first raised by the EU in 1997 (European Union, 2005, fiche 970254).

Tomatoes and cucumbers – fireblight Japan has barred the importation of tomatoes and cucumbers from Belgium because a small amount of tobacco is also grown in Belgium. The Japanese authorities argue that Belgium tobacco might be infected by tobacco blue malt and that the tomatoes and cucumbers might be carriers of the blue malt fungus. As a result, a Belgian farm growing tomatoes or cucumbers that is located 80 km from the tobacco fields can't export to Japan but a French farm that is 10 km across the border is able to do so (European Union, 2005, fiche 040056).

Failure to recognize that the EU has an integrated system for sanitary and phytosanitary regulation As a result, each EU member state must negotiate separate bilateral agreements with Japan on agricultural regulation (European Union, 2006, fiche 040049).

2.1c Foreign access to service markets

Telecommunications policy The issue is whether the Japanese telecommunications market will continue to be dominated by the overwhelming market power of the dominant carrier group, the Nippon Telephone and Telegraph Corporation (NTT). The Japanese government initiated a limited set of reforms in 2001. However, the USTR argued, foreign access to the Japanese telecommunications market remained tightly limited by the market power of NTT (98 per cent market share) and the weakness of the Ministry of Public Management, Home Affairs, Posts and Telecommunications (MPHPT). The Ministry is hemmed in by political and industry interests that inhibit the development of pro-competition policies.

These conditions contribute to a series of anti-competitive practices. NTT imposes high charges and onerous conditions for carriers that want to connect to the NTT system. The Ministry also allows NTT regional carriers to engage in discriminatory pricing to ensure that non-NTT carriers are unable to compete. Foreign carriers that wanted to develop their own right of way were faced with very high charges for using NTT poles, ducts and conduits. The process followed by NTT in establishing charges for outside telecommunications carriers lacked transparency and was seemingly arbitrary.

Japan has started collecting a "universal service fee" from all carriers to fund phone service in rural areas. The NTT regional carriers are the only telecommunications service providers eligible to receive the subsidies. To an extent, this program offsets the promised reforms in connection charges.

DoMoCo, a subsidiary of NTT, is the dominant wireless provider in Japan. It was recognized as a dominant carrier under the Telecommunications Business Law in 2002. However, DoMoCo has not been required to justify its rates, as the law seems to require. On a more positive note, Japan has made telecommunications spectra available to new entrants to the Japanese mobile telecommunications market (European Union, 2005, fiche 010001; United States, 2002, pp. 204–205).

It was hoped that the telecommunications reforms, when completed, would open up Japanese telecommunications markets for outside, including foreign, service providers. In principle, the interconnection charges imposed by NTT on outside service providers have been lowered and rationalized, but the implementation of the reforms has been postponed until 2010 (United States, 2007, pp. 305–306).

However, the measures adopted failed to address the overwhelming market position of the NTT. Interconnection rates are still very high (United States, 2002, pp. 204–205). By 2007, Japan had still not instituted dominant carrier regulations or insisted on competitive interconnection rates. NTT has also been able to cross-subsidize competitive services from earnings made in protected markets (United States, 2007, pp. 305–306). The EU basically concurs (European Union, 2005, fiche 0010001).

Information technologies The United States and Japan have created a separate IT Working Group under the Regulatory Reform Initiative. However, the United States argued in 2002 that progress was being limited by the lack of a robust legal framework. There were no clear-cut liability rules for internet service providers. There was no explicit intellectual property protection for "temporary copies" created in the RAM of a computer. The lack of authorization for digital signatures limits the development of internet commerce and paperless transactions (United States, 2002, pp. 207–209).

In the 2007 Report, the United States Trade Representative acknowledged that the Japanese government had addressed many of these issues. However, concerns were raised as to whether the implementation of the reform initiatives would: a) encourage private sector self-regulation; b) provide meaningful opportunities for the private sector to comment on draft rules and to participate effectively in government advisory groups; c) adhere to the principle of technology neutrality; and d) insure that the policies and rules are consistent with international practice (United States, 2007, pp. 307–308).

Entry limits to the electrical energy market The cost of electric power in Japan is the highest in the industrialized world. The US argues that the costs can be substantially reduced if the Japanese government allowed the emergence of genuine competition in the non-fuels procurement process. Foreign companies often face discriminatory standards and specifications, which are generally design-based rather than performance-based. Each of Japan's ten power companies uses a separate set of standards and specifications. Information on requests for proposals is not easily available for foreign suppliers, and specifications and drawings are usually published only in Japanese (United States, 2002, p. 243). A few reforms were made in the electric energy market but the net effect was minimal (United States, 2007, p. 335).

Foreign access to insurance services Japan's private insurance market is the second largest in the world. Services are provided by a mix of private insurance companies, public insurance carriers and mutual care societies. The private companies are regulated by the Financial Services Agency (FSA). The FSA is also responsible for regulating the securities industry.

The FSA in Japan has undertaken significant steps to deregulate Japanese financial markets. Nevertheless, a significant number of problem areas remain. Review times for new products should be speeded up. There is a fear that solvent US carriers will be asked to provide more support for insolvent Japanese insurers. The US was also opposed to a proposed expansion of the subsidized postal insurance program (European Union, 2002, fiche 960206; United States, 2002, p. 234; United States, 2007. p. 328).

Limited foreign rights to offer accounting services Public accounting services can only be offered by certified public accountants (CPAs). To qualify as a Japanese CPA, a foreigner must take a special CPA exam; this was last offered in 1975 (United States, 2002, p. 236; United States, 2007, p. 331).

Limited foreign rights to offer legal services Japan has allowed foreign lawyers to open offices and advise clients in Japan since 1987. However, contacts between Japanese lawyers and foreign lawyers are strongly discouraged. Foreign participation in the Japanese bar associations is limited. Foreign law firms are barred from hiring Japanese lawyers to advise domestic clients (United States, 2002, p. 236). Some of these restrictions may be eased with the implementation of reforms allowing Japanese lawyers to work with foreign lawyers that were implemented on 1 April 2005 (United States, 2007, p. 331).

Limited foreign access to civil air landing slots US access to Japanese civil aviation markets has been limited by extremely high airport costs and enduring limits on traffic rights, operational flexibility and pricing. In 1998, Japan and the US signed a Memorandum of Understanding on civil aviation. Several US carriers were granted increased landing and transit rights as a result of these discussions. These benefits have been substantially negated by a subsequent increase in international landing fees, which were already among the highest in the world. Landing fees for domestic flights, which only benefit Japanese carriers, were reduced. Both sides agreed to hold further negotiations in 2001, but no substantive progress has been reported (United States, 2002, p. 243; United States, 2007, p. 335).

Limited access to port transportation services The Japanese Harbor Transportation Association (JHTA) has undue power to regulate market entry and to impose high costs. Japanese law protects the JHTA by preventing new service providers from entering the market unless it can be proven that there is an insufficient supply of services. The JHTA, a private group, has been able to set port rates and to force carriers that want to enter the Japanese market to prove that there is unmet demand for sea transportation services. In 1997, the US Federal Maritime Commission imposed a $100 000 fine on each Japanese ship arriving in the US from Japan. As a result, Japan agreed in 1997 to reform the port services sector. However, these reforms have not lessened the ability of the JHTA to set fees and limit market access (United States, 2002, p. 246; United States, 2007, p. 336).

US access to Japanese construction projects These problems include "rampant bid-rigging, unreasonable restrictions on the formation of joint ventures, use of vague and discriminatory qualification and evaluation criteria, and the structuring of individual procurements so that they fall below the thresholds established in international agreements" (United States, 2002, p. 228; United States 2007, pp. 324–325).

Problems with foreign investments Cross-border mergers and acquisitions are more difficult in Japan in part because of different management techniques, a general lack of transparency in government decision making, and a cautious attitudes towards foreign investors. The scarcity of qualified lawyers, accountants and auditors is another barrier. Target companies have not been not required to disclose any anti-takeover measures they may have adopted or explain why they were taken. Proxy voting arrangements are not well developed (United States, 2002, pp. 337–339).

On 1 May 2006, major reforms were introduced to the Japanese Commercial Code that addressed some of these concerns. However, it was not clear by the end of 2006 that the reforms would effectively open Japanese investment markets to foreign interests (United States, 2007, pp. 314–315).

2.2 Domestic Regulation Issues

2.2a Standards and technical requirements

Product definitions: liquor Japanese classifications of liquors are not consistent with international practice, as endorsed by the International Federation of Wines and Spirits and EU Regulation 1576/89. This has created problems for European liquor exports to Japan (European Union, 2004, fiche 980123).

Marine recreational craft Japan has developed standards and systems for marine craft safety assurance that are unique in the world. These requirements are, in general, not consistent with the international practices promulgated through the International Maritime Organization and recognized by governments and insurers worldwide. These idiosyncratic requirements, coupled with the insistence of the Japanese government that every craft be inspected individually, create major barriers for American companies that are interested in exporting boats to Japan (United States, 2007, p. 319; United States, 2002, pp. 222–223).

2.2b Regulation of pharmaceuticals and medical devices

Arbitrary pharmaceutical price controls Pricing in the Japanese medical market is essentially controlled by the government reimbursement policies. In 2002, Japan initiated a "foreign reference pricing" system, which bases reimbursements on the prices for similar goods in the US, the UK, Germany and France. This approach fails to recognize the costs of doing business in Japan (United States, 2002, p. 210).

The Japanese government recognizes the need to promote the importation of new drugs and devices into the Japanese market and has discussed the need for pricing flexibility. However, the implementation of these proposals has been lagging (United States, 2007, pp. 309–310).

Restrictions on approvals of dietary supplements Dietary supplements composed of vitamins, minerals, herbs and non-active substances have traditionally been classified as drugs in Japan. They are therefore subject to the full drug review process. Manufacturers are allowed to claim that their products confer nutritional and health benefits, if they have scientific data to back this up. However, there are no clear definitions on the types of data that are needed to support these claims (United States, 2007, p. 227; United States, 2007, p. 323).

Restrictions on energy drinks The European Union argues that Japanese standards defining energy drinks are unnecessarily restrictive. They are defined as vitamin-containing health supplements to be packaged in a maximum size of 100 ml without carbonization. Maximum permissible levels are set for the major active ingredients. As a result of these restrictions, European energy drinks can't be sold in Japan (European Union, 2005, fiche 020081).

Cumbersome cosmetics regulations The regulations governing the introduction of new cosmetics in the Japanese market are significantly different from US and EU practices. These differences add substantially to the cost of entering Japanese markets (European Union, 2005, fiche 960115; United States, 2007, p. 323).

Entry restrictions for foreign medical technology In the past, Japan has imposed a series of restrictions on the introduction of foreign pharmaceuticals. Products generally had to undergo clinical testing for the Japanese market, even though similar tests had already been conducted for approval in the US or EU markets. The review period could take over a year.

Japan introduced a series of reforms in 2000 that were intended to alleviate these problems. Review periods were nominally limited to one year and foreign clinical data was to be accepted. In practice, the usefulness of these reforms has been limited. The Japanese government can still stop the clock and ask for additional clinical information (European Union, 2005, fiche 050034; European Union, 2006, fiches 160117 and 06005). These problems emerge in the approval process for medical devices as well as for pharmaceuticals (European Union, 2005, fiche 050035; United States, 2007, pp. 309–310).

Restrictions on food additives The United States opposes Japanese policies regarding food additives. Japan has a more restrictive food additive list that is inconsistent with international practice, as defined by the FAO/WHO Experts Committee on Food Additives. As a result, many food preparations have to be approved on a case-by-case basis. Some of the banned additives are also used in traditional Japanese dishes without restriction (European Union, 2005, fiche 970254; United States, 2002, pp. 226–227; United States, 2007, p. 322).

2.2c Intellectual property rights

Scope of patent protection According to the USTR's 2002 report, the Japanese patent system offers inadequate protection for patent holders. Patents in business processes are not recognized. The patent litigation process is very slow, there is no way to compel discovery and the protection for confidential information is inadequate (United States, 2002, pp. 231–232).

After 2002, Japan took several steps to improve the administration of intellectual property laws. The management of patent infringement cases was improved and timetables were speeded up. However, the basic complaints were still carried over from the 2002 Report (United States, 2007, p. 325).

Inadequate internet copyright laws Japan does not have adequate copyright protection for materials on the internet and in other electronic formats. There is inadequate copyright protection for "temporary copies". As a result, music that is broadcast in a digital format that can be easily downloaded is not covered by Japanese copyright laws. Despite new legal efforts to combat copyright infringement, piracy was still a major problem (United States, 2002, pp. 232–233; United States, 2007, pp. 326–327).

Arbitrary trade mark recognition "Well known" trademarks are to be accorded greater legal protection in Japan. Unfortunately, the employees in the Patent Office are prone to make arbitrary *ex officio* determinations as to which trademarks are well known (United States, 2002, p. 233; United States, 2007, p. 327).

Open trials on trade secrets Because of the constitutional ban on closed trials, Japanese trials involving trade secrets are open to public view.

This has substantially weakened Japanese legal protection for trade secrets (United States, 2002, p. 234). Partial reforms were introduced in 2003, but the basic problem has not been resolved (United States, 2007, p. 327).

Weak border enforcement of IP rights Under a 1997 Supreme Court decision, Japanese authorities allow the parallel importation of patented products. In effect, a patent holder does not have the right in Japan to block the importation by some other agency of his or her products as long as they have been patented in another country (United States, 2002, p. 234; United States, 2007, p. 328).

Weak protection for geographical indicators Articles 22 to 24 of the TRIPS Agreement obliges WTO members to provide legal means to prevent the misuse of geographical indicators. In the 2002 Report, the United States Trade Representative suggested that Japan had not developed the legal tools needed for the task (United States, 2002, pp. 233–234).

The 2007 Report stated that the concern had persisted. However, the Japanese government had announced that three Japanese terms would be registered as geographical indicators for wines and spirits, and that the National Tax Agency was to protect these labels in the territories of WTO members. The Report stated that they had no information as to how this was to be done or how foreign companies could register their geographical indicators for protection in Japan (United States, 2007, p. 327).

2.2d Business regulation issues

Antiquated corporate codes Japanese incorporation laws limit corporate flexibility in responding to commercial situations (United States, 2002, pp. 217–218). The USTR recommends measures to promote board independence, the use of outside auditors and the use of share exchanges to facilitate mergers and acquisitions.

The US also suggests that Japan reforms its arcane arbitration laws to meet contemporary business needs. The process of civil litigation should be modernized to facilitate quicker, cheaper and better judicial decision making. Court review of government procedures and decisions should be strengthened and streamlined. The USTR 2007 Report describes the results of the Japanese regulatory reforms. The promise seems to be more significant than the results (United States, 2007, pp. 314–315).

Failure to police and punish anti-competitive practices The Japanese Fair Trade Commission (JFTC) has frequently been criticized for a failure to aggressively police anti-competitive practices. In part, this reflects a lack of bureaucratic independence. The JFTC is an agency within the Ministry of Public Management, Home Affairs, Posts and Telecommunications. The Ministry is responsible for promoting a number of the key industries in which anti-competitive practices have been prevalent. Budgets and fines are modest. The investigative powers of the JFTC are limited; it does not have the authority to conduct compulsory searches and seizures. The fines imposed seem to be relatively minor in comparison with the financial resources available to the cartels being regulated. It can't reduce criminal penalties for companies that cooperate with an investigation. It rarely initiates criminal proceedings against even flagrant violations of the anti-trust laws. It is exceedingly rare for private companies to win lawsuits against competitors for anti-competitive behaviors (United States, 2002, pp. 213–214).

Some of these factors were addressed in the 2006 amendments to the Anti-Monopoly Law. However, the effectiveness of these changes had not been demonstrated by 2007 (United States, 2007, pp. 311–313).

Lack of transparency in government rule making The Japanese government has recognized the need for greater transparency and more opportunities for public comment in government decision making. These concerns were the subject of the Three Year Program for Promoting Regulatory Reform, which included strengthening the public comment procedures. However the practical impact was limited. The USTR argued that most regulations were initially developed in cooperation with the affected interest groups behind closed doors. The public comment period was short and few comments seemed to have any effect on the draft regulations being considered. Little effort had been made to implement the transparency regulations in government agencies. There were few venues in which interested parties can participate in the development of regulatory proposals. The grounds for judicial review of regulatory decisions were very limited (United States, 2002, pp. 215–217). The reforms that came into effect in April 2006 alleviated some of these concerns but did not fully solve the problem (United States, 2007, pp. 313–314).

Anti-competitive practices in the auto industry US access to Japan's automobile market has been hampered by overly restrictive regulations, non-transparent rule making and lackluster enforcement of anti-trust laws. These issues are being addressed by the Automotive Consultative Group, which was organized in 2001. However, comparatively little progress was reported by 2007 (United States, 2002, pp. 242–243; United States, 2007, pp. 333–334).

Table 8.2 Japanese trading issues raised in 2007 but not in 2002

Type of barrier	Complainant		WTO
	US	EU	
1. Import-related issues			
a. Sanitary, phytosanitary restrictions			
Unnecessary fumigation for cherries	x		
Restrictive pests standards		x	
2. Domestic-related issues			
a. Standards and certifications			
Building products	x		
Marine craft	x		
b. Medical, pharmaceutical regulation			
Cosmetics and quasi-drugs	x		
Food additives	x		
c. Market regulation issues			
Review of fair competition in marketing	x		

3. ISSUES RAISED IN 2007 BUT NOT IN 2002

A list of the issues raised in 2007 but not in 2002 is set forth in Table 8.2.

3.1 Import-related Issues

3.1a Sanitary and phytosanitary issues

Cherries Japan has required cherries exported from the US Pacific Northwest to be fumigated with methyl bromide to ensure that they are not infested by the codling moth. However, US research has shown that sweet cherries are not hosts to codling moths. The US has further offered Japan an opportunity to review the quarantine security system that is used in the Northwest, which offered better assurances of pest-free produce than the methyl bromide fumigation (United States, 2007, p. 321).

Unreasonable restrictions on pests Japan's Ministry of Agriculture, Forestry and Fishery often bans the importation of agricultural products that may carry pests that are already present in Japan. They further require plant-exporting countries to develop pest forecasting systems that are equivalent to the one in place in Japan. These requirements are not based on the recommendations of the International Plant Protection Convention, which is the international authority on the issue. Finally, Japan bans imports from all parts of an exporting country if there is a report of an outbreak of a pest in any part of it. This rule ignores the effectiveness of internal containment procedures in the exporting countries (United States, 2007, p. 311).

3.2 Issues Relating to Domestic Regulation

3.2a Standards and technical requirements

Building products The US government is concerned that Japanese regulations governing indoor air quality and chemical emissions from building materials may be overly restrictive in the case of some wall coverings (United States, 2007, p. 321).

Marine craft The Japanese system for inspecting and qualifying marine craft is unique in the world. Japanese rules are complex and vague and subject to arbitrary interpretations. As a result, each vessel must be inspected separately, which creates an enormous burden on exporting companies (United States, 2007, p. 319).

3.2b Pharmaceuticals and medical devices

Cosmetics and quasi-drugs Both the US and the EU complain about Japanese limits to the introduction and marketing of cosmetics and "quasi-drugs", which would be handled as over-the-counter sales in the US. The approval process is slow and non-transparent, and manufacturers are barred from making verifiable claims about the effectiveness of their products (United States, 2007, p. 323).

Food additives Japan requires exporters to disclose the names and percentages of all ingredients, including food additives, as well as a description of the associated manufacturing processes. This is a burdensome process that creates the risk of unnecessary disclosure of trade secrets (United States, 2007, p. 318).

3.2c Business regulation issues

Fair competition in marketing The US argues that the introduction of legitimate innovative marketing techniques, such as give-aways and lotteries, has been impeded by the rules of the Japan Fair Trade Council. The JFTC further limits market innovations by supporting industry-developed "fair competition codes" (United States, 2007, p. 332).

4. ISSUES RAISED IN 2002 BUT NOT IN 2007

A list of the issues raised in 2002 but not in 2007 is set forth in Table 8.3.

4.1 Import-related Restrictions

4.1a Sanitary and phytosanitary requirements

Ban on dairy products from Spain Japan has banned the importation of dairy products form Spain because of bovine spongiform encephalopathy, including milk, milk products, semen, derived cattle embryos, hides, skins, gelatin and collagen. These materials are not regarded as carriers of BSE by the OIE (European Union, 2004, fiche 040064).

Limits on foreign racehorses The European Union argues that the restrictions placed on racehorses with foreign experience against participating in Japanese races is an unjustified barrier to trade (European Union, fiche 960108).

Excessive use of fumigation The US complained that Japan imposed excessive fumigation requirements; they were imposed on lettuce, avocados and fresh flowers, which generally do not survive the process. These fumigation requirements were justified by the need to keep out pests, most of which were already present in Japan and not under effective regional control. The Japanese government liberalized the fumigation policies in 2002; however these changes did not address many problem areas (United States, 2002, p. 225).

Bans on importing fresh peppers and eggplants Japan has argued that the ban on imported peppers and eggplants (aubergines) was necessary to prevent the introduction of tobacco blue mold into the country. The US has argued that there is no evidence that these plants are carriers of tobacco blue mold (United States, 2002, p. 225).

Fresh apple quarantine requirements Japan has imposed burdensome quarantine restrictions to prevent fireblight on mature, symptomless apples. To qualify for export rights, US orchards have to undergo fireblight inspections at three times during the growing season. There must be a 500 meter fireblight-free buffer zone around all orchards producing export fruits. To meet Japanese export requirements, apples must also be treated with chlorine after harvesting.

The US insists, and says that Japanese scientists agree, that mature,

Table 8.3 Issues raised in 2002 but not in 2007

Type of barrier	Complainant		WTO
	US	EU	
1. Import-related issues			
a. Sanitary, phytosanitary requirements			
Ban on dairy products from Spain		x	
Limits on foreign racehorses		x	
Excessive use of fumigation	x		
Fresh bell peppers and eggplant		x	
Fresh apple quarantine requirements	x		
Ban on fresh potatoes	x		
Standards for organic foods	x		
b. Foreign access to domestic service markets			
Entry limits into natural gas markets	x		
c. Government procurement			
Computers	xi		
2. Domestic-related issues			
a. Standards and technical requirements			
Unjustified ban on tandem motorcycles	x		
Requirements for marine recreational craft	x		
b. Intellectual property issues			
Vagueness of copyrights impede enforcement	x		
Open trials on trade secrets		x	
Inadequate internet copyright laws		x	
Narrowly defined scope for patents		x	
c. Restrictive business practices			
Collusion in domestic steel markets	x		
Collusion in domestic paper markets	x		
Collusion in domestic flat glass markets	x		
Bid rigging in construction, architecture contracts		x	
d. Limitations in policies, enforcement			
Lack of transparency, input in rule making		x	

asymptomatic apples are not fireblight carriers and that all of these restrictions constitute unwarranted trade restrictions. The US asked for WTO consultations over this issue under the DRU process. (United States, 2002, p. 224).

Ban on fresh potatoes Japan has imposed a similar ban on fresh potatoes imported from the US in order to keep out golden nematode and potato wart. Potato wart is not found in the US. The Japanese ban extends to potatoes grown in regions that are free of the golden nematode. The Japanese government also bans the importation of peeled potatoes, which can't be carriers of either disease (United States, 2002, pp. 224–225).

Standards for organic foods Japanese laws limit rights to import organic foods to government-licensed importers. Japan has been slow to recognize organic certifications issued by the US Department of Agriculture (United States, 2002, p. 226).

4.1b Foreign access to domestic service markets

Limited entry into natural gas markets Japan's natural gas markets are subject to many of the same anti-competition impediments that characterize the electrical market. A limited series of pro-competition reforms in the natural gas market were implemented in 2001. However, the liberalization has not been sufficient to attract any foreign gas company to enter Japanese markets (United States, 2002, p. 210).

4.1c Foreign access to government procurement

Computers Although US companies are world leaders in computer technology and have established strong positions in the Japanese private sector markets, their share of government purchases is minimal. Enactment of the Bilateral Computer Agreement in 1992 has failed to make an appreciable difference in the situation (United States, 2002, pp. 227–228). However, this issue was not carried forward to the 2007 USTR report so it may have been resolved.

4.2 Restrictions Related to Domestic Regulations

4.2a Standards and technical requirements

Unjustified ban on tandem motorcycles Japan's ban on tandem motorcycles is the last vestige of a more general set of restrictions on motorcycling. The government was studying the issue, but the ban had not been lifted by the time of the 2002 USTR Report (United States, 2002, p. 245). However, this issue was not carried forward to the 2007 USTR report so it may have been resolved.

4.2b Business regulation issues

Collusion in Japanese steel markets US steel producers have argued that the five leading Japanese steel companies coordinate output, pricing and market allocation goals with the approval of the Ministry of the Economy, Trade and Industry (United States, 2002, p. 247).

Anti-competitive practices in domestic paper markets US exporters argue that their access to the Japanese paper market is substantially limited by anti-competitive arrangements among Japanese paper companies. Under the 1992 US–Japan agreement, *Measures to Increase Market Access for Paper Products*, Japan agreed to introduce transparent corporate procurement guidelines, to introduce new Anti-Monopoly Act compliance programs, and to encourage key segments of the Japanese market to use more imported paper products. Japan also agreed to provide market information and low-interest loans to foreign paper exporters. The Agreement expired in 1997, with little progress in expanding foreign participation in Japanese paper markets (United States, 2002, pp. 245–246).

Anti-competitive practices in domestic flat glass markets Japan's four major flat glass manufacturers have maintained roughly constant market shares through informal agreements and tight control over distribution channels. These issues were to be addressed in the 1995 Bilateral Flat Glass Agreement. Little progress was reported in the 2002 Report (United States, 2002, pp. 243–244).

REFERENCES

Notes: The EU references are arranged by fiche number, the United States references are arranged by date and page number.

European Union, Directorate General Trade (2002), "Insurance", Fiche 960107, *Market Access Database.*

European Union, Directorate General Trade (2005), "Japan: cut flowers", Fiche 960107, *Market Access Database.*

European Union, Directorate General Trade (2005), "Exporting live horses", Fiche 960108, *Market Access Database.*

European Union, Directorate General Trade (2005), "Pigmeat", Fiche 960109, *Market Access Database.*

European Union, Directorate General Trade (2005), "Cosmetic registration", Fiche 960115, *Market Access Database.*

European Union, Directorate General Trade (2005), "Pharmaceuticals", Fiche 960117, *Market Access Database.*

European Union, Directorate General Trade (2005), "Japan food additives", Fiche 970254, *Market Access Database.*

European Union, Directorate General Trade (2005), "Japan: MRL law revision under Food Sanitation Law", Fiche 970255, *Market Access Database.*

European Union, Directorate General Trade (2004), "Liquor: product definition", Fiche 980123, *Market Access Database.*
European Union, Directorate General Trade (2005), "Plant health facilities", Fiche 00002, *Market Access Database.*
European Union, Directorate General Trade (2005), "Anti-competitive regulatory framework in the telecoms sector", Fiche 010001, *Market Access Database.*
European Union, Directorate General Trade (2005), "Import restrictions on energy drinks", Fiche 020081, *Market Access Database.*
European Union, Directorate General Trade (2006), "Japan: beef, beef products and processed animal proteins", Fiche 040045, *Market Access Database.*
European Union, Directorate General Trade (2006), "Japan: pot plants in approved growing media", Fiche 040049, *Market Access Database.*
European Union, Directorate General Trade (2005), "Japan: tomatoes and cucumbers – fire blight", Fiche 040056, *Market Access Database.*
European Union, Directorate General Trade (2006), "Japan: dairy products", Fiche 040064, *Market Access Database.*
European Union, Directorate General Trade (2005), "Japan: pig meat – classical swine fever", Fiche 040069, M*arket Access Database.*
European Union, Directorate General Trade (2005), "Leather and leather footwear (tariff quota)", Fiche 050015, *Market Access Database.*
European Union, Directorate General Trade (2005), "Burdensome clinical trials", Fiche 050034, *Market Access Database.*
European Union, Directorate General Trade (2005), "Difficulties in processing time for registration", Fiche 050035, *Market Access Database.*
European Union, Directorate General Trade (2006), "Product approval processes", Fiche 06005, *Market Access Database.*
European Union, Directorate General Trade (2007), "Japan: fresh fruit and vegetables – all import issues", Fiche 070244, *Market Access Database.*
United States Trade Representative (2002), "Telecommunications", *Report on Foreign Trade Barriers*, pp. 204–205.
United States Trade Representative (2002), "Sectoral regulatory reform: information technologies', *Foreign Trade Barriers*, pp 207–209.
United States Trade Representative (2002), "Natural gas", *Foreign Trade Barriers*, p. 210.
United States Trade Representative (2002), "Medical devices and pharmaceuticals", *Foreign Trade Barriers*, pp. 210–212.
United States Trade Representative (2002), "Antimonopoly law and competition policy", *Foreign Trade Barriers*, pp. 213–215.
United States Trade Representative (2002), "Transparency and other government practices", *Foreign Trade Barriers*, pp. 215–217.
United States Trade Representative (2002), "Commercial law", *Foreign Trade Barriers*, pp. 217–218.
United States Trade Representative (2002), "Distribution and customs clearance", *Report on Foreign Trade Barriers*, pp. 218–219.
United States Trade Representative (2002), "High tariffs on beef, citrus, dairy and processed food products", *Report on Foreign Trade Barriers*, p. 219.
United States Trade Representative (2002), "Rice importing system", *Report on Foreign Trade Barriers*, pp. 219–220.
United States Trade Representative (2002), "Wheat import system corn for industrial use", *Report on Foreign Trade Barriers*, p. 220.

United States Trade Representative (2002), "Fish products", *Report on Foreign Trade Barriers*, p. 221.
United States Trade Representative (2002), "Pork import regime", *Report on Foreign Trade Barriers*, p. 221.
United States Trade Representative (2002), "Wood products and housing", *Report on Foreign Trade Barriers*, p. 221.
United States Trade Representative (2002), "Marine craft", *Report on Foreign Trade Barriers*, pp. 222–223.
United States Trade Representative (2002), "Leather/footwear", *Report on Foreign Trade Barriers*, p. 223.
United States Trade Representative (2002), "Ban on US poultry", *Foreign Trade Barriers*, pp. 223–224.
United States Trade Representative (2002), "Fresh apples: quarantine restrictions for fireblight", *Report on Foreign Trade Barriers*, p. 224.
United States Trade Representative (2002), "Import policies: ban on imports of livestock products due to BSE", *Report on Foreign Trade Barriers*, p. 224.
United States Trade Representative (2002), "Ban on fresh potatoes", *Report on Foreign Trade Barriers*, pp. 224–225.
United States Trade Representative (2002), "Ban on fresh bell peppers and fresh eggplant", *Report on Foreign Trade Barriers*, p. 225.
United States Trade Representative (2002), "Excessive use of fumigation", *Report on Foreign Trade Barriers*, p. 225.
United States Trade Representative (2002), "Biotechnology", *Report on Foreign Trade Barriers*, pp. 225–226.
United States Trade Representative (2002), "Standards, testing, labeling and certification: new standards for organic foods", *Report on Foreign Trade Barriers*, p. 226.
United States Trade Representative (2002), "Restrictive food additive list", *Report on Foreign Trade Barriers*, pp. 226–227.
United Sates Trade Representative (2007), "Dietary supplement", *Foreign Trade Barriers*, p. 227.
United States Trade Representative (2002), "Government procurement: computers", *Report on Foreign Trade Barriers*, pp. 227–228.
United States Trade Representative (2002), "Construction, architecture and engineering", *Report on Foreign Trade Barriers*, p. 228–229.
United States Trade Representative (2002), "Patents", *Report on Foreign Trade Barriers*, pp. 231–232.
United States Trade Representative (2002), "Copyrights", *Report on Foreign Trade Barriers*, pp. 232–233.
United States Trade Representative (2002), "Trademarks", *Report on Foreign Trade Barriers*, p. 233.
United States Trade Representative (2002), "Geographic indications", *Report on Foreign Trade Barriers*, pp. 233–234.
United States Trade Representative (2002), "Border enforcement", *Report on Foreign Trade Barriers*, p. 234.
United States Trade Representative (2002), "Insurance", *Foreign Trade Barriers*, p. 234.
United States Trade Representative (2002), "Trade secrets", *Report on Foreign Trade Barriers*, p. 234.
United States Trade Representative (2002), "Professional services", *Report on Foreign Trade Barriers*, p. 236.

United States Trade Representative (2002), "Investment barriers", *Report on Foreign Trade Barriers*, pp. 237–239.
United States Trade Representative (2002), "Autos and auto parts", *Report on Foreign Trade Barriers*, pp. 242–243.
United States Trade Representative (2002), "Civil aviation", *Report on Foreign Trade Barriers*, p. 243.
United States Trade Representative (2002), "Electric utilities", *Report on Foreign Trade Barriers*, p. 243.
United States Trade Representative (2002), "Flat glass", *Report on Foreign Trade Barriers*, pp. 243–244.
United States Trade Representative (2002), "Other barriers: motorcycles", *Report on Foreign Trade Barriers*, p. 245.
United States Trade Representative (2002), "Paper and paper products", *Report on Foreign Trade Barriers,* pp. 245–246.
United States Trade Representative (2002), "Steel", *Report on Foreign Trade Barriers*, p. 247.
United States Trade Representative (2002), "Sea transportation: ports", *Report on Foreign Trade Barriers*, p. 246.
United States Trade Representative (2007), "Telecommunications", *Report on Foreign Trade Barriers*, pp. 305–306.
United States Trade Representative (2007), "Sectoral regulatory reform: information technologies", *Foreign Trade Barriers*, pp. 307–308.
United States Trade Representative (2007), "Medical devices and pharmaceuticals", *Foreign Trade Barriers*, pp. 309–310.
United States Trade Representative (2007), "Agriculture", *Foreign Trade Barriers*, p. 311.
United States Trade Representative (2007), "Antimonopoly law and competition policy", *Foreign Trade Barriers*, pp. 311–313.
United States Trade Representative (2007), "Transparency" *Reports on Foreign Trade Barriers*, pp. 313–314.
United States Trade Representative (2007), "Commercial law", *Reports on Foreign Trade Barriers*, pp. 314–315.
United States Trade Representative (2007), "Distribution and customs clearance", *Report on Foreign Trade Barriers*, pp. 315–316.
United States Trade Representative (2007), "Rice stocks release program", *Report on Foreign Trade Barriers*, pp. 316–317.
United States Trade Representative (2007), "Pork import regime", *Report on Foreign Trade Barriers*, p. 317.
United States Trade Representative (2007), "Wheat import system corn for industrial use", *Report on Foreign Trade Barriers*, p. 317.
United States Trade Representative (2007), "Fish products", *Report on Foreign Trade Barriers*, p. 318.
United States Trade Representative (2007), "High tariffs on beef, citrus, dairy and processed food products", *Report on Foreign Trade Barriers*, p. 318.
United States Trade Representative (2007), "Proprietary ingredient information disclosure requirements for imports", *Report on Foreign Trade Barriers*, p. 318.
United States Trade Representative (2007), "Leather/footwear", *Report on Foreign Trade Barriers*, p. 319.
United States Trade Representative (2007), "Marine craft", *Report on Foreign Trade Barriers*, p. 319.

United States Trade Representative (2007), "Wood products, housing and building materials", *Report on Foreign Trade Barriers*, p. 319.

United States Trade Representative (2007), "Standards, testing, labeling and certification: beef", *Report on Foreign Trade Barriers,* p. 320.

United States Trade Representative (2007), "Standards, testing, labeling and certification: enforcement of maximum residue limits", *Report on Foreign Trade Barriers*, pp. 320–321.

United States Trade Representative (2007), "Standards, testing, labeling and certification: building size, design and wood products", *Report on Foreign Trade Barriers*, p. 321.

United States Trade Representative (2007), "Phytosanitary issues", *Report on Foreign Trade Barriers*, p. 321.

United States Trade Representative (2007), "Biotechnology", *Report on Foreign Trade Barriers*, pp. 321–322.

United States Trade Representative (2007), "Restrictive food additive list", *Foreign Trade on Barriers*, p. 322.

United States Trade Representative (2007), "Cosmetics and quasi-drugs", *Reports on Foreign Trade Barriers*, p. 323.

United States Trade Representative (2007), "Nutritional Supplements", *Reports on Foreign Trade Barriers*, p. 323.

United States Trade Representative (2007), "Poultry", *Foreign Trade Barriers*, p. 323.

United States Trade Representative (2007), "Construction, architecture and engineering", *Report on Foreign Trade Barriers*, pp. 324–325.

United States Trade Representative (2007), "Patents", *Reports on Foreign Trade Barriers*, p. 325.

United States Trade Representative (2007), "Copyrights", *Reports on Foreign Trade Barriers*, pp. 326–327.

United States Trade Representative (2007), "Geographic indicators", *Reports on Foreign Trade Barriers*, p.327.

United States Trade Representative (2007), "Trade secrets", *Reports on Foreign Trade Barriers*, p. 327.

United States Trade Representative (2007), "Trademarks", *Reports on Foreign Trade Barriers*, p. 327.

United States Trade Representative (2007), "Border enforcement", *Reports on Foreign Trade Barriers*, p. 328.

United States Trade Representative (2007), "Insurance", *Reports on Foreign Trade Barriers*, p. 328.

United States Trade Representative (2007), "Professional services", *Report on Foreign Trade Barriers*, p. 331.

United States Trade Representative (2007), "Investment barriers", *Report on Foreign Trade Barriers*, pp. 331–332.

United States Trade Representative (2007), "Anti-competitive practices', *Report on Foreign Trade Barriers*, p. 332.

United States Trade Representative (2007), "Autos and automotive parts", *Report on Foreign Trade Barriers*, pp. 333–334.

United States Trade Representative (2007), "Business aviation", *Report on Foreign Trade Barriers*, p. 335.

United States Trade Representative (2007), "Electric utilities", *Report on Foreign Trade Barriers*, p. 335.

United States Trade Representative (2007), "Transportation", *Report on Foreign Trade Barriers*, p. 336.
World Trade Organization (2007), "Japan: measures affecting imports of pork", *Dispute DS 66*.
World Trade Organization (2007), "Japan: tariff quotas and subsidies affecting leather", *Dispute DS 147*.

9. A comparative perspective

1. INTRODUCTION

There are four major purposes behind this exercise. The first is to assess whether the avenues of free trade are being clogged by a mounting pile of non-tariff trade barriers. The second goal is to say something interesting about the similarities and differences in the non-tariff trade barriers attributed to the three countries. The third goal is to think about how the legal and institutional machineries supporting free trade could be strengthened, if it is necessary. Finally, we want to see whether there are any plausible relationships between national differences in the political contexts of government decision making and the patterns of trade restraints attributed to each of the three governments.

We will be looking first at comparisons among the three states with respect to the complaints raised against them. This may give some clues about national differences in trade policy. The second set of comparisons looks at the complaints raised by each state against the others. Our goal is to look into national differences in patterns of diplomacy.

2. COMPARISONS BY COUNT

Three major conclusions jump out from this analysis. First, trade complaints are piling up faster that they can be resolved. This is particularly true for the WTO Dispute Resolution Process. Second, the United States seems to be the odd man out in this process. Substantially more trade complaints are filed by and against that country than against the other two. Third, there does not seem to be any relation between the overall level of protectionism and the frequency with which trade complaints are generated for a particular country.

Table 9.1 summarizes the data on the overall number of cases raised in the five-year period, the number that were resolved and the number that persisted for the three countries. The data cover both national complaints and the WTO cases.

According to these data, relatively few trade issues were resolved within

Table 9.1 The aggregate counts of trade complaints

	Years raised				Number of WTO cases		
	2002 and 2007	2007 only	2002 only	Total	As complainant	As respondent	Total
European Union	18	9	18	45	17	37	54
Japan	45	7	21	73	12	8	20
United States	48	25	4	77	31	23	54
Total	111	41	43	195	60	68	128

five years. The number of persistent trade issues was almost four times greater than the number of resolved complaints. Secondly, the number of complaints seems to be piling up. The number of new complaints is over one and a half times larger than the number of resolved complaints. This is particularly true for the United States, which registered the greatest number of new complaints and the smallest number of resolved issues. In fact, the number of resolved issues is slightly larger than the number of new issues for the European Union and Japan.

The exceptionalism of the United States emerges in several other aspects of these data. The United States was virtually tied with Japan in the total number of trade complaints registered against it. The number of WTO cases filed against a country is probably a better measure of the seriousness with which a complainant country regards a trade issue. Here, the United States has far more cases filed against it than the other two countries.

There are also national differences in the subject areas in which trade issues are raised for each of the three governments. Rough counts by topic area are set forth in Table 9.2. The results for the country that was the object of the greatest number of trade issues are set out in bold.

Overall, there are national differences in the trade barriers discussed in this work. The trade issues raised about Japanese practices seem the most egregious, the Americans are somewhat more trade tolerant and the complaints about the European Union seem to be the least serious.

3. PERSISTENCE AND RESOLUTION

In Chapter 1, we raised the issue of the effectiveness of the trade agreements and the WTO trade Dispute Resolution Process. The short answer is simple: the Uruguay Round agreements and the WTO Dispute Resolution Process are important tools for the defense of free trade. However, they are not adequate to prevent the gradual erosion of free trade commitments.

The available evidence suggests that trade issues that have been publicized are rarely settled through bilateral negotiations. Evidence from the European Union's Market Access Database is testimony to the persistence of trade issues over time. Comparisons between the fiche number (which is based in part on the year the issue was first considered) with the current date on the fiche (which is based on the last time the issue was reviewed) can be used to establish the minimum period of time a trade issue has remained unresolved.

Examples from EU complaints about US trade practices are summarized in Table 9.3. The data are based on frequency distributions on European Union fiches that were last reviewed in 2006 on issues raised

Table 9.2 Issue counts by subject area

Issue	Respondent			Total
	US	EU	Japan	
Import-related				
Trade administration	8	6	**19**	33
SPS requirements	7	10	**23**	40
Access to service markets	10	6	**14**	30
Government procurement	**7**	1	1	9
Safeguard issues	**13**	1	0	14
Domestic-related				
Standards, technical requirements	5	**10**	4	19
Pharma, medical devices	3	1	**13**	17
Market regulation	5	0	**7**	12
Intellectual property	10	8	10	28
Export-related				
Export barriers	**3**	1	0	4
Export incentives	**8**	1	0	9
Total	79	45	91	215

Table 9.3 On the persistence of EU–US trade issues

Number of issues that date back to:	
1996	12
1997	1
1998	5
1999	3
2000	0
2001	1
2002	1
2003	0
2004	1
2005	0
2006	26
Total	50

Source: EU fiche listings in the References section for Chapter 4.

about trade practices in the United States. The data suggest that almost a quarter of the issues raised by the European Union about the United States are at least ten years old. This conclusion highlights the importance of the WTO Dispute Resolution Process.

This review of trade barriers among our three countries also highlights some of the features of the Dispute Resolution Process. It seems to be effective and widely used, but it is lengthy, convoluted and heavy-handed. Most disputes are only resolved after repeated appeals and delays and immediately before a credible threat of international retaliation. Data on the DRU cases discussed in this book are set forth in Table 9.4.

The first conclusion that jumps out from Table 9.4 is, again, American exceptionalism. Every case included the US as either a respondent or a complainant. There were no cases in the DRU system with decisions made between 2002 and 2007 that just involved the EU and Japan. Most of the cases were between the US and the EU.

A second conclusion is that the DRU system seems to be a clunky way to resolve trade disputes. Out of the 23 cases listed in Table 9.4, only six of them were resolved before a panel came to a decision. They are DS 174, DS 260, DS 262, DS 316, DS 319 and DS 347. We assume that this reflects the limited utility of government-to-government negotiations as a route for resolving disputes. The remaining cases went to at least a decision. A majority of these decisions (13) were appealed. The losing partner resisted compliance with the appellate decision in 7 of the 13 cases. The time required for cases that went from complaint through the appeal process was substantial, averaging close to five years.

The data in Table 9.4 are summarized by time and outcomes in Table 9.5.

4. WHAT ISSUES WERE RAISED AND WHEN?

We asked in Chapter 1 whether there are any identifiable differences among the issues that persisted through 2002 and 2007, were dropped after 2002 or emerged for the first time in 2007. A list of the major issues that were raised against each government in 2002 and 2007 is set forth in Table 9.6.

A list of the major issues that seemed to have been "settled" after 2002 is set forth in Table 9.7. Most of the issues listed in the table fall into one of three patterns. Some of them remained unresolved and were, in effect, relabeled in later years. This is the best interpretation of the issues listed under Japan. There is no evidence in the 2007 reports of any significant liberalization of Japanese markets in the areas listed in Table 9.7.

The second pattern covers issues that were either of minor importance to begin with or were resolved through the passage of time. This includes

Table 9.4 Timelines and outcomes of the WTO dispute resolution cases

EU against the US	
DS 108: taxation of foreign sales corporations	
1997: panel > anti-US > appeal > anti-US > compliance disputed	2005
DS 136, 162 (Japan): Anti-Dumping Act of 1916	
1999: panel > anti-US> appeal > anti-US > compliance disputed	2004
DS 160: business music exemption to copyrights	
1999: panel > anti-US > compliance disputed > resolved	2003
DS 176: rejection of Cuban trademark rights	
2000: panel > pro-US > appeal > anti-US > awaiting compliance	2003
DS 212: use of "same person" rule in anti-dumping cases	
2001: panel > anti-US > appeal > anti-US > compliance disputed > consultations > awaiting compliance	2005
DS 213: countervailing duties on German flat steel	
2001: panel > anti-US > appeal > anti-US > compliance	2004
DS 217: Anti-Dumping Act of 2000	
2001: panel > anti-US> appeal > anti-US > arbitration > retaliation	2007
DS 248, 249 (Japan), 262: anti-dumping on imported steel	
2002: panel > anti-US > appeal > anti-US > compliance	2003
DS 262: sunset review of anti-dumping duties on steel products	
2002 no panel	2007
DS 294, 322 (Japan), 350: zeroing methodology to calculate dumping margins	
2004: panel > anti-US > appeal > anti-US > compliance disputed	2007
DS 320: continuing use of zeroing methodology	
2007: panel; no report yet	
DS 317, 353: subsidies for large civilian aircraft	
2005: panel > discussions, no results > refiled complaint > panel	2007
DS 319: determination of anti-dumping margins	
2004: consultations requested, no action	
DS 320: removal of US retaliations on beef hormone dispute	
2005 panel > no report	2007
N = 14	

Table 9.4 (continued)

Japan against the US	
DS 184: anti-dumping on Japanese hot-rolled steel	
2000: panel > anti-US > appeal > partial reversal > awaiting compliance	2005
DS 224: anti-dumping sunset review on steel from Japan	
2002: panel > pro-US> appeal > pro-US	2004
N = 2	
US against the EU	
DS 16, 27, 158: banana wars	
1995: panel > anti-EU > appeal > anti-EU > compliance disputed	2007
DS 26: hormone treated meats	
1996: panel > anti-EU > appeal >anti-EU > compliance disputed	2007
DS 174: restrictions on use of geographic indicators	
1999: panel > partly supported > compliance	2005
DS 260: safeguards on imported steel	
2002: requested panel > deferred	2007
DS 291: restrictions on biotech products	
2003: panel > anti-EU > awaiting compliance	2007
DS 315: uneven enforcement of customs requirements	
2004: panel > anti-EU > appeal > awaiting compliance	2007
DS 316, 347: large civil aircraft subsidies	
2004: panel > pending > suspended	2007
N = 7	
Japan against the EU	
EU against Japan: there were no WTO disputes arising from issues discussed in this study	
US against Japan: there were no WTO disputes arising from issues discussed in this study	

Table 9.5 Aggregated timelines and outcomes

	Awaiting decision	Awaiting compliance	Compliance accepted	Compliance Disputed	Retaliation
US	4	2	3	4	1
EU	2	2	1	2	
Mean time since filing					
US	2.6 years	3.5 years	3.5 years	4.8 years	6 years
EU	3.3 years	4 years	6 years	12 years	

Table 9.6 Major issues raised in 2002 and 2007

European Union
The banana wars
Restrictive sanitary and phytosanitary measures
Content restrictions in media content and geographic indicators
Product safety requirements
Anti-dumping rules
Aircraft development subsidies
Japan
Quantity and distribution restrictions on imported agriculture
Restrictive sanitary and phytosanitary measures
Excessive regulation on pharmaceuticals and medical devices
Weak protection for intellectual property rights
Failure to police anti-competitive practices in business
United States
Barriers to government procurement
Violations of international anti-dumping rules
Unilateral enforcement of trade rights
Ideosyncratic intellectual property rules

most of the issues listed for the European Union in Table 9.7. European standards for aircraft hush kits and fertilizers probably would have a significant market impact. However, issues concerning the standards for gas connectors, anchor bolts and roofing shingles would have only minimal impact on US–EU trade overall.

The third pattern covers issues listed in Table 9.7 that were resolved in large part through the WTO Dispute Resolution Process. This covers the changes in United States policies regarding foreign sales corporations and the imposition of countervailing duties on imported steel products.

Table 9.7 Issues that appeared only in the 2002 lists

European Union
MRAs and PECA agreements
Standards for fertilizer, aircraft hush kits, gas connectors, anchor bolts, shingles
SPS requirements for BSE, gelatin, animal by-products, plant quarantine
Accounting, legal auditing, tourism, utilities services
Government contracting
Japan
SPS requirements on racehorses, apples, potatoes, fumigation
Approvals for veterinary drugs
Standards for organic foods, food additives, motorcycles, boats
Limits on professional services and e-commerce
Restricted access to markets for gas, glass, paper, steel, semiconductors, construction services
Erratic enforcement of intellectual property rights
Lack of transparency in government rule making
United States
Foreign sales corporations
Countervailing duties on steel
Sunset provisions on countervailing duties
Restrictions on foreign legal services

Missing from this analysis are lists of significant issues that have been resolved outside the WTO process through bilateral negotiations. From this we conclude that the WTO Dispute Resolution Process is necessary in large part because government-to-government discussions on trade barriers seem to be relatively fruitless, at least after governments have gone public with their complaints.

The next task is to analyze the major issues that arose for the first time in 2007. The issue summary is set forth in Table 9.8. The major trade restraints attributed to the United States were based on a series of security initiatives taken by the government after the 9/11 attacks and the Enron debacle. The other issues listed for 2007 would seem to have minimal trade impact. The trade issues attributed to the EU and Japan in 2007 are generally consistent with the patterns described for 2002 and 2002/2007.

These data support a modification of the conclusions based on just the number of trade issues listed in Table 9.1. Although old issues are not being resolved very rapidly, new ones are not emerging at a dangerous rate. The major new threats to international trade seem to come from the development of new regulatory programs that are not necessarily intended

Table 9.8 Issues raised for the first time in 2007

European Union
Customs administration and EU enlargement
Restrictions on wood packing and genetically modified organisms
Restrictions on food supplements
Standardization and the metric directive
Japan
Limits on advertising, electricity markets, aviation services
United States
New security, transparency requirements
Regulation of foreign banks in the US
Standards for HDTV, cruise ships, pressure equipment

to limit international trade. We cannot expect that governments will place a moratorium on new program development. The long-term prospects for the gradual erosion of free trade are still troubling.

5. IS THERE AN INTERNATIONAL CONSENSUS ON TRADE ISSUES?

An analysis of the frequencies with which any two of our three countries bring the same trade complaints to the third country will give a rough indicator of the extent to which there is an international consensus as to what constitutes a trade issue. The data are summarized in Table 9.9. The numbers after the slash refer to the number of issues under that heading. The number before the slash refers to the number of the cases in which the two potential complainants were in agreement; for example, the entry "1/4" for United States trade administration means that the European Union and Japan both raised an issue in only one out of four cases. The numbers in this table are aggregates for all three tables, 2002/2007, 2007 only and 2002 only.

Table 9.9 again highlights American exceptionalism. The entries in which the two countries are in agreement at least half of the time are highlighted in bold. There was more agreement between the EU and Japan about US trade restrictions than between the US/EU or US/Japanese pairings. EU/Japanese consensus was especially strong in the critiques of US tariff policies, government procurement policies, access to service markets, anti-dumping rules, claims of unilateral rights to take action against trade restrictions and US export subsidies. We note that these are the major

Table 9.9 Trade issues by subject and extent of international agreement

Complainants	EU/US	EU/Japan	Japan/US
Respondent:	Japan	US	EU
1. Import-related			
Trade administration	3/9	1/4	2/5
SPS issues	3/22	1/9	1/5
Access to services	2/13	0/12	0/6
Government procurement		0/5	0/1
Safeguard issues		**9/13**	0/1
2. Domestic-related			
Standards and tech. requirements	0/5	**2/4**	2/10
Pharma and medical devices	5/13	0/3	0/1
Intellectual property	0/10	**4/9**	1/8
Market regulation	0/7	0/5	
3. Export-related			
Export impediments		0/3	
Export subsidies		**3/5**	0/2

areas in which the number of complaints against the US was particularly high. The lowest level of consensus on international trade issues was between the US and Japan. The only area in which the two countries were in even general agreement was in protesting EU actions in the area of standards and technical requirements. Table 9.9 also points up the extent that the US and EU go their own ways in determining what issues to highlight. The EU and US were not in agreement more than fifty percent of the time on any of the issues raised against Japan. Japan and the US did not agree even half the time on any of the issues raised against the EU.

Both the EU and the US are far more aggressive in making complaints against each other. The EU though, has far fewer complaints against Japan than does the US. We will discuss the relation between the US trade complaints about Japan and Japanese reform movements in Chapter 10.

6. HOW SERIOUS ARE THE TRADE COMPLAINTS?

A core issue is whether the number of trade issues raised against a country is actually a reflection of the extent to which trade restrictions have been levied by the government. It could be, for example, that complaints are generally raised against bona fide trade barriers. If so, then we would expect to see:

1. More complaints > less trade

It is also possible that the process of international trade becomes the cause, rather than the result, of international trade. This might happen, for example, if the trade restrictions emerge as a result of domestic resistance to foreign competition. If so, then:

2. More trade > more complaints

Most of the issues raised about the restraint of trade are at least loosely based on alleged violations of international trade agreements. It is also possible that these agreements do not address the most serious trade restraints. If so, then we would expect to see:

3. No relation between trade complaints and trade levels.

Which hypothesis is the most consistent with the data? One approach is simply to compare data on trade/GNP with the number of complaints. If the complaints are indicative of trade problems, then we would expect the countries receiving the greatest number of complaints to have the lowest level of trade as a fraction of GDP. On the other hand, the complaints may simply be a consequence of trade. If so, then a greater number of complaints would be associated with a higher level of trade penetration, not a lower one.

We can also look at the export/import ratio as an indicator of trade policy. Countries that emphasize mercantilism would be likely to push exports and restrain imports. These results would be consistent with an export/import ratio of greater than 1.00. Countries that valued free trade would probably be far more tolerant of export/import ratios of less than 1.00.

The data are set forth in Table 9.10. We are looking at import data because that is where most of the problems arise. The European results are based on trade data for the largest 16 EU counties. We are only looking at trade with countries outside the EU, since intra-EU trade occurs within one comprehensive set of trading rules. The complaint count is based on the sum of complaints for 2002 and 2007, 2002 only and 2007 only.

The two indicators listed in Table 9.10, imports as a percentage of GDP and the imbalance between exports and imports, point to the same conclusions. The United States has the highest level of import penetration and the lowest ratio of exports over imports. These data suggest that it has the most open economy. In contrast, imports in Japan constitute the lowest fraction of GDP among the three governments and it has the greatest surplus of exports over imports. This suggests that the Japanese economy

Table 9.10 Measures of trade liberalization and the number of trade complaints

	GNP ($t)	Imports	Imports/ GNP (%)	Exports/imports (in ratio)	Issues
Japan	4.3	0.38	8.7	1.70	69
EU	13.0	$1.13t	8.8	0.92	45
US	13.2	1.9	14.5	0.54	78

Note: GNP and import values are in trillions of US dollars.

Source: United States (2007).

is the most closed to foreign goods of the three. The data for the EU on both indicators fall between these two extremes. This suggests that the European economy is more open to foreign trade that the Japanese but less so than the United States.

Comparisons between the number of trade complaints for the three governments and the measures of trade transparency suggest that there is no gross relationship between the two indicators. The greatest number of trade complaints was lodged against the US, which also has the lowest export/import ratio and the greatest level of trade penetration. These two simple measures suggest that the more cosseted economies, such as Japan, are less likely to generate trade complaints than apparently more open economies, such as the United States. In other words, the frequencies of trade complaints do not seem to be an accurate indicator of the level of actual trade restraints.

These data are generally consistent with other estimates of non-tariff trade barriers. In the 2008 World Bank analysis of trade patterns, The United States ranked 11th out of the top 20 nations in lowest import protection and 8th out of the top twenty countries in the liberalization of trade in services. Neither the European Union nor Japan ranked on either list (Islam and Zanni, 2008). The overall level of protectionism in the United States declined significantly between 1984 and 1990. Congress then started placing more emphasis on tightening up the anti-dumping rules (Hufbauer and Elliott, 1994).

A conclusion that there is no apparent relation between the number of trade issues raised against a country and the extent to which that country has an open economy does not necessarily mean that the trade issues are frivolous. Hypothesis 2 suggests that the stresses created by free trade could be a motive for imposing additional trade restraints. If so, then we would expect to see more restrictive policies in more open economies.

The question then is, how trade restrictive are the policies alleged in the trade barrier complaints? For the purpose of this exercise, we will assume that the complaints are, in general, factually correct. The first step in assessing the extent of trade restrictions will be to organize the specific complaints into patterns. The *de minimus* issues will be dropped from the analysis and the major issues for each country will be grouped according to target market and regulatory purpose. Complaints that have been made against all three countries in roughly the same form will also be dropped from the analysis. All issues raised throughout the five-year period will be considered. The results are set forth in Table 9.11.

There is no clear methodology for assessing the seriousness of non-tariff trade barriers. In reality, the impact often depends on the commercial context in which they emerge. Some types of barriers, such as inconsistent product standards, generally have a disproportionate impact on smaller manufacturers. Other barriers, such as idiosyncratic anti-dumping rules, depend on government execution. Finally, the unwillingness of a government to police monopolistic business practices may leave no formal policy record for analysis.

The reader is therefore invited to estimate the extent to which these policies constitute significant trade barriers. The relevant criteria include:

- The value of the affected trade
- Whether the impact is to directly limit trade value or to raise product costs
- Whether any cost increases affect capital or marginal costs
- Whether any trade limitations are immediately applicable or contingent on other factors.

Table 9.11 suggests that the trade restraints attributed to Japan cover the widest range of goods and would be expected to have the most serious consequences. Japanese agricultural trade is directly limited by a wide range of marketing and tariff restrictions. A host of sanitary and phytosanitary restrictions would have the effect of substantially raising the costs of imported foodstuffs. The widespread development of market-sharing arrangements among domestic producers under government sponsorship would be expected to severely limit market opportunities for a wide range of imported products and services. In effect, foreign entry into a wide range of Japanese markets would only be possible with the support of established Japanese companies. This conclusion is consistent with an earlier econometric analysis of Japanese protectionism (Sazanami, Urata and Kawai, 1995).

The trade constraints listed in Table 9.11 for the United States are more complex. The constraints on bidding for government procurement seem to

Table 9.11 Trade issues that could have potentially significant impacts

1. United States
    - Government procurement issues
        - Buy America policies
        - Special business set-asides
    - Unilateral enforcement of trade rights
        - Exon-Florio Amendment
        - Section 301
    - National security issues
        - Export Management Systems
        - Container security requirements
        - Sarbanes-Oxley Act
    - Safeguard policies
        - 1916 Act
        - Helms-Burton Act
        - Zeroing methodology
        - Hyde Amendment
        - Byrd Amendment
        - Carousel rule
        - Steel cases
    - Export subsidies
        - Farm subsidies
        - Aircraft subsidies
        - Foreign sales corporations
2. European Union
    - Agricultural import restrictions
        - The banana wars
        - BSE restrictions
        - GMO restrictions
    - Environmental regulations
        - RoHS
        - WEEED
        - EUP
        - REACH
3. Japan
    - SPS requirements
    - Marketing restrictions on agricultural goods
    - Limits to service market entry
        - Telecommunications
        - Insurance
        - Energy
        - Investments
    - Limits to government procurement
        - Construction, computers,
    - Collusive business practices

present an absolute bar to foreign participation for a substantial portion of this business. Government purchases, in turn, constitute a significant percentage of total GDP in the United States. On the other hand, all three governments and most of the EU member states set forth significant exceptions when they signed the Government Procurement Agreement during the Uruguay Round of GATT.

The US anti-dumping policies constituted the most serious issues in US trade practices for Japan and the EU. These were repeatedly and vigorously challenged through the WTO Dispute Resolution Process. The EU and Japan were also very concerned about US claims of unilateral rights to the extraterritorial enforcement of unilateral trade policies.

However, the effect of both sets of policies is contingent on US willingness to use them. The provisions of Section 301 and the Carousel Rule haven't aroused much international opposition, probably because these tools for remedying alleged trade violations have rarely been used. The opposition of Japan and the EU to US anti-dumping policies became far more serious when the US used them as the basis for filing a number of anti-dumping cases against foreign steel producers. The WTO cases against the United States on anti-dumping policies were largely resolved when the US dropped the steel cases.

The impact of European product requirements, such as CE Marking and the environmental initiatives, is more complex. These initiatives impose new costs on all companies covered by these acts, domestic and foreign alike. However, the requirements will have to be built into all operations for the domestic companies but only for the export operations of the foreign companies. Since it is likely to be more difficult and expensive to manage two sets of business regulatory requirements than one, the impact of these requirements is likely to be more burdensome for foreign companies than for domestic ones. In effect, the security initiatives impose a capital cost on producers that is likely to fall more heavily on foreign producers than on domestic ones.

The most important trade restrictions attributed to the European Union fall into yet another pattern. Several trade restrictions imposed limits on the value or volume of trade. The trade restrictions that were the subject of the banana wars directly limited the number and value of bananas that could be shipped to Europe from the traditional sources of supply used by American companies. The effect of the Media without Frontiers directive, which requires at least a 50 per cent European origin on mass media, depends on the potential demand for non-European media. We can assume though, that the directive would not have been passed if people did not consider the possibility that non-European mass media might constitute more than half of the total content in some contexts.

More commonly, EU trade restrictions have a major impact on the capital costs of product development. The requirements of the product safety and environmental directives, CE Marking, RoHS, EUP and REACH, affect how a product is designed, manufactured, tested and documented. The cost per unit for a small manufacturer can be very substantial. The cost of compliance for a multinational enterprise, with production runs in the millions, is likely to be far more manageable. Any increases in marginal costs are likely to affect large foreign and domestic manufacturers equally. In summary, the costs of the European product regulation initiatives are likely to be felt most strongly by smaller, especially foreign, companies. The impact of the European product regulation initiatives on larger manufacturers should be significantly less severe.

Earlier studies of European protectionism also concluded that food safety was a major issue and that the EU placed significant restrictions on trade in agricultural products (Messerlin, 2001). However, they also concluded that European anti-dumping initiatives can be used for protectionist purposes (Messerlin, 2001; Fischer, 2000).

7. TRADE ISSUES AND THE POLITICS OF TRADE REGULATION

One of the questions raised at the beginning of this work was whether the political economies of the three governments had an impact on the types of trade restraints developed in each region. The results are far from scientific since the analyses for the three governments in Chapters 3, 5 and 7 were developed in full knowledge of the trade issues and are laden with value judgments. Nevertheless, the results of comparisons between processes and results may be instructive.

For the United States, it was argued that the basic ideology of government places more trust in the free market than in the effectiveness of government regulation. Government becomes more like an agent of last resort. However, the United States has lost a lot of manufacturing jobs since the 1990s. Some cities have experienced significant population declines in response to economic reversals and de-industrialization. In government, power over trade policy is divided between the president and Congress. The president, as the official representative of the government, has primary power over international negotiations. The Congress is under a lot of pressure to support the commitments made by the president, especially in the area of mutual tariff reductions. On the other hand, congressional representatives represent local constituencies not the national interest. A more protectionist perspective would be expected. Congress controls legislation. In the area of international trade, this involves a lot of control over anti-dumping policies and the unilateral enforcement of asserted trade rights.

These considerations suggest that US trade barriers would probably be developed by Congress in response to local industrial dislocations. The legislative histories and even the names of such acts as the Exon-Florio Amendment, the Byrd Amendment, the Hyde Amendment and the Berry Amendment suggest that these were developed as Congressional initiatives and not in response to presidential pressures. This pattern is consistent with the second hypothesis presented above. Many of the trade barriers attributed to the United States seem to have been developed as a reaction against the pressures of free trade.

The Japanese pattern of trade governance is quite different. It was argued in Chapter 7 that Japanese governmental and business practices reflect the exceptional importance of hierarchical relationships, where the subordinate owes total devotion to the superior and the superior owes an ongoing concern for the interests of the subordinate in return. Senior government bureaucrats have a senior role over business executives. Most sectors of the Japanese economy are led by specialized government agencies. The role of the Diet in setting policy is comparatively minor and most government regulatory initiatives are developed by the bureaucracies in ways that are far from transparent.

These observations, which were largely taken from an OECD report on the Japanese economy (Organisation for Economic Co-operation and Development, 1999), almost exactly parallel the types of issues raised about Japanese trade barriers. This pattern best matches hypothesis 1: the issues raised about Japanese trade practices seem to be the major source of constraints on international trade in the Japanese economy.

The relation between the political economy of the European Union and the pattern of European trade issues falls into yet another pattern. It was argued in Chapter 5 that the government of the European Union is heir to the idea of a sovereign state that is concerned about the welfare of its subjects. Most policy initiatives are developed by government experts. Business involvement in the policy process through either politics or lobbying is comparatively minor.

These observations suggest that we would see the development in Europe of comprehensive sets of regulatory policies without any major attention being paid to potential trade impacts. These conclusions fit the issues raised about the trade impacts of the European product safety (CE marking) and environmental initiatives (RoHS, WEEED, EUP and REACH). There is no evidence that these initiatives were intended as trade restraints.

There is another set of EU trade issues which seem to be very protective of community traditions and safety. These include the banana wars, the BSE regulations, the opposition to GMOs, the Media without Frontiers directive, limitations on the use of geographic indicators and the insistence on traditional wine-making techniques. These policies are consistent with the argued role of the EU as the community protector. However, they were also intended as trade restraints from the very beginning.

We therefore conclude that the relation between the decision processes and policy outcomes in the European Union on the product safety and environmental initiatives best fits hypothesis 3: there is little evidence that these policies were adopted because of their potential trade impacts. Hypothesis 1 best fits the "community protective" initiatives since the goal was to limit trade in the affected areas.

8. HOW EFFECTIVE ARE THE TRADE SUPPORT SYSTEMS?

The core issue in all WTO dispute resolution processes is whether a country has acted in violation of the commitments made in signing trade agreements. The subject jurisdiction of the WTO process is therefore limited by the effective scope of the GATT agreements. This is surprisingly limited. Japan, for example, has been maintaining the most restrictive set of trade policies among the three governments under discussion. It is also the country that has been brought up on charges before the WTO the fewest times. The reason is simple: there is no agreement covered by the GATT/WTO that commits signatory countries to the enforcement of open, competitive, free-market economies.

The United States, in contrast, has both the most open economy and has been brought up on charges before the WTO the most often of the three governments. There is again a reasonable explanation for this pattern. The anti-dumping policies of the United States were clearly in violation of the requirements of the GATT Agreement, the Anti-Dumping Agreement, the Countervailing Duties Agreement and the Safeguards Agreement. The government of the United States also demonstrated a willingness to use the authority claimed under domestic law in the anti-dumping steel cases.

To some extent, the effectiveness of the WTO Dispute Resolution Process is limited by the unavoidable vagueness of the agreement terms. The SPS Agreement, for example, commits signatory states to base their sanitary and phytosanitary requirements on "scientific analysis" and to avoid measures that are "unnecessarily" trade restrictive. The intrinsic ambiguities of these terms led to the beef hormone disputes between the

United States and Europe. The United States successfully prosecuted the European Union before the WTO on the grounds that no scientific basis had been shown for the European policy (DRU 26). The European Union then sued the United States for maintaining the retaliatory measures that had been authorized under the original action on the grounds that it had shown a scientific basis for the original policies (DS 320).

To generalize from these examples, the Dispute Resolution Process seems best suited to resolve government commitments to take specific actions or to implement concrete procedures. It is less suited to adjudicate compliance with agreements to adopt general policy preferences. Finally, the issue of enforcing internally competitive markets through transparency in policy making leading to arm's-length relations between government and business is not even addressed.

9. NATIONAL POLITICS AND THE EMERGENCE OF TRADE COMPLAINTS

There are several factors that help reconcile the observed patterns of trade disputes, especially the WTO complaints, with the patterns of national policy. One apparent anomaly is Japan's lack of involvement as a defendant in the WTO Dispute Resolution Process. The tight cartelization of Japanese markets is probably the most serious trade obstacle in the list. It clearly generated a lot of complaints, especially from the United States. However, it was not a subject of the WTO Dispute Resolution Process.

A review of Chapter 2 suggests an answer. None of the trade agreements address the need for transparency and neutrality in government rule making or the need to enforce free competition and arm's-length pricing in the private sector. More generally, there is little in the agreements that would make the mercantilism implicit in the Japanese system the basis for a WTO grievance. Of course, there is a need to achieve an international consensus on economic policy and Japan is not alone in following these practices. The very diversity of the international marketplace has probably made it next to impossible to achieve an actionable consensus on the most basic economic and political policies.

Similar comments can be made about the European trade barriers. On one hand, bananas turned out to be actionable, since the EU tariff quotas were in direct violation of several GATT agreements. On the other hand, it probably would have been a lot harder to have prosecuted the EU for SPS restraints. The SPS Agreement calls on countries to use "scientific evidence" and not to be "unnecessarily restrictive". These are general terms which implicitly delegate authority over their interpretation to the responsible government. Given the sensitivity of issues such as BSE, it would be hard to prove that the EU was not relying on scientific evidence. The lack of specificity in the terms of the governing agreements seems to have complicated the process of enforcing them.

Finally, the EU was criticized for the trade restrictions that were to emerge with the enforcement of the new environmental requirements, the RoHS, WEEED and EUP directives and the REACH regulations. These could create a substantial trade impact on a wide range of goods. However, no WTO complaints were filed on the basis of these policies.

The most likely explanation for this state of affairs is not hard to see. The EU government has every right to pass legislation protecting the environment as long as it is not unnecessarily trade restrictive. In fact, the original GATT agreement provided explicit authority for governments to take measures protecting national health and welfare, even if they were trade restrictive. Furthermore, there are no agreements in the WTO arsenal that would provide for international coordination of new legislative initiatives, even if the result might be a regime that was unnecessarily trade restrictive. The national notification provisions of the Technical Barriers to Trade agreement are intended to provide advance notice of new policies. However, the impact of this provision has been minimal. See Chapter 2 for a more detailed analysis of these agreements.

The United States presents yet another picture. The preceding comments about the lack of an international venue for mitigating the trade effects of new legislation apply equally well to the security measures enacted after the attacks of 9/11. However, other US policies seem to be overtly protectionist or to simply defy international agreements. These include, for example, the various government procurement set-asides, the US anti-dumping rules and the assertion of a right to unilaterally enforce a number of trade policies affecting other countries.

REFERENCES

Fischer, T. (2000), *The United States, The European Union and the "Globalization" of World Trade: Allies or Adversaries?* Westport, Conn., Quorum Books.

Hufbauer, G. and K. Elliott (1994), *Measuring the Costs of Protection in the United States*, Washington, Institute for International Economics.

Islam, R. and G. Zanni (2008), *World Trade Indicators 2008: Benchmarking Policy and Performance*, Washington DC, The World Bank.

Messerlin, P. (2001), *Measuring the Costs of Protection in Europe: European Commercial Policy in the 2000s*, Washington, Institute for International Economics.

Organisation for Economic Co-operation and Development (1999), *Regulatory Reform in Japan: Enhancing Market Openness Through Regulatory Reform*, Paris, OECD.

Sazamani, Y., S. Urata and H. Kawai (1995), *Measuring the Costs of Protection in Japan*, Washington, Institute for International Economics.

United States, Department of Commerce (2007), *Statistical Abstract of the United States*.

10. Prospects for reform

1. THE ARGUMENT THUS FAR

In Chapter 1, it was argued that market expansion is an essential tool for economic development. Free trade has been the public ideology for most developed trading states. For most countries, public commitments to free trade have been backed up by the ratification of GATT, membership in the World Trade Organization and widespread acceptance of a series of trade agreements covering specific aspects of the trading process that were negotiated during the Uruguay Round.

However, the effectiveness of the GATT trading system is being eroded by a mounting pile of non-tariff trade barriers. Some of the barriers are examples of outright protectionism (particularly in Japan and the United States) and some of them are by-products of domestic regulations that were probably not intended to limit trade (particularly in Europe and the United States).

New issues are emerging at a faster rate than old ones are being resolved. The two major tools for dispute resolution are bilateral negotiations and appeals to the WTO Dispute Resolution Process. Unfortunately, there is little evidence that negotiations are likely to be very effective and the Dispute Resolution Process is time-consuming and generally contentious.

Would it be possible to develop a more effective system for protecting free trade?

2. PROSPECTS FOR REFORM AT THE NATIONAL LEVEL

If governments are truly committed to free trade, then why do these trade barriers emerge in the first place? If we want to mitigate the effects of trade restrictions, a good place to start would be to reduce the probabilities that they will emerge in the first place.

Acceptance of the legal concept of "sovereignty" can lead to confusion in this area. The idea of a "sovereign state" connotes the existence of a unified process for making decisions and a single entity for adopting policies. This idea of the unitary state carries over to the treaty process. A president may sign a treaty but the "government" then has to ratify it. A president is only the representative of the collective machineries of government.

The realities of modern government are quite different. Inevitably, many different agencies are going to be involved in developing and enforcing policies. Many agencies will be independent sources of authority and will be able to proceed more-or-less independently of the other government decision makers. The results in international trade are the emergence of many small policies than can override any overall commitment to free trade.

In the United States, the president and Congress are the competing centers of authority. The president is basically the guardian of United States commitments to free trade. The United States Trade Representative, who works directly for the president, takes the lead in negotiating international agreements, especially on tariff reductions. However, the members of Congress represent their home districts, which are often feeling the pinch from trade dislocations. The American anti-dumping policies and preferences for unilateral enforcement of international trade policies were generally passed by Congress over the objections of an unwilling president (Fischer, 2000).

A different pattern of decentralization was seen in the European Union. Each directorate general has a different policy jurisdiction. The directorates general commonly form close working alliances with their counterparts in member state governments, who, in turn, can have a say in the specialized meetings of the Council. The European Union does not have an executive office with broad policy powers. The result tends to be policy fragmentation. DG Trade is the guardian of the EU's commitment to free trade. However, it has little control over the policies developed by, for example, DG Enterprise, DG Environment or DG Health. As a result, the EU may adopt policies for the internal free market that have a potentially avoidable impact on international trade.

The Japanese pattern of policy decentralization resembles what is found in the European Union. Each major sector of the Japanese economy is regulated by a specialized agency of the Japanese government. Senior government officials are expected to take the lead in protecting the interests of the business sectors that fall within their jurisdiction. The Diet is weak and coordination across bureaucratic agencies has only limited effectiveness. The results are seen in the proliferation of local oligopolies in the Japanese economy under the approving sponsorship of the supervising government agencies. Under these conditions, any formal commitments by the government to the principles of free trade are largely meaningless.

There is no obvious strategy for mitigating the impact of government decentralization on overall trade policy. Often, there are constitutional barriers to policy reform. In the United States, for example, Congress controls virtually all legislative authority. Powers have been delegated to the president to deal with those aspects of international trade policy that require speed and consistency. A blanket delegation of powers to the president to review all legislation for potentially adverse trade impacts seems quite unlikely.

There are also issues of expertise. Complex issues, such as the management of sanitary and phytosanitary programs, should be handled by government agencies that have highly specialized competencies. Inevitably, the tasks of balancing trade liberalization against other community interests will have to be handled by the experts.

Finally, it is not at all clear that an aggressive policy of trade liberalization would receive broad political support. Would a broad commitment to free trade outweigh a promise of enhanced security in the United States after 9/11? Would free trade be more important than protecting the security of the food supply in Europe after the BSE scares? If not, then the prospects of amending these policies to promote free trade would be uncertain, at best.

Apart from the pluralistic decision-making processes, governments have to respond to national issues with programs that may have significant collateral impact on international trade. Given the complexities of modern life, we can expect that governments will continue to develop new initiatives such as Sarbanes-Oxley, the Patriot Act and the European environmental initiatives. Given a global community of sovereign states, we can't expect any one sovereign state to voluntarily slow the pace of policy formation to await the development of an international consensus on what constitutes acceptable measures. The development of new policies, in short, is always likely to go more rapidly than the development and ratification of new international agreements governing these policy initiatives. Again, it seems unlikely that governments will generally be willing to forestall needed domestic legislation so that arrangements can be worked out to mitigate the possible impact on international trade.

However, it might be possible to develop some process that would require each country to make a full evaluation of the trade barriers associated with each initiative in the context of the aggregate benefits of free trade. An example of this approach is the environmental impact statement (EIS) that must be filed in connection with all significant Federal initiatives (United States, 1969). However, the EIS requirement had the strong support of an environmental movement that aggressively used the courts to enforce the requirement. It is not clear that free trade could garner similar support in most countries.

Requiring the development of a "trade impact statement" would therefore seem to be an unlikely prospect. Given the complexity of modern regulatory programs, the analytical task could be formidable. More importantly, national security and public safety concerns are likely to trump free trade preferences. As we mentioned in Chapter 1, GATT expressly allows the signatory states to adopt trade-limiting practices in the interests of public welfare. We may well be swallowed up by this exception.

Requiring countries to develop trade impact statements for new initiatives would not address the problems of legacy policies. A significant number of trade issues were simply legacies from a simpler time when countries were less linked by trade. A basic issue for the US is the continued reliance on imperial units of measurement instead of the metric system that is almost universally used elsewhere. Although this issue did not loom large in the US–EU disputes, the failure of the US to adopt the metric system has made virtually any attempt to lower barriers caused by national differences in standards and technical requirements irrelevant. See *The Failure to use the Metric System*, in Chapter 4 Section 2.2a, and *The Metric Directive*, Chapter 6 Section 3.2a. Other legacy issues affecting US trade are the 1916 Anti-Dumping Act, the Hilmer Doctrine and the First to Invent Doctrine on patents. The development of specialized wine production techniques and geographic indicators are probable legacy issues for the EU.

We assume that legacy trade barriers were not initially intended to limit trade. The 1916 Anti-Dumping statute was, obviously, intended to limit trade. However, it was clearly not intended as a way around the WTO rules, which did not exist when the 1916 Act was passed.

This does not necessarily mean that it would be easy to reverse or remove legacy trade barriers. It may be difficult to change a legacy policy because important collateral commitments were based on the assumption that the policy would be continued. For example, generations of European vintners have relied on approved wine production techniques. Liberalizing the requirements could create competition they could not easily meet. In the US, laws, standards, technical regulations, designs and products have been based on the use of English units for hundreds of years. As a result, a change to the metric system could be very painful.

3. PROSPECTS FOR REFORM THROUGH INTERNATIONAL DIALOG

Another strategy might be to improve the international coordination of national efforts in program development.

One focus would be the specialized intergovernmental agencies. Groups such as the FAO, the OIE, the IPPC and the Codex Commission are intended to reduce international trade barriers through the direct involvement of the relevant agencies in the exchange of information and expertise. This has two inherent drawbacks. There are a lot of policy areas that are not covered by this system. Furthermore, the need to exchange information and expertise suggests that outcomes are important and there may be few set answers. These factors would leave substantial room for unilateral decision making.

The missing element in this analysis is a consideration of the decision-making incentives facing the national regulatory authorities in agriculture. Their agenda emphasizes the need to protect the safety of national food supplies. Negotiations over agricultural exports may be affected by overly restrictive SPS policies on imports. However, different agencies are handling these two policy areas, especially in the EU. There are few consequences for a too cautious policy choice. This is less true in the US, where the US Department of Agriculture is intimately involved in both policing SPS requirements and in promoting US agricultural exports.

Another approach would be to encourage international business-to-business dialog in the policy development process. This approach is already being implemented at two levels. Under the Technical Barriers to Trade Convention, signatory states are obliged to notify each other on pending measures that could affect free trade. The member countries are also required to publicize these notifications and to provide a forum for public comment. In the United States, NCSCI, the National Center for Standards and Certification Information, is the contact and dissemination point.

This initiative hasn't worked as well as the proponents had hoped. Governments tend to emphasize the smaller issues such as pending changes in standards or technical requirements, in their notifications. The larger trade issues raised by policy initiatives are not covered by the system. Furthermore, the notifications are generally ignored by private business. Unless business becomes involved in the process, the government generally lacks both the expertise and credibility that are needed to successfully lobby a foreign government over a notification issue.

The governments of the United States, the European Union and Japan have also developed formal, ongoing channels to discuss the trade and investment implications of potential policy initiatives. These initiatives are more promising.

The establishment of first the EU–US High Level Regulatory Cooperation Forum and then the Transatlantic Economic Council (United States, 2008) was one of the major achievements of the 2005

US–EU Summit. The goals are to avoid future difficulties by promoting a mutual understanding of problem definitions and response priorities, not necessarily to resolve current disputes. The major priorities are in the areas of liberalization of capital markets, investment controls, money laundering, enhancing trade, travel and security, defending intellectual property rights, competition policy and government procurement. The strategy is to promote ongoing contacts between the regulatory agencies in the two governments that have similar responsibilities (European Union, 2005).

Similar arrangements between the governments of Japan on one hand and the United States and the European Union on the other were discussed in Chapter 7. The US–Japan Structural Initiative Talks led to the development of the Framework for a New Economic Partnership in 1990. An Office of Trade and Investment Ombudsman was created in 1994 to address problems faced by individual exporters. Japan launched the Deregulation Action Programme in 1995 to implement some of the initiatives that were discussed in the talks (OECD 1999). However, familiar problems seem to have emerged in the US–Japan negotiations. Negotiations in different issues areas have often involved different government agencies with different constituencies and objectives. The level of coordination among participants on either side has been limited (Naka, 1996).

The evidence presented in Chapter 8 highlights the limited success of these efforts on the opening up of the Japanese economy. The OECD report on the Japanese economy (1999) suggests two reasons for the comparative failure of these efforts. The Japanese government participation in these reform discussions was partly in response to foreign pressure and partly to chart a way out of a persistent recession. These efforts failed in large part because foreign pressure did not provide a strong basis for developing a domestic consensus in favor of reform and because the prime minister's office was not able to force compliance by the semi-autonomous regulatory agencies.

It is too early to determine whether the US–EU dialog will come to a similar fate.

4. PROSPECTS FOR REFORM: STRENGTHENING THE WTO

It was argued in Chapter 9 that there are two limitations to the WTO Dispute Resolution Process. It tends to be long and contentious and the agreements it serves to enforce don't address the most basic issues concerning the proper role of government in business. Can either issue be addressed effectively?

Consider how the contexts of WTO trade disputes might bias the positions of the parties and the outcomes of the process. In Chapter 1, the contrast between free trade and mercantilism was discussed. We argued that trade liberalization is likely to provide diffuse benefits to a larger number of people at the expense of more serious benefits and costs to a far smaller number of people. The decision between free trade and mercantilism can rest on whether we focus on maximizing the aggregate benefits to the many or on mitigating the associated pain to the few.

The decision process could play a role here. In the WTO rounds, the governments are asked to balance their interests over a wide range of tariff items and trade issues. The participants are likely to focus on maximizing the magnitude of the aggregate benefits. The use of the "most-favored nation" (now called "normal trade relations") principle also has an impact on outcomes. The basic MFN principle is "a benefit to one is a benefit to all". The implicit corollary is "a barrier against one has to be a barrier against all". This principle substantially raises the costs of imposing protective barriers against imports from a particular country. General support for principles of free trade would be a logical consequence.

In contrast, consider the WTO Dispute Resolution Process. The only issues on the table are the protectionist decisions of the accused country, the agreements they are alleged to have violated and the economic consequences of the protectionism. The immediate consequence of a successful prosecution is not trade liberalization but further protection. The complainants will be authorized to impose their own trade barriers with an economic effect that is roughly comparable to the trade barriers that the defendant had imposed in the first place. The final stage then, is negotiations between successful complainant and unsuccessful respondent on whether they are both willing to remove their trade restrictions. At least one side, the respondent, may well want to maintain its trade restraints. In other words, the discussions start with trade restrictions and the scope of liberalization benefits is limited to the products being protected. This is also an adversarial system. Outcomes are at least implicitly recorded as "I won, you lost". Compromise could well be considered by the combatants as a partial failure. This is not a system that is likely to produce ringing endorsements for free trade (Conybeare, 1987).

Our brief review of the WTO cases filed by the US, the EU and Japan against each other also highlights another pattern: national arguments in the Dispute Resolution Process are pushed very aggressively and defended almost always to the end. This has the hallmark of zero-sum games, not the search for a shared middle ground. This is what we would expect to see in mercantilist competition, and not with the search for a free-trade consensus. Other observers have commented that the search for a high-minded route to a common welfare often comes down to charges of bad faith in the disputes over specific trade policies and decisions (Gavin, 2001; Troutman, 2004).

There are a few steps that could be taken to limit the incentives to pursue a mercantilist agenda and to encourage a larger, pro-free trade perspective. At present, for example, the interpretation of the agreements is based on both the negotiating records and the rulings of previous dispute resolution findings. This is, in short, a common law approach. It may enhance predictability but it ignores the underlying trade realities.

This approach could be modified by the addition of a new "trade impact statement" that would assess the trade impacts of alternative rulings. This could be developed by two existing WTO groups, the Trade Policy Review Body and the Goods Trade Body that are discussed in Chapter 2. A trade impact statement could remind the disputants what is at risk in their disputes.

A more fanciful step would be to revise the penalties that could be awarded by a dispute resolution panel to include forced trade liberalization by the defendant rather than the imposition of new voluntary restrictions by the complainant. Under present rules, the imposition of trade restrictions by the defendant nation is met by the addition of new restrictions by a successful complainant against the defendant. This seems to be going in the wrong direction.

Mandated trade liberalization would address another problem with the present system, the relative powerlessness of smaller countries. Penalties are imposed in the form of permission for the complainants to impose new barriers against defendant countries. However, the economic impacts of trade bans between larger and smaller countries are quite disproportionate. A US ban on Caribbean coffee imports could be an economic death sentence for many small countries in the region. A Caribbean ban on general imports from the US would be insignificant for the US (Troutman, 2004).

The situation would be reversed if the penalties could take the form of WTO-mandated trade liberalization. If the Caribbean country was required to open up new markets for US goods as a price for a violation, the impact on the US economy would be negligible. However, if the US was required to open up additional domestic markets for Caribbean imports, the benefit to the islands could be substantial.

We can also consider the agreements that the WTO Dispute Resolution Process is intended to enforce. In Chapter 9, we argued that the process seems to work more effectively in enforcing agreements that involve commitments to specific procedures and concrete steps. It does not work as well for enforcing agreements involving commitments to general philosophies and broad principles. Given the complexities of contemporary regulatory issues, and the diversity of opinions and approaches that can be found in the global village, an international consensus on clarity and specificity will probably be hard to develop.

They probably have to be couched in general terms. It is likely that the more specific the language, the harder it will be to achieve an international consensus. Support for generality may well mask a lack of consensus on the details.

This is particularly true regarding principles governing the relations between business and government. Somewhere at some time, someone in government has cozied up to business for mutual benefit in virtually every society. The differences between, for example, Sweden and Nigeria, may be one of degree rather than of kind. Conventions that criminalize anti-competitive behaviors have not been popular. The lack of enforcement for the US Foreign Corrupt Practices Act and the Inter-American Convention Against Corruption are examples of this phenomenon. GATT is understandably silent on this subject. Given this, it is hard to see how the Japanese could be brought to task for rigging domestic markets under existing agreements.

It is also true that the agreements may have to be applied to a wide, and initially unanticipated, range of fact situations. Any attempt to draft an agreement that is sufficiently detailed to cover all imaginable situations is likely to come undone when it has to be applied to situations that were not initially imaginable. Generality and an appeal to reason may well be the only way to go. The problem is that the definition of what is reasonable may well be situation- and culture-bound.

As a result of these processes though, debates over the implementation details for these agreements tend to be shifted to international litigation before the WTO, a process that is not likely to encourage a broad respect for trade and the general good.

5. STRENGTHENING INTERNATIONAL INSTITUTIONS

In essence, the global economy has grown in complexity and scope to a point where free trade can't be easily protected by the trade defense mechanisms that are currently available. It will not be easy to develop procedures and agreements that could be more effective in defending free trade.

The most logical way to minimize the future development of international trade barriers is to strengthen the machineries for coordinating national policy initiatives. Here is another paradox of free trade. While strong governments may be an enemy of free trade, centralized governments are also necessary to protect it.

Systematic trade liberalization has occurred on three occasions in recent history. At the national level, the Northern victory in the American Civil War led to the development of a true free market within the United States under the policy leadership of the Federal government. On a regional level, the creation of the European Union led to the emergence of a free market within Europe and a central government strong enough to maintain it. On the international level, the acceptance of GATT, and the negotiation of worldwide tariff reductions between 1947 and 1994, marked a period of substantial liberalization of trade in the global marketplace.

Unfortunately, the broad acceptance of market liberalization has depended on the reality or immediate threat of catastrophe. For the American Union, it was the Civil War; for Europe and the World it was World War II and the subsequent threats of Soviet invasion and nuclear annihilation. Fortunately for the world, the Soviets are gone and the threat of general nuclear war is over. Will common sense now be a sufficiently strong basis for maintaining a global commitment to free trade?

Nevertheless, there may be lessons to be learned on how best to construct a multi-state free market involving major economies. Both the US and the EU offer an example of the successful coordination of policies across different levels of government. In the US, it was the creation of "marble cake" federalism in ways that allows the Federal government to provide policy leadership at the state level. In the EU, the acceptance of subsidiarity as a governing principle and the acceptance of the comitology process supported the expansion of EU authority into areas that had been under member state jurisdiction. The two examples have many features in common. Planning is initiated at the "higher"-level government. Subordinate-level governments participate directly in the planning, help enactment processes and have significant voices in program implementation. Successful implementation generally contributes to the political successes of the political leadership of the subordinate-level governments.

The continuing problems encountered with the further liberalization of global trade may be contributing to the proliferation of free trade agreements (Cleaver, 1997). The United States, for example, has signed twelve of them and has ratified nine (Shaffer, Agusti and Earle, 2008, pp. 274–275). Free trade agreements generally resolve some of the problems associated with global trade liberalization. Generally, they have involved a dominant country, often the United States, and a much smaller partner state. The European version of the process is represented by the accession of relatively poor and isolated Eastern European states to EU membership.

In these negotiations, the restricted number of partners tends to limit the range of issues that have to be worked out. The asymmetry in power between the partners facilitates the negotiation process. The success or failure of a Central American Free Trade Agreement could have a major impact on El Salvador but only negligible consequences for the United States.

Unfortunately, as we pointed out in Chapter 1, international trade and the global economy are based on the developed states. The proliferation of side agreements with minor states may represent the re-emergence of economic blocks rather than the continuing liberalization of global commerce.

Perhaps our most feasible option is just to muddle through the inherent contradictions between the requirements of free trade and the capabilities of international institutions. The consequences are likely to emerge in the form of creeping complexity of "free" market regulations and the gradual division of the global marketplace into regional alliances.

Perhaps the answer will be found in the formation of strong regional arrangements, such as the EU and MERCOSUR. Both the European Union and the United States have been aggressively pursuing the development of free trade agreements with many countries (Messerlin, 2001). Hopefully, this would not lead to building dikes among these regional arrangements but to dredging the harbors within each group. The arguments advanced at the beginning of this chapter would suggest that regional free trade would not be as effective as global free trade, even if it is a lot better than across-the-board mercantilism.

6. IN CONCLUSION

Perhaps the strongest lesson to be drawn from this study is the realization that the incentives in government for protectionism are strong and that free trade is the anomaly. The disasters of two world wars and the threats implicit in the Cold War pushed the major powers to make a commitment to free trade. We may have to wait for new disasters to befall us and new threats to emerge before that commitment is likely to return. Until then, progress towards effective reform at the national, bilateral and international levels may be unlikely.

REFERENCES

Cleaver, T. (1997), *Understanding the World Economy*, London, Routledge.

Conybeare, J. (1987), *Trade Wars: the Theory and Practice of International Commercial Rivalry*, New York, Columbia University Press.

European Union, Directorate General Trade (2005), *Implementation of the Economic Initiative of the June 2005 EU–US Summit: Joint EU–US Work Programme*, Brussels.

Fischer, T. (2000), *The United States, the European Union and the "Globalization" of World Trade; Allies or Adversaries?* Westport Conn., Quorum Books.

Gavin, B. (2001), *The European Union and Globalization: Towards Global Democratic Government*, Cheltenham UK, Edward Elgar.

Messerlin, P. (2001), *Measuring the Costs of Protection in Europe: European Commercial Policy in the 2000s*, Washington, Institute for International Economics.

Naka, N. (1996), *Predicting the Outcomes in the United States–Japan Trade Negotiations*, Westport Conn., Quorum Books.

Organisation for Economic Co-operation and Development (1999), *Regulatory Reform in Japan: Enhancing Market Openness through Regulatory Reform*, Paris, OECD.

Schaffer, R., F. Agusti and B. Earle (2008), *International Business Law and its Environment* (7th edn), Mason, Ohio, Cengage Learning.

Troutman, L. (2004), "The WTO: The Institutional Contradictions" in Mike Moore (ed.) *Doha and Beyond: The Future of the Multilateral Trading System*, Cambridge, Cambridge University Press, pp. 19–25.

United States (1969), *The National Environmental Policy Act of 1969*, 42 USC 4321 et seq.

United States, Mission to the European Union (2008), "U.S., E.U. meet to advance economic cooperation" at http://useu.usmission.gov.

Index